Improvisational theater may seem a far cry from modern business, but in fact it is highly relevant. By looking through that particular lens this book offers a different way to engage with and respond to the complexities and uncertainties of leading organizations into an era when creativity and change are of paramount importance. This book wears its well-grounded learning lightly and is confident enough to sidestep the more stultifying academic conventions and focus on clear communication. And therein lies a great deal of its value.

—*Marshall Young, Director, Oxford Strategic Leadership Programme, University of Oxford*

Everything's An Offer

How to do more with less

BY ROBERT POYNTON

ILLUSTRATED BY GARY HIRSCH

On Your Feet
2008

Text © 2008 Robert Poynton
Everything's An Offer: How to do more with less

Illustrations © 2008 Gary Hirsch

ISBN13: 978-0-615-22618-7

The moral right of the author has been asserted. So there.

Published by On Your Feet
Portland, Oregon, U.S.A.
www.oyf.com

Printed in the United States. In Mattoon, Illinois, the self-declared
bagel capital of the world.

Printed on recycled paper (recycling and reuse being a fine
example of using everything as an offer).

Cover design by Gary Hirsch.
Interior design by Abbey Gaterud.
Text set in Sabon LT Std and Optima LT Std.

For news, further information, podcasts, T-shirts and other details
related to the book, visit www.everythingsanoffer.com.

This book is dedicated to everyone who sometimes feels like an impostor.

Table of Contents

PART 1

An Unlikely Story

1   Making God Laugh

One Saturday in late November 1996, I bought a T-shirt that changed my life. This is not the kind of thing that ought to happen to any sensible, grown-up person. T-shirts are meant to do little more than cover your torso or carry an amusing slogan, they are not supposed to have life-changing properties, yet for me, the purchase of this particular T-shirt was a pivotal moment.

A remarkable number of people have a story of this kind. A car accident, a last-minute trip, a missing guitar or one last beer turns a life on its head and leads to a great friendship, new job, marriage, divorce, research grant, business, invention or who knows what. Stuff happens. Nobody has a script for their life. Much of the time we are borne along on currents that we only dimly perceive. The idea that we can plan our lives with certainty and security is largely an illusion. Hence the old joke:

"How do you make God laugh?"

"Show him the plan."

The T-shirt punctured that illusion and catapulted me into a world I knew nothing about. In this new yet strangely familiar world, I quickly discovered that apparently magical creative power can be based on method and discipline. I learned that there are other ways to engage with a complex, shifting and unpredictable reality than trying to pin everything down. Fascinated, I set out to explore how to apply what I was learning to everyday life and work. This book charts what I have learned on the journey and the story begins with a T-shirt.

I bought it in Portland, Oregon, at the Saturday crafts market under the Burnside Bridge. I had only wandered in to keep out of the rain and was rather half-heartedly looking for Christmas presents to take back to Europe when my eye fell on a stall selling outrageously colorful hand-painted T-shirts. I immediately knew I had to have one. However, they weren't cheap, so I agonized over which of the lurid, cartoon-like images I wanted most. The cat-eating fish won the day and twenty-eight dollars later I was the proud owner of an original, airbrushed, Gary Hirsch design.

I knew from past experience that an original T-shirt can create an impact out of all proportion to its cost, so as I wandered off through the drizzle I wondered if I could convince the man behind "Catfish" to paint a special shirt I could give to the corporate clients I worked for (as a facilitator, consultant and trainer). The artist's phone number was on the packaging so later that day I gave him a call, fully expecting him to be out or to make his excuses. I was wrong on both counts—he was not only there but interested and available so the following day two bald guys with glasses met at the Three Lions Bakery on Southwest Twelfth and Morrison to talk about a T-shirt.

It was a curious chain of events that led me to be in Portland at all. A few months earlier a surprise call from Nike had hauled me out of a meeting. I had recently done some communications consulting for them so I assumed they were calling about follow-up, but much to my surprise I was invited to deliver a talk at their prestigious Design Camp on Orcas Island just north of Seattle. This event was strictly for designers and the convention was such that the solitary outside speaker should be famous or important or both. Unfortunately for Nike the famous, important guy had dropped out late in the day (as famous, important people can) so they asked me instead.

I was told that my speech should be about "creative problem solving." While I nervously wondered what that meant and whether I was qualified to speak about it, I discovered there were a number of other requirements. The previous year's speaker, against whom I would inevitably be compared, was a Harvard professor and Grateful Dead fan (which made him not only eminent, but interesting as well). He had been brilliant, insightful and funny and, as a counterpoint, had moved people to tears by recounting his wartime experiences.

My heart and self-esteem sank. I desperately tried to think of something to say that would make me sound smart, but my floundering search was interrupted by a question from the people at Nike:

"What are you going to wear on your feet?"

This plunged me further into confusion. I could tell that "shoes" was not a good answer but nonetheless I was wrong-footed. It took me a few seconds to realize that this was not an obsessive preoccupation with dress code, but an entirely logical question for a company that shod half the world.

"A pair of waxy black Doc Martens," I said, pleased with a response that seemed inoffensive enough. The feeling of satisfaction was fleeting. A painful silence was followed by another question which made it quite clear that they had been looking for a rather different answer.

"What kind of trainers do you wear? Do you run, play basketball, soccer?"

Feeling desperate, I clutched for any chance to recover. As a kid I had first come across Nike in my skateboarding phase when the coolest thing in the world would have been a pair of blue suede Nike high-tops of the kind worn by Tony Alva and the other Dogtown boys. I thought this might be my chance to get some so I asked if they happened to have any. This was also the wrong thing to say. The main effect of the request for a pair of twenty-year-old shoes was to display my ignorance of Nike's commitment to innovation. I may as well have asked a baker for a loaf of bread he baked in the spring of 1976. Fortunately the mention of skateboarding allowed me to scrape by since this was an area they were just moving into. I was told I would get a pair of their latest skate shoes on arrival.

I clearly hadn't made a great first impression. Furthermore, I was being asked to deliver something with the substance of a university lecture and the entertainment value of a best man's speech so I decided to use a selection of video clips from comedy shows I *knew* to be funny to illustrate the ideas I wanted to talk about. Nervously clutching my materials, I arrived at Orcas Island, VIP-style, by seaplane. It was a beautiful journey but I didn't enjoy it much because the closer I got, the more of an impostor I felt. Even during the speech I was uncomfortable—the shoes Nike provided were an American nine (not an English nine), making them painfully tight. Thankfully, I was saved by the video clips which delivered the much-required humor in spades. Not only that, but they had got me thinking.

In particular I was entranced by the clips from the improvised TV show *Whose Line is it Anyway?* With the speech finally over, I wondered: What kind of ability did it take to perform like that? How could these people invent intricate stories so effortlessly while I sweated over every word of a prepared script? How could they respond to anything that hit them without missing a beat while I fumbled over a slide that stuck? How did they know what to do without consulting each other? How could they make everything fit together so well? How could they be so productive and so cheerful under such pressure? The more I thought about it, the more extraordinary it seemed.

Thus a few weeks later when I turned up in the Three Lions Bakery to meet Gary Hirsch to talk about a T-shirt, these questions were lurking in the back of my mind. When, by way of introduction, Gary mentioned that as well as making artwork, he also performed improvised comedy, they all popped up again. Here I was in the company of someone who could satisfy my curiosity so I *had* to ask "how do you do that?" To my great surprise (and his great credit) Gary immediately replied, "Oh, it's really not hard. With a bit of practice anyone could learn," and he launched into an energetic explanation of how improvisers do what they do. I was hooked. Quite unintentionally, Gary had catapulted me into the world of improvisational theater.

He suggested that the extraordinary thing about improvisation isn't how much talent it takes, but how little. He described how universal a phenomenon it is, pointing out that we all improvise all the time. He explained that what you see on stage is not based on a prodigious memory, complicated system or innate genius but on a small number of simple rules or practices. As he talked I began to make connections with my own experience. I started to see why the advertising agencies where I had worked were not as creative as they claimed to be. I could see manifold connections with the ecology and complexity science I had recently been studying, which all of a sudden seemed to make much more practical sense. I even got new insight into why conversations in the kitchen can be so productive.

I also started to see parallels with some deeper questions that I often struggled with. Those questions revolved around a sense of frustration I felt when my own personal satisfaction seemed out of kilter with the way things were organized. I didn't see why work had to be dull or dispiriting so much of the time. Why couldn't it be more playful? Why was it so difficult to get anything done, particularly something new or different? Why was there so much emphasis on conformity, safety and control—regardless of the circumstances? Why were things so compartmentalized? Why did numbers seem to matter more than feelings? Why did we accept so much collateral damage—to other people and to the living systems that support us—as a cost of doing business? Why couldn't you make money and have fun? Gary didn't address any of these questions directly, but there were enough implicit clues in what he said to put me in a state of high excitement.

The sense of promise was so palpable that even as Gary talked, I started to ask myself "What could I do with this?" and as it happened, the timing was impeccable. A few weeks earlier another client of mine, an advertising agency, had asked me to come up with ideas to help them animate a moribund off-site meeting. The situation was the very opposite of that I had faced with Nike. The previous meeting had been awful: "bitchfest" was the word someone used. The agency, desperate to avoid a repeat, was happy to entertain *any* idea that might help make it more energetic, more productive and, heaven forfend, even fun.

Gary had said that anyone could improvise so I took him at his word. Less than half an hour after first meeting him, I asked if it would be possible to run an improv workshop for a group of advertising executives.

"Sure," he replied, as if the question were so obvious that he found it mildly boring. It seemed that nothing could faze this man.[1]

----

1   I later learned that nothing could have been further from the truth. Gary was, in fact, behaving like a character in the Jim Jarmusch film *Night on Earth*. A casting agent who believes she has discovered a new star (a taxi driver played by Winona Ryder) calls her business partner from the back of the cab and, trying not to give the game away, utters the line "I know I sound calm, but I assure you, I'm hysterical."

A few days later I left Portland armed with a battered copy of Keith Johnstone's book *Impro* and a homemade video of an improv show with which to sell the idea to the client. Ten weeks later we were in Tempe, Arizona, running an off-site meeting that no one would describe as a "bitchfest." In fact, it immediately led to four more engagements and before long the sporadic workshops turned into a business.

More than ten years later, the adventure that started with a T-shirt is still romping along. On Your Feet, the idiosyncratic little company that emerged from this episode, has what one potential customer described as "an implausibly good client list." (GE, Philips, Nike, Oxford University's Saïd Business School, the BBC and Orange are among the blue-chip companies I have worked with.) Whether you measure it in terms of money, relationships, learning or personal satisfaction, what flowed from the episode with the T-shirt has been extraordinarily productive and not just for those of us who are intimately involved. The A to Z of people we have worked with runs from accountants to Zen priests (passing through park rangers, salesmen and teachers, to name but a few). It is no exaggeration to say that tens of thousands of people have benefited in all sorts of different ways.

It is an unlikely story. So unlikely, in fact, that people sometimes think it is an embellishment of the truth. Actually this is only a fraction of it. Were I to tell the whole story I doubt that anyone would believe it. (I have to admit it seems pretty farfetched to me and I was there.) However, to notice only the amusing improbability of it all is to miss the most significant point. Just because events unfolded in a way that no one planned doesn't mean that what happened was down to luck, coincidence or some unfathomable mystical process. As the famous Liverpool footballer Kenny Dalglish is said to have quipped: "You don't get lucky, you get in position."

The people in this story did plenty of things to "get in position." It made a huge difference that they were willing to ask unusual questions, go out on a limb, say yes instead of no, admit failings, embrace mistakes and so on. For example, the people at Nike took a risk on an unknown speaker. The ad agency acknowledged the failure of the previous meeting and became open to any possible alternative. Gary said yes to something before he knew exactly what it was or how to do it and said yes in a way that inspired confidence, even though the idea was only half-formed. I was willing to act on a hunch by giving him a call. When we met, both of us quickly let go of our prior agendas. We allowed ourselves to be changed by what emerged in the conversation and to explore something quite different from what we had met to discuss (T-shirt design).

Neither chance nor necessity were responsible for this chain of events. It hinged on how the people involved behaved and that behavior had consequences extending far beyond what anyone intended or imagined. It is itself an example of improvisational practice in action. The result was that significant value was created out of nothing.

This is a stark contrast to what might have happened. Imagine Gary and I had behaved in a more conventional manner. If so, instead of going straight to the question in the Three Lions Bakery, I would have e-mailed him a "request for proposal" some days after our meeting. While he sweated over how to capture the playful simplicity of improv in written form, I would have had plenty of time to imagine potential problems, drowning my original enthusiasm, so that when his twenty-page submission finally arrived, I would have pushed it to one side, worried about whether this was the right moment to put my reputation at risk by proposing it to the client. This might have been the normal way for each of us to behave, but had we done so, nothing would have ever come of it.

The habit of trying to create order by predicting, controlling or constraining what happens can be a barrier to action and creativity. The trouble is that we are addicted to control. It is such an automatic response that we often fail to realize there is any other way to think or act. For example, filmmaker Robert Rodriguez was able to make an award-winning film (*El Mariachi*) on his own with only a few thousand dollars (a story he tells in his book *Rebel Without a Crew*). He made up for the lack of resources by doing everything himself and using anything he had around him—including a turtle, a guitar case, a pit bull terrier and a small town in Mexico. In short, he was very improvisational. But once the film was made and he started getting interviews with agents and studios in Hollywood, everyone assumed he must have had a proper crew, a decent budget and all the normal paraphernalia associated with making a movie. It simply didn't occur to them that there was any other way to make a film that looked as good as *El Mariachi*. And because it wouldn't occur to them, the studios could never have done it.

The same is true on a wider scale. Innovation is one of the most powerful mantras of contemporary business. Everyone wants new stuff and they want it now. New ideas, new relationships, new technologies, new products, new conversations, new markets and new ways to do business altogether. Yet generally, they try to produce new stuff in the same old ways—by setting goals, creating systems and carefully measuring results. Most people are aware, however dimly, that this familiar approach won't achieve the desired effect but it is so deeply ingrained that they aren't aware of any other way to behave. Thus they continue to work harder at what they *do* know, which normally leads to more of the very behavior, systems and processes that get in the way of anything new actually happening. The way companies are organized does not support, guide or reward creative behavior.

I became sharply aware of this recently. I was part of an On Your Feet team facilitating an off-site meeting with a group of high-flyers from a large technology company and the CEO came along to address them. True to his engineering roots, he arrived precisely on schedule and spoke earnestly about the pressing need to become more creative, innovative and imaginative. Dressed in an immaculate grey suit, he insisted, without any discernible irony, that the entire culture of this large, conservative organization needed to change in order for that to happen. It was a familiar refrain. These same themes crop up time and again at conferences and meetings like this all over the world: namely that the future will not be like the past, old methods won't work, uncertainty and complexity are growing, boundaries blurring and the speed of change is increasing.

However, what struck me this particular day was what the CEO (let's call him Norman of Big Technology Inc.) *wasn't* able to say. Norman admitted that he couldn't tell his audience *how* to do what he was asking. He explained that it wasn't simply about plugging in a new system, developing a new technology or rolling out a new training program. He stated clearly that however much power or authority he might have, he could not personally supply an answer. To my ear this was not only true but unusually frank. Such honesty was refreshing, but at the same time it also felt rather unsatisfactory. There was a gap between the abstract concepts he was talking about and the everyday reality of the people in the room. He hadn't given his audience any clues about what they could actually *do* to bring about the change he was describing. Nor had he explored, or even touched on, what might be in it for them personally (apart from more pressure and stress).

As I sat in the wings, I realized why I continue to be excited about the practices of improvisation even after all this time. It is because they give you something to do that can fill this gap. The practices provide a structure that is easy and quick to grasp. That structure is very open but nonetheless provides constant guidance and support. It doesn't give you a prescriptive plan, it gives you something to navigate by that helps you to make your own choices. It is this practice that enables improvisers to embody exactly the qualities that business leaders like Norman identify as critical: flexibility, adaptability, co-creativity, collaboration and so on. The practice is what makes it possible for improvisers to make more with less in no time at all and glean an enormous amount of personal satisfaction from doing so. And as Gary pointed out in the Three Lions Bakery, this practice is within the reach of all of us. It is something you can put into action, on your own, in your own way, for your own purposes, whenever you wish. To work with the ideas we will explore here you need no permission, no task force, no marketing campaign or formal training. You don't even have to tell anyone you are doing it. This means that while the practice of improvisation may not be an answer, it is a great response.

This response, though personal, could make an enormous difference to organizations (and on a grander scale, to society). Whatever the formal structure, it is how people talk and act that determines what an organization is capable of, what it is like to work for (or with) and what it is really worth. This elusive quality is not captured in a balance sheet or organizational chart because it emerges from the complex web of relationships among the people involved. That web, as Norman correctly pointed out, cannot be controlled from a central point, so you cannot mandate creativity or flexibility. Frustrating though this may be to the part of us which is addicted to control (more about this in Chapter 14), it means that if we change the nature of our own relationships, we can change the organization. Indeed, if we want to change the nature of the organization, we *have to* change the nature of our own relationships. This book is an exploration of how we might use ideas and methods derived from improvisational theater to facilitate that change.

In the introduction to *A General Theory of Love*, a poetic take on the science of emotion, psychiatrist Thomas Lewis, MD, suggests that "every book, if it is anything at all, is an argument: an articulate arrow of words, fledged and notched and newly anointed with sharpened stone, speeding through paragraphs to its shimmering target."

I prefer to think of this book as an invitation if only because the idea of spending several hundred pages arguing with you (or shooting arrows at you) isn't very appealing. Nonetheless it seems like a good test to submit to, so in a nutshell, the argument of this book goes like this:

"Stuff happens and you can choose how to use it."

Though brevity has its virtues, I suspect that this is a somewhat blunter arrow than Dr. Lewis had in mind. If we allow the argument to be expanded a little, it would go like this:

Life is too complex to control and it is often fruitless and demoralizing to try. However, that doesn't mean resigning yourself to fate. Inspiration can come from the most unlikely sources. One such source is improvisational theater. It is based on a method that can help you navigate through circumstances which are beyond your control—circumstances which, let's face it, are staggeringly common. This method promotes adaptability, flexibility and creativity and comprises a small set of simple practices that can help you to communicate and build relationships or ideas, even when everything is in flux.

The heart of this practice can be summed up in six words: let go, notice more, use everything. Trite though that may sound, a small set of simple behaviors can help you find unexpectedly valuable and fulfilling opportunities remarkably often. These won't necessarily be the opportunities you expect, but they will be there nonetheless.

More than ten years after the serendipitous meeting with Gary in the Three Lions Bakery, I know from experience that my original hunch was right. The practices have proved to be of great value to me in a wide variety of situations over a long period of time. It is both highly economical and deeply satisfying to discover that one can continue to learn from the iteration of a few simple ideas, deepening your understanding as you go.

Moreover, there is breadth here, as well as depth. As an ever-increasing range of people with different interests and experiences encounter these practices they uncover new insights and new ways to use them. This learning process has been driven by curiosity as interested people—be they clients, friends or family—ask my colleagues and me questions. Questions like:

How can you help us motivate and engage (and therefore keep) the fast-track individuals in our organization?

Our meetings suck. How can we make them shorter and less tedious?

We launched a new set of values and nothing has changed. What can we do?

How can our leadership team use stories and storytelling more effectively?

Do you do couples counseling?

Can you summarize a two-day conference for us in ten minutes?

How can salespeople collaborate with customers?

How do I keep a relationship healthy when I frequently have to say no?

How can we help a group of managers share knowledge better?

Where can I get some of those fabulous giant Post-it notes you use?

Can you help us prepare for the uncertainties of moving to a new building, equipped with ground-breaking technology?

And, perhaps, most often:

Where can I get one of those T-shirts?[2]

This is just a dozen of the hundreds of questions we have been asked. Improvisational practice has something to say about all of them because although it comes from comedy, it works with the fundamental building blocks of communication and relationships. Many of the questions straddle the professional and the personal. For example, "How do I keep a relationship healthy when I frequently have to say no?" came from a sales team but it is a very pertinent question for anyone who is a parent (or a child). This crossover is to be expected—at home and at work, communicating and living in relationships is essentially what human beings do.

Since most of my experience comes from working with business organizations, you will find many work examples and stories in the pages that follow, but the lessons can be applied to any relationship, however personal (hence questions about couples counseling). As one participant rather elegantly put it after a workshop: "I know the company paid for that, but it was for me."

Exactly what will be in it for you personally, I cannot say. Improvisation relies on structure, but that structure is coupled with great individual freedom. A coherent story, rather than a chaotic series of unconnected ideas, is created by the interplay between the two. A similar principle applies to this book. It has a structure—sixteen chapters organized in four sections—but I could easily have chosen a different structure. The reader always has the freedom to hop about, go backwards or start at the end, remaking the book as they pursue their own questions. To make this easier, it may help you to know what is where.

This chapter is the first of three that make up Part 1—"An Unlikely Story." Together

- -

2   The original "Catfish" T-shirt is buried at the bottom of a drawer, but we often wear other Gary Hirsch designs in workshops, which frequently prompts this question. If you are curious or if you would like to get one of your own, have a look at www.oyf.com or Gary's own Web site www.doodlehouse.com.

they explain how widespread and important improvisation is, tracing the connection between the abilities improvisers display on stage and those we all need if we are to prosper in the modern world.

The essence of the method is explained in Part 2 ("Let Go, Notice More, Use Everything: A Fundamental Grammar of Relationships and Communication") which introduces what I call the "foundational" practices and gives examples and illustrations of how to apply each of them. It comprises eight chapters, the last of which looks at how to start your own practice.

Part 3, "Shaping Stories," shows you how to look in a more "macro" way at a relationship or a story and introduces three different tools that can be used to manage the flow of any relationship or process.

Part 4, "Improvisation and the Joy of Uncertainty," is more philosophical and explains how the way of being encapsulated in the improvisational practice is increasingly important to our individual and collective well-being (and why this is a challenge). The final chapter ("Going Native") uses stories to put flesh on the bones of these ideas and to paint a picture of what a more improvisational world might look like.

Hopefully this will enable you to find your own way around if you want to. If you don't, then rest assured that there is a certain logic to the order I have used which seems to work well for plenty of people.

At this point in our history, human beings face a barrage of disorienting, uncontrollable changes—both creative and destructive. Whether we do so with trepidation or delight will depend on how well we prepare. Contradictory though it may sound, I want to suggest that the practice of improvisation applied to life (rather than the theater) will help you prepare even when you don't know what's coming. Thus in a way, this book is a manual for life in the twenty-first century.

Wherever you apply it, this practice could help you and those with whom you have relationships become more effective, more fulfilled, more creative and, in some sense, more alive. While I understand why Gary told me in the Three Lions Bakery that there is no secret to improvisation, there is, in fact, something magical going on here—something that requires no analysis, argument or cleverness, just a willingness to play. What you stand to gain are a few basic ideas that could make your life easier, simpler and more fun. Those ideas can help you to do more with less—less material, less energy, less effort and less stress.

    This means that, yes, this book could change your life. There, I have said it now. Cliché though it is, I am not going to apologize because it's true, and not just for me or the group of blessed and rather eccentric people I work with who use this stuff to make a living. A seemingly trivial detail, like the purchase of a twenty-eight-dollar hand-painted T-shirt, might, out of nothing, turn out to have an influence that you cannot possibly imagine.

2 💡 Only the Dead Don't Improvise

I am sitting in the shade of the porch. Above my head are the chestnut beams that support a roof made of reused, lichen-spotted tiles. At my back is a hand-built stone wall, expertly crafted out of granite blocks that fit together like the pieces of a giant jigsaw puzzle. Five years ago this was nothing more than a steep hillside overgrown with bracken and brambles three kilometers outside the small town of Arenas de San Pedro in the Sierra de Gredos of central Spain. You might well ask how an Englishman like me came to live in such an out-of-the-way spot. It's a question I sometimes ask myself. After all, I never planned to live in rural Spain, but then how often does life correspond to the plan? Even the house we built here is only partly the result of planning. And were you to examine the plans, you would not find the porch where I am sitting at all.

Building is normally a frustrating business. Everything from a kitchen extension to an Olympic stadium seems to suffer from complications, delays and unexpected costs. When we began to build this house I assumed that the best way to counter this was through careful forethought and attention to detail. With this in mind, once we had bought the land, the first thing we did was commission a proper topographical survey where men with red and white poles, hard hats and strange tripods spent a number of hours taking careful measurements. Based on that survey the house was designed to take advantage of the slope that ran from one end of the plot to the other so that it became taller along its length.

One gray autumn morning, the architect (Jojo), his friend (Pablo) and I laboriously marked out the foundations with stakes and hairy string. Having driven a hundred miles and worked for several hours, it was a realization as dismal as the day itself to discover that, at crucial points, the slope did not correspond to the topographical plan. Nor was it a little bit off. The discrepancy was nearly two meters. Vertical meters.

I felt deflated. This wasn't what was supposed to happen. It had been difficult enough to get three of us to the site on a day when it wasn't tipping with rain. We had yet to break ground and things were already going awry. I responded swiftly by looking around for someone to blame and within moments my sense of righteous indignation at the incompetence of Spanish surveyors was rising.

However, in my heart I knew that it wasn't the surveyor Chuchi's fault. His plan reflected the overall slope but the surface was irregular, with humps, bumps, trenches and hollows which meant that specific points could vary substantially. To avoid these errors you would have needed to take hundreds of measurements and I would have been the first to balk at the cost. Even had Chuchi been incompetent, the scapegoat strategy would have been useless in any practical sense. Laying into him would have given me momentary relief but it would not have changed the lay of the land. There was more of a slope than we thought and however much we wished there wasn't or blamed someone for not telling us about it, that wasn't going to change.

Meanwhile Jojo (the architect) was unperturbed. In fact, he actually seemed to be enjoying himself. Seeing there was more depth than we had thought, he suggested that we take advantage of it and put the garage underneath the house instead of alongside. Once mentioned, it seemed obvious. It would make use of the unanticipated gap, tuck the garage out the way and make the garden bigger. In fact, it was much better than the original plan. It made such good sense, I was thrilled.

I was also bemused. This was all so different from what I had imagined. It was disorienting that something which had taken so long to plan could so quickly and radically start to be transformed and I asked Jojo if we were allowed to do this. He interpreted my question literally and explained that, while theoretically we ought to resubmit the plans, in practice not even the Castilian authorities (punctilious upholders of Philip II's enthusiasm for bureaucracy) would require it for a change of this nature.

But that wasn't really what I meant. I was struggling with the fact that despite the painstaking preparation, despite months spent developing detailed technical drawings and submitting them to the appropriate authorities in duplicate, carefully labeled in neat yellow folders with important-looking stamps, the reality was turning out to be remarkably plastic. My assumption that we should try to anticipate and resolve problems before they occurred by thinking everything through as carefully as possible was already being challenged. I began to realize that there was more to the process of building than I had anticipated. Some adjustments were required in my way of thinking, as well as in the position of the garage.

The garage was just the first of many adaptations and innovations we would come up with over the next year and a half. Some of these ideas occurred in response to a problem. For example, the basement, which now acts as home to two chainsaws, a compressor, five mountain bikes and a hundred liters of olive oil, was the result of bad weather.[1] Working with stone in wet weather is difficult if not dangerous, so when it started to rain, Jose Luis (the foreman) decided to dig the trenches under the house for the plumbing instead. However, that autumn Arenas de San Pedro lived up to its nickname as "the urinal of Gredos" and it kept raining for weeks. So Jose Luis, Basilio and Tomas kept digging until they had created a large, open and unanticipated cellar. Being city dwellers we had failed to realize how important such a space would be. Jose Luis, being a local, knew it would be indispensable. By this stage of the process he also knew that we trusted his judgment, so he simply took the initiative, thereby making up for a shortcoming of the plan.

- - - - - - - - - - - - - - - - - - -

1   In Spain a family is reckoned to use about a liter of olive oil a week. That's right—a week. This accounts for the three hundred million or so olive trees there are in Spain, almost ten trees per person.

Other improvements came about as a result of using what we had. Tomas tipped the earth that was dug from the basement-to-be over the edge of a narrow path that ran along the downhill side of the house. As the digging proceeded the narrow path became a wide path and eventually a terrace where you can now sit comfortably and drink a beer in the afternoon sun.

Some changes were the result of seeing opportunities that would not have been visible from the draftsman's table. One day I was standing on the scaffolding admiring the view toward the snow-capped peaks of Gredos. "What a shame we won't be able to stand here when the scaffolding comes down" I mused. That thought led to an elevated section of garden just where the scaffolding had been.

Many of the best ideas—like the porch—emerged from the work itself. As he finished the top of one stone wall, Basilio became worried that rain would seep into it and through a series of conversations with several different people, the original idea (of a horizontal pergola) evolved into a sloping tiled roof, which not only protected the stone wall but created the shady porch where I am now sitting. It is beautifully integrated into the structure, but the fact is, this porch was improvised.

The mental adjustment required to make all these ideas happen was to realize that plans, however meticulous they may be, are only part of the story, even with things as tangible as wood, stone and cement. I had to learn firsthand on the building site what the best architects, engineers and builders already know from experience. Namely, that the inevitable gap between what you anticipate and what actually happens is an opportunity as well as a problem. In that gap lie all kinds of possibilities—to adapt and improve the thing you are making, to create a better fit or to allow the circumstances to suggest more appropriate alternatives. Plans are the first word, not the last, and departing from them is not a sign of weakness or failure. Whatever you are making, the most effective and rewarding projects require a great deal of creative adaptation.

In this respect building is not unusual. A meeting may have a detailed agenda but the conversation it yields will be improvised. If everything is scripted (or could be), then it will not be a very satisfying meeting. Any conversation worth having is branching and fluid. We instinctively flex, adapt and extemporize and it is this quality that makes conversation rewarding. It is what enables us to learn, create connections or get to new ideas that we wouldn't have thought of alone. This applies to personal conversations as much as to business conversations.

The need for creative adaptation is ubiquitous. All kinds of everyday activities are highly improvised. Imagine you are enjoying a conversation with a friend so much that you invite them to stay for dinner. The food, as well as the talk, will be improvised, at least to some degree. If you simply open the fridge and conjure a meal from whatever you find there, you are obviously improvising. But even if you set out to follow a recipe, the natural variability of ingredients and the large number of factors involved means that there will always be something you have to work around: the peppers take longer to roast than you expect, you have parmesan not pecorino and only one leek. Good cooks do more than follow recipes.

Turn on the television while you cook and there's a good chance you will see an improvised event pulling in a massive audience—the most popular sports, such as football (soccer) or basketball, are highly improvised. They regularly provide compelling drama without anyone having to work on a script. As the viewing figures demonstrate, there are few more economical ways to engage an audience.

However, improvisation isn't just about fun and games, it can be a matter of life and death. In the theater of war it is well understood that improvisational ability is critical to success in battle. As long ago as the summer of 1805, Admiral Lord Nelson, commander of the British Fleet at the Battle of Trafalgar, was conscious that the ability to work quickly and flexibly under pressure could be a strategic advantage as well as a tactical necessity. He was so convinced that his officers and men would respond better than their enemy to the mayhem of a sea fight that he deliberately sought to create havoc. Nelson explained this idea to Captain Richard Keats in his garden at Merton some months in advance of the battle: "I think it will surprise and confound the enemy. They won't know what I am about. It will bring forward a pell-mell battle, and that is what I want."[2] Events proved him right. Nelson deliberately upset the normal order of battle and gave his ships a high degree of autonomy to act as they saw fit. Despite being outnumbered, the British won the battle convincingly with a fraction of the casualties suffered by the French and Spanish.

On land things may have changed a lot since Nelson's time when thousands of men used to face each other across a field armed with muskets and literally kick up the "fog of war," but technological advances do nothing to remove the metaphorical equivalent. Radar, reconnaissance drones and infrared cameras do not change the fact that information is always incomplete and hazy. Events still change quickly, results are unpredictable and a lot is at stake. The U.S. Department of Defense, in collaboration with IBM, have coined the term "sense and respond" as a counterpoint to "command and control" to describe the kind of operational flexibility that is critical to modern warfare.[3]

A well-known military maxim says that "no plan survives first contact with the enemy." Generals and their strategic planners know that no commander, however powerful, can see everything that is coming. The experience of soldiers on the ground bears this out. I once had a participant in a workshop who had seen active service in the Israeli army. "Once the shooting started, it was all improv," he said. Things look similar even from the safe distance of the computer-modeling suite. The Dupuy Institute uses sophisticated models and analysis to forecast the outcome of battles, yet even they recognize that "the mother of all intangibles is initiative, or the ability of lower-ranking soldiers to improvise on the battlefield."[4]

How much we rely upon improvisation becomes evident when you eliminate it. I

- - - - - - - - - - - - - - - - - -

2   Adam Nicolson. *Men of Honour: Trafalgar and the Making of the English Hero*. (London: HarperCollins, 2005), 195.

3   "Transforming the military through sense and respond." IBM White Paper, 2005.

4   "And now, the war forecast." *Economist Technology Quarterly*. 15 September 2005.

grew up in England during the 1970s—a period when the United Kingdom suffered from dreadful industrial relations. A tactic that was commonly employed by unions was the "work to rule." The idea was that by strictly following the regulations but doing nothing beyond them, employees could bring an organization to its knees (for example, by refusing to work overtime or following safety regulations to the letter). As a school-boy I thought it was cool that you could wreck things without doing anything "wrong." As an adult it suggests to me that rules and regulations don't capture what is really needed to make something work.

I was reminded of this recently when working with a global delivery company. Someone happened to say, "You know, a number-four-sized package fits really neatly into the number nine slot if you put it in sideways." This spawned an animated conversation about the idiosyncratic tricks and twists that make life simpler, easier or quicker, even in the discipline-driven world of parcel delivery. One got the sense that these little improvisations were an important part of what made the system actually work and that without them, the hi-tech hub would, like Britain's factories in the 1970s, grind to a halt. Thus improvisation isn't just about making do, it is often critical to making things work at all. Moreover, the most useful, pleasing or distinctive features (like the porch of our house) don't necessarily figure in the plans or the manual.

Improvisational theater may still seem an unlikely source of inspiration, but the circumstances improvisers face are remarkably familiar. They work with scarce resources, under massive time pressure, in unpredictable circumstances. They produce a constant stream of innovation using a cocreative and collaborative method. They know how to thrive on constant change without showing signs of stress or strain, delivering an enormous amount of satisfaction to their customers and to themselves. These abilities are not taught in business schools, yet they are not minor themes. Perhaps it is assumed that such skills can't be taught? Or perhaps the academic approach of most business schools means they simply aren't looking in the right place.

Look closely at the theater and what you see is that improvisation offers far more than a quaint metaphor. Improvisers embody a long list of qualities required to succeed in the modern economy. These days it isn't just people in so-called "creative" business-es that have to be able to generate a stream of new ideas. Every day, existing ways of making and doing things become obsolete—the competition you will face tomorrow probably doesn't exist today. This applies to the individual as well as the organization and it is as true for journalists and software engineers as it is for factory workers. In *The World is Flat*, best-selling *New York Times* journalist Thomas L. Friedman points out that people all over the globe now compete against each other. In this "flat world" if you aren't able to create new possibilities then someone is going to eat your lunch or, more likely, provide an alternative arrangement to meals altogether.

Our understanding of the relative importance of competition and collaboration is also shifting. The traditional view is that business is based on voracious, testosterone-fuelled competition and that this is the natural state of affairs. Yet our view of nature is heavily colored by wildlife documentaries which, just like any other drama, include a disproportionate amount of blood, gore and sex for the simple reason that it makes "good telly." If you talk to scientific ecologists, the natural basis for this assumption doesn't look quite so clear. Stephan Harding, ecologist at Schumacher College in De-von, England, maintains that in the wild it is difficult to identify competition hap-pening. Adjacent species rub shoulders more than they lock horns. It seems that life is more like golf than boxing—you primarily compete against the course itself. Other players are on the course with you and at some level you may be competing with them, but you are rarely locked in mortal combat. Untrammeled competition is not the all-pervading state of affairs it is often taken to be and collaboration and competition are not opposing alternatives. In fact, organisms often need to be able to collaborate in or-der to compete.

What holds in ecology also seems to be true in the economy. Increasingly, economic success depends on the ability to create and sustain a complex and shifting web of col-laborative relationships. The dramatic advances that technology brings, many of them unexpected and unforeseen, accentuate this. As local supply chains metamorphose into global supply webs, the economic interdependence of different companies (and countries) becomes ever more tightly woven. As freeware and the open-source movement mushroom, it becomes easier for individuals and small companies to connect and form alliances that enable them to compete with (or even outperform) the big ones.

As more functions are outsourced, the hard boundaries of an organization start to blur, as do the definitions of what constitutes a competitor (or for that matter, an industry). This makes a mockery of the classical model of strategy with precise demarcations and well-defined competitors that can be subjected to rigorous analysis. "Insourcing" accelerates the collaborative tendency inwards. When a partner like UPS takes responsibility for an entire logistics operation (like Web sales) from start to finish, the point where one organization ends and the other begins becomes a little bit fuzzier. Collaboration thus becomes fundamental.

This way of working is intrinsic to improvisational theater. Improvisers always work in a collaborative way: building on suggestions and taking direction from their customers, exchanging and developing ideas from any quarter and weaving them into a coherent whole. This cocreative process is very fluid, which means that improvisers take constant change in stride. Indeed, as we shall see later on, if not enough change is occurring, they will strive to create it. People in business also face constant, rapid and unpredictable change, but they tend to react differently and talk about change as if it were possible to isolate, contain, control and plan for. The implicit hope is that given the right system or enough data we will be able to wrestle all this change to the ground.

Improvisers take a much more intimate view. If they don't engage with the changes that occur on stage, they look wooden and flop. They know they can't deflect or duck change and that without it, they won't create any action. Yet surely the same is true in business? Change doesn't happen "out there" in the market (which is, after all, just an abstraction). It assails you personally. A new piece of software renders your job obsolete. An organizational restructuring changes where you go to work, who you talk to and what you talk about. Because change comes home to roost in the everyday relationships of individuals, the knowledge and experience of the improviser can help each of us become more adept at dealing with the personal consequences of change.

Responding creatively to change means you have to be prepared to work with the unknown. Improvisers respond by being playful. Though this might seem trivial, playfulness is one way to develop a tolerance for ambiguity and uncertainty. Play and games are a means that humans have developed for exploring the unknown (hence military war games) and improvisation is one of many ways we can learn how to adopt a more playful attitude with serious benefit.

Another universal feature of the contemporary world is the excruciating pressure of time (as a Polish saying puts it: "sleep faster, we need the beds"). No one is exempt from this particular pinch. Not so long ago the president of a New York advertising agency called me with a plea for help. "Could you do some thinking for me?" she said. "I just don't have time to think any more." I was surprised that a CEO, of all people, wouldn't have time to think but time pressure affects everyone. Since you can't create more time, you need to become more comfortable and effective with the little that you do have. Improvisers embody this quality too. They are quite accustomed to working at the very limit—in real time (and with their customer watching).

The parallels continue. Everyone needs to be able to engage an audience. More and more people expect their opinions to matter, they are better informed and they have more choice than ever before. Whether you are literally selling a product or metaphorically selling a policy or an idea, you need to be skilled at engaging an audience. The same is true for individuals as well as organizations. Our personal success depends, in no small part, on how well we are able to engage the attention and energy of the people around us.

Last but not least there is the matter of stories. In the past few years businesspeople have begun to realize how powerful it can be to communicate using stories. Story is the improviser's product and they succeed or fail by their ability to create engaging narratives and characters. Their take on story is particularly relevant because they do not so much tell stories as cocreate them—just like people in organizations.

This portrait of the modern world is a remarkable likeness for the improvisational stage (and vice versa). With so many close parallels, the question is, how do improvisers do all of this and what can that teach the rest of us?

What we stand to learn here is not only useful but rewarding. I can't think of many people who enjoy themselves at work as much as improvisers. However, having fun is not just a question of quality of life, important as that may be. In my experience, people are more productive when they are having fun (I know I am). There is scientific evidence to back me up: show people a comedy film and their ability to perform a creative task is significantly improved.[5] Thus what's on offer here from improvisers is a virtuous circle—a neat set of new-economy practices that can help you enjoy yourself more, which in turn, can help you do better work.

It should be no surprise that improvisation is very widespread since life itself is a process of creative adaptation. As Charles Darwin himself observed: "In the long history of humankind (and animal kind too) those who learned to collaborate and improvise most effectively have prevailed." That didn't change when we discovered agriculture, split the atom or invented double entry bookkeeping.

Nonetheless, although improvisation is tightly woven into everything we do, it often gets forgotten, ignored or overlooked. There is a widespread belief that improvising is what you do when all else fails. In this light, it becomes synonymous with "winging it" or "b.s." rather than an important skill which can be developed and learned.

I certainly had a blind spot. When we started building the house my enthusiasm for improvisation was already a few years old, but until I became intimately involved, I didn't see much of a connection with construction and assumed that improvisation was of negligible importance to the process. That assumption was logical enough. A house is a concrete thing even if it's made from straw bales. It is tangible and lasting. It costs a lot of money. There is a lot at stake—you don't want the roof to leak, the walls to crumble or the foundations to subside. The construction process is highly regimented:

----

5   Alice M. Isen, "Positive Affect and Decision Making," in *Handbook of Emotions*, ed. Michael Lewis and Jeannette M. Haviland-Jones (New York: Guilford, 2000), 417-435.

detailed plans have to be approved by the appropriate authorities, who have legions of restrictions and obligations you must comply with. It seems only sensible that building ought to be a highly controlled and rigorous process.

Yet I learned from firsthand experience that the physical structure of stone, brick and wood that makes up our house in reality (versus the abstract version that appeared in the plans) is the result of the interplay between two different forces: planning and improvisation. Neither one alone would have been enough. Designing the load-bearing structure required rigorous analysis and meticulous calculations. On the other hand, without the fluid and ingenious process of adaptation to real, sometimes awkward circumstances, the process would have stalled as soon as something unanticipated happened, like the miscalculation of the slope or the basement-producing rain. Interesting opportunities would have been missed. The ability to improvise well was intrinsic to achieving a good result.

There are close parallels with management. There is a widespread assumption that what happens in organizations is determined by rational deliberation, planning and strategy, which neatly echoes the assumptions I held about building. Generally accepted management practice (GAMP), which, by definition, represents the dominant thinking, paints a picture of solid structure and neat coordination. Yet, as Marshall Young, Fellow of Strategic Leadership at Oxford University's Saïd Business School says, "GAMP is a myth." What we experience is a meandering path littered with blind alleys, false starts and misunderstandings. There is a yawning gap between what actually happens and how we describe it. As a senior manager from a telecommunications business said to me once, "I have been watching myself very closely for the past month or so and I have come to the conclusion that your premise is right—management is, in the main, improvisation."

If so, then the education and training that most of us receive is woefully incomplete. The continued emphasis on the intellect, with its academic, written, abstract approach, leaves us ill-prepared to deal with a complex, changing, interconnected world. It doesn't develop or train our whole selves; it doesn't invite us or help us to use our bodies, our emotions or our intuition and by ignoring them, writes them off as irrelevant or inferior. Yet if we are prepared to abandon such a narrow approach there is plenty we can do to train and develop our other faculties, even if that means opening up to the possibility of learning from a group of people we normally regard as a bunch of comedians.

3   📕   Less to Remember

Imagine you are part of an organization where you can depend upon people to listen to each other. Not a place where people just stay quiet while others speak, but where they really listen and then act upon what they hear. Throughout this organization people face difficulty with grace. They invite and accept contributions from all kinds of people, including customers, suppliers and staff from different departments and levels.

Their systems are simple and few. People don't get stuck on their own particular agendas. They learn quickly from each other, which makes turf wars rare. This also allows ideas to flow easily back and forth between different individuals and teams who make simple additions that quickly become better ideas. The ingenious solutions they come up with are often the result of using existing materials, ideas, people or technologies in a novel way or for an unexpected purpose. As a result sophisticated new products are regularly and rapidly developed by building on suggestions from customers. This happens fast enough for those customers to see things changing in response to their needs. As a result they can become enthusiasts who offer yet more ideas, improvements and feedback.

Wouldn't that be a satisfying organization to be involved with, in any capacity? Unlikely though it may sound, this is an accurate description of an improv ensemble at work. A team of people get up on stage, where their every move is highly visible, with the aim of entertaining their audience. They have no opportunity for rehearsal, hardly any props, no costumes, no set and no director or writer to help them out (or pass the buck to). Yet they regularly deliver not just customer satisfaction but customer delight. Theirs must be one of the few businesses that can make this claim with a straight face—people literally applaud and laugh out loud.

Nor is this just a flash in the pan. Improv groups can deliver an original product—week in, week out—over the long term.[1] Like anyone they have good days and bad days, but they know how to create the conditions required to deliver a satisfying performance. Despite the many imponderables, a skilled improv group can guarantee a result—their creativity is sustainable.

This is not just about comedy. People laugh at improvisation not because it is funny, per se, but because they find it joyful. There is an important difference. If you go to an improv show and watch the audience rather than the players, what you will see is that they aren't laughing at jokes. For example, imagine a troupe of performers working together to create a single, coherent story using a dynamic where each improviser can only say one word at a time. It begins like this:

"You—should—always—surf—near—the…"

There is a long pause until finally, the last player says "ocean." You wouldn't expect this to be funny and yet the audience goes berserk. This is a real example. People often laugh loudest at something that seems obvious, even banal, which might seem strange until you realize that it is the *way* the improvisers work together that people really respond to. What you see on the improv stage is people being good-natured with each other, while putting themselves at risk. They support each other in difficult circumstances and do whatever they can to help each other connect ideas and make the thing work. This is so satisfying to watch that you can't help but laugh.

----

1   Brainwaves, the performing group that Gary belongs to (which is distinct from On Your Feet, the consulting company), has existed for over twenty years. London's Comedy Store Players have been playing to packed houses for over twenty-five years.

So to paraphrase basketball coach Phil Jackson: There is more to life than improvisational comedy—but then there's more to improvisational comedy than improvisational comedy.[2] We don't just laugh at things that are comic, we laugh to express joy or delight and we laugh when we see things fit. The laughter that accompanies improvisation is an expression of emotional satisfaction. We love the experience of watching people who are able to make sense and order where there could just as easily be chaos or conflict. The comedy may have some useful side effects—like making it a participative and enjoyable method to play around with—but for our purposes here, it is just a vessel and not the main point.

Improvisers are masters of creating flow. They know how to produce and connect a stream of ideas with impetus and direction, no matter how awkward the circumstances. They create distinctive characters, complex relationships and a plot with a beginning, middle and end, solving seemingly insurmountable problems as they go. Even when that flow is interrupted by new instructions or suggestions, they will keep going, not by ignoring the suggestions but by finding a way to incorporate them. If the flow falters, the story will languish, the audience will lose interest and the improvisers will be left isolated and exposed. So when a glitch or a gap occurs, improvisers will quickly find a way to use it. They don't control things any more than a surfer controls a wave, but they are magnificent surfers.

In the relationships and interactions that matter to us, we all need to be able to create flow. Without it, you are literally and metaphorically going nowhere. Any conversation, process or relationship needs flow if it is to yield a satisfying result, whether you are coming up with new ideas, negotiating a price, giving feedback on an experience or trying to resolve a misunderstanding. Psychologist Míhaly Csíkszentmihályi goes further—he suggests that being in a state of "flow" is closely related to happiness or optimal experience.

- -

2   In *Sacred Hoops*, a book about his time with the Chicago Bulls, Jackson said, "There is more to life than basketball, but then there's more to basketball than basketball."

If you aren't able to generate any flow it is very hard to influence what happens to you. An untethered boat, with no forward speed through the water, is at the mercy of wind and tide. It will just drift, helplessly. If you want to be able to steer a boat, you need water to be flowing past the hull and the rudder. In nautical terminology the minimum speed needed to be able to steer is known as "steerage way." Something similar occurs to us in the sea of human interactions. Unless we are able to generate some kind of forward momentum, we will be carried along by the winds and currents of peer pressure, market forces or genetic inheritance, unable to influence our own fate.

This raises the question "*How* do improvisers generate flow?" The most familiar method—break a problem into its component parts and analyze what to do—won't work. However quickly you think, there isn't time to process all the possible responses and work out what the best one would be. Being smart or clever in the conventional sense is not enough. In fact, on the improv stage, trying to be clever often does more harm than good (an idea we will explore more thoroughly later on). Improvisers need a more efficient method than trying to cram thousands of possible scenarios into their brains.

A similar difficulty bedeviled attempts by engineers to make robots walk. Robots with large centralized "brains" can become paralyzed when trying to process everything around them. As a result, they would spend their time "not walking, but worrying about getting the layout of the yard right."[3] Robot engineers (and their robots) took a great step forward when, instead of trying to give their machines a central processor clever enough to analyze everything, they provided each leg with a little processing power of its own and some simple rules to follow (rather like the reflexes in our own bodies).

Improvisers have arrived at a similar solution. As Gary explained on that pivotal day in the Three Lions Bakery, what they have is a practice made up of a small set of simple rules (or individual "practices") that can be applied in any situation. These rules, coupled with the high degree of autonomy they allow each other, are what enable

----

3   Kevin Kelly, *Out of Control: The New Biology of Machines, Social Systems & the Economic World*. (Reading, MA: Perseus Press, 1995), 35.

improvisers to coordinate a highly complex set of actions beautifully. Their method is simple enough to be remembered easily, flexible enough to be applied universally and allows them to generate endless variety and novelty.

Improvisation is thus a compelling demonstration that you don't need complicated systems to produce complex results. This is not intuitively obvious. Most people assume that a rich and complicated series of ideas or events must be the result of an intricate and complicated process. The science of complexity suggests otherwise. Complexity theory demonstrates, for example, that the beautiful and extraordinarily complex movement of a flock of birds can be emulated realistically on a computer using a small number of simple rules, like "keep someone on your left" or "if you get more than a certain distance away from the next bird, move closer." Birds instinctively follow the particular rules that create the complex patterns we see in the sky, presumably through some kind of genetic inheritance. The computer animators that seek to emulate them try different combinations of rules and program in the ones that work best.

The improvisers' rules are also the result of systematic study. Actors and directors have devoted considerable time and energy to exploring what works. Indeed, in some respects the theater resembles a laboratory. You have an idea, try it out, get feedback, learn something as a result, incorporate that learning into what you know and try something else (or try the same thing again to see if you can come up with a general pattern). The results may not be scientific but they are empirical—they have been verified through considerable observation and experience.

Many of the most acute observations have been made by director Keith Johnstone. In the 1960s Johnstone worked at the Royal Court Theater in London and his foray into improvisation began when he was asked to write a script in a ridiculously short period of time. He faced the artistic equivalent of the squeeze that many businesspeople face today so he set about discovering easier, quicker ways to work. The debt to Johnstone is enormous because the clarity and simplicity of his ideas make it easy to apply them beyond the theater. This legacy gives improvisation some substance—substance that Marshall Young of Oxford University refers to as "intellectual keel."

That keel is made up of a set of practices. A practice is, by definition, something you do. Expressing these basic ideas as a set of practices (rather than principles) is deliberate. It forces you to recognize that it isn't enough to think about them, talk about them or organize them in a grid on a PowerPoint slide. You have to act.

Practice is not only something you do, but something you keep doing. If you want to be really good at something you are never done with practice. The best footballers in the world still practice their passing. The best musicians still play scales. Tiger Woods, they say, still practices three-foot putts for two hours a day (perhaps in homage to fellow golfer Gary Player's maxim: "The more I practice, the luckier I get."). There are some skills that you cannot be too good at. The practices of improvisation are that fundamental. They are the passing or putting of human interaction.

Consider listening, for example. If you're an improviser you always have to practice listening. Attending closely to what is said is vital because it is your primary source of information. You don't need to discuss how important listening is. You don't do it once and stop. You listen to your colleagues, to the audience, to any other sounds in the theater (a bang or a squeak might be useful in your story). From moment to moment, from one show to the next, an improviser has to practice listening constantly.

The simplicity of this can be disarming. People accustomed to engaging primarily with the intellect can find themselves hankering after some more elaborate theory instead of an uncomplicated, repeated practice. Rather like the flock of birds, it can be hard to believe that something more complex isn't required and it is easy to get caught up in a clever argument over words and definitions. But while highfalutin debate might sound grand, from the improviser's point of view, all it does is cause delay. It puts off the moment when you move into action or commit to a choice.

I am reminded of a story about a famous Italian pasta chef who was being interviewed on television. When asked about the secret of his pasta he simply held up his stubby-fingered hands and waved them in the direction of the camera, indicating that the answer lay in the hand itself, not in an abstract idea or recipe. The gesture said more powerfully than any words that there wasn't any point in *talking* about pasta; it was a question of touch, manipulation and feel. The secret, if there was a secret, was the subtle craft derived from practice and experience.

Anything worth learning requires practice. Learning to speak a language, play the guitar, make bread, be a parent, weight a pass, interpret a balance sheet—these things all require practice. The reverse is also true. There are few things worth doing that won't be improved through practice. Snakes and Ladders doesn't take much practice, but then it's hardly up there with chess, is it?

This emphasis on practice means that discipline is more important to improvisation than unfettered freedom or sheer creative brilliance. This is true in two ways. On the one hand it requires discipline to practice: you have to be determined and committed. On the other hand, the set of practices also constitutes an "activity or experience that provides mental or physical training," so they are a "discipline" in this sense as well.

Most people don't associate discipline with improvisation or creativity in general, yet it is fundamental. This was brought home to me by Chris Riley, former Chief Strategic Officer of advertising agency Wieden+Kennedy. He once engaged my colleagues Gary Hirsch and Brad Robertson to run a workshop for a client of his at very short notice.

Having had so little time to prepare, Gary and Brad had to shape the workshop as they went along. Throughout the day they were constantly making and revising decisions about what to do. Even so, each section of the day ended bang on time. In Chris's closing remarks he asked the group what they thought was the most important quality that Gary and Brad had displayed in delivering the workshop. People said things like "energy," "imagination" and "creativity," as most people would. Chris then gave his own view. "Discipline," he said.

Thus the enviable ability that improvisers display—to be able to create flow regardless of the circumstances—is the result of practice and discipline. One performer claimed he could capture the whole method in only three words: "Just say yes." My own summary requires rather more words. Six to be precise. Those six words are: let go, notice more, use everything.

These three couplets mark out the territory within which the specific practices lie and we can represent this visually in a simple diagram, like this:

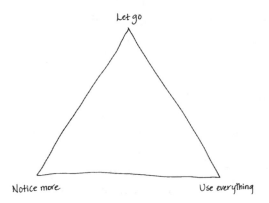

However, since each of these phrases is also an action, you could start practicing now, without even getting into specifics. In the very next conversation you have, you could let go of trying to control the outcome, devote more attention to what other people say or make an effort to use anything that happens to feed the flow of the conversation—including interruptions, disagreements or misunderstandings that you might normally ignore. A small shift perhaps, but one that, if taken to heart, can create a big difference.

The advantage of this simple practice is that you have less to remember. It relieves the pressure of keeping up with the explosion of new ideas that abound in the management literature (or the self-help books). You can exchange the restless search for a quick fix for the quiet patience of a practice. Whatever happens, you can go back to the same simple, familiar ideas and apply them again. Over time you deepen and internalize your understanding, so that you can bring these ideas to bear quickly and easily, without even thinking about them consciously.

However, if that's all there is to it, this would be a pamphlet rather than a book. Simple though these ideas may be, they are not without their subtleties. There is also a danger of oversimplifying. For example, without further qualification the idea of "letting go" might sound reckless. Making sense of it requires more explanation—of what it pays to let go of.

Therefore the aim of the next six chapters is to flesh out the basic ideas. Each one will identify and examine a particular element of the improvisational practice and explain how it connects to the others. Important terms will be defined. None of these are very technical, but improvisers do use familiar words in particular ways that it is helpful to understand. We will look at how these practices play out in the "laboratory" of the stage and, through stories and examples, connect them to organizational and personal issues exploring how you might take advantage of them.

However, before plunging into the particulars I want to make three suggestions to help you get more out of what follows. They are:

Start where you like.

Play around with what's here.

Bring your own stuff to play with.

Let's take each of these in turn.

Start where you like

The order of the next six chapters has a certain logic, but that doesn't mean you have to read them (or apply them) in that order. You can start anywhere—any piece of practice is as good a beginning as any other. This allows you to follow your interest (or your instinct) and start working with any idea that attracts you for whatever reason.

This is possible because these practices are all connected. There is no single linear sequence of practices. They are more like a hologram, where you can elicit the whole from any individual piece. Can anyone really say where "listening" ends and "being present" begins? I know I can't. You can imagine the body of practice as a single house with various doors. Enter through whichever one you like.

Play around with what's here

I would encourage you not to show too much respect or deference. You might re-name a practice if it makes more sense to you that way. You might add things of your own, ignore bits that don't interest you or apply them to something I don't even mention.

I want to stress this because once I start to label the practices, organize them and write about them at length, it is easy to slip into thinking that this is the way things are. It isn't. It is just how I describe them. Words in print tend to give the illusion of preci-sion and permanence, but in the grand scheme of things everything is temporary. It is all work in progress.

This is not an attempt to be modest. Playfulness is at the very heart of this work and if you take what I say too seriously, you are less likely to play around with it and ar-rive at something new. That would be a shame. Ever since the serendipitous collision in the Three Lions Bakery we have seen how different people make different connec-tions to great effect. I remember one occasion, shortly after On Your Feet started, when, at the end of an idea-generation workshop, a beautiful young woman asked, "Do you do relationship counseling?" Neither Gary nor I knew what to say or where to look, so she continued: "I have the feeling that if I had known some of this stuff awhile back, I wouldn't be divorced." Her comment got us thinking about how to apply improv practices to personal relationships, which at the time was something we had not really considered.

Bring your own stuff

The third thing to be aware of is that you will need to put the practices to work on your own stuff. In isolation these practices won't tell you what to do. They cannot tell you what you want. They don't spell out specific steps for dealing with confused customers, inventing new widgets or calming fractious children. There aren't differ-ent versions for managers, software engineers or parents. They offer general rules and leave you free to find your particular solutions, specific to the time and place you find yourself in. I can illustrate with examples or stories, but in the end, you have to work out what is important to you and then plug these practices in. You have to supply your own situations, relationships, difficulties, interests and desires.

You can think of the practices as scaffolding. In construction, scaffolding is fundamental. It provides a strong and flexible structure. Building would be hard without it. Nonetheless it doesn't tell you what to build. The same applies here. These practices won't provide you with a prescription, formula or specific answer.

I mention this because although it seems obvious that the search for definitive answers is naïve, our language and behavior still betrays a hunger for them. I often catch myself falling into this trap. For example, I remember one occasion when I was visiting friends in La Guardia, in the heart of Spain's most important winemaking region, La Rioja. I was in a vineyard with Juan Carlos López de la Calle, one of Spain's foremost winemakers and listened, rapt, as he demonstrated how to prune the ancient vines.[4] Juan Carlos explained how these particular vines, almost a hundred years old with a tap root drilling dozens of meters into the earth, produced very few, but very fine grapes, so it was important to take special care when pruning. I asked if the idea was for the grapes to receive the sun or the shade. Juan Carlos straightened up, pruning shears in hand. "Ah," he said, leaving a lengthy pause. "Grapes are like people. They want sun when it's cool and shade when it's hot."

In my eagerness I had automatically posed the question in a way that presupposed there was a single answer that he, the authority, could provide which would enable me to do the "right" thing. We find great relief in external sources of authority, be they books, bosses, experts or belief systems. When we are told what to do it absolves us of responsibility, makes life easier and, on occasion, allows us to blame someone else.

The practices in this book won't do that for you and I know from experience that this can frustrate people. Any honest answer to the question, "What should I do when

- - - - - - - - - - - - - - - - - - -

4   Artadi's Viña El Pison 2004 (one of López de la Calle's wines) was awarded a maximum one hundred points by wine authority Robert Parker.

I get back to the office on Monday morning?" will invariably begin, "It depends…"
What it depends on is context and only you can supply the details of your own context.
Where is the sun? Has it rained? Do you want more grapes or better grapes?

You might wonder why I am being so scrupulous. Why not give you a series of steps,
clearly spelled out and neatly numbered? While being definitive obviously sells (and has
done for a long time if the Ten Commandments are anything to go by), it is not what I
am interested in doing. Life is messy and often the more life there is, the messier it gets
(think of a jungle or a house full of children).

One way to deal with the mess is to simplify things, much as I did with the triangu-
lar diagram above. We draw maps. We categorize, divide and write lists of neatly numbered principles. Often that's extremely useful, but as Alfred Korzybski, founder of
General Semantic Theory, famously pointed out, "The map is not the territory." When
economists start with the assumption that human beings always act rationally, it's not
surprising they end up with some odd results. It might make things simpler to ignore the
fact that we are emotional, but it leaves out much of what matters most.

I don't want to do that. What I am interested in is the messy, changing, interconnected and unpredictable reality we face every day and in what we can do with that.
What the practices of improvisational theater promise is a way to work with reality, not
a way to tidy it up. An improviser wouldn't call it a mess anyway. They would call it an
offer.

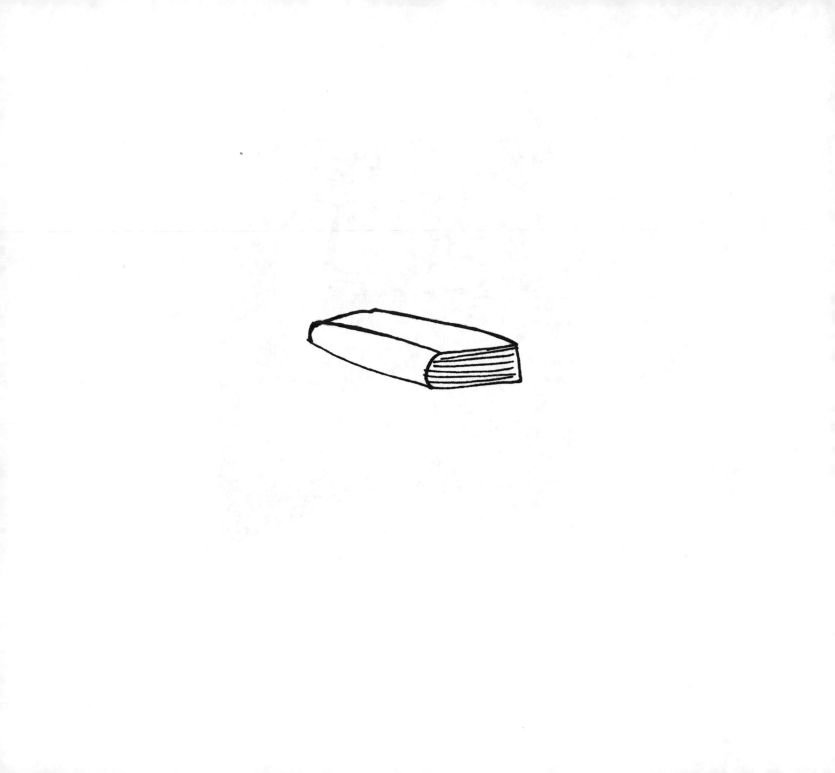

PART 2

Let Go, Notice More, Use Everything

A Fundamental Grammar of Relationships and Communication

4   Free Stuff Everywhere

Two days after its launch, the command module of the Apollo 13 space mission suffered a sudden explosion. No one knew what had happened but one thing was clear—the crew were quickly running out of oxygen. The engineers back in Houston had to find some way to remove the carbon dioxide from the air the crew were breathing, using only what the astronauts had on board, or the consequences would be dire. All they had was an assorted collection of spacesuits, hoses, cables and tape. None of the pieces were designed for the task but there was nothing else to work with.

The engineers scrutinized what they had very closely and focused on the intrinsic qualities of the objects and materials they had regardless of their normal use. Was it sticky, or bendy, did it react with carbon dioxide, was it waterproof, etc.? They had to let go of existing labels and be prepared to see new possibilities in anything. Remarkably, they managed to do it and the crew were able to breathe easily again.[1]

In the language of improvisation, the NASA engineers saw everything as an offer. Like the NASA team, improvisers on stage are in a tight spot. They too have to make do with what they have; they can't send out for spare parts (or ideas) and they can't afford to wait. So improvisers take this simple idea of regarding anything and everything as an offer to heart and make it a fundamental piece of practice.

- - - - - - - - - - - - - - - - - -

1   In the film version of the story they literally tear up the plan to achieve this. Ground control asks, "Have you got a copy of the flight plan?" When the crew say they do, they are told, "Then rip the cover off." "With pleasure," replies astronaut Jack Swigert (played by Kevin Bacon).

To an improviser an offer is anything and everything you can take and use to further the story. On stage the most obvious offers are the things other actors say but offers can be physical as well as verbal. If you proffer your hand I can take that as an offer, shake it and say, "It's a deal then," "Good luck, Corporal Standish" or anything else that could conceivably go with a handshake. There are lots of different ways that any particular offer could be taken and used. Offers also come from the audience (for example, the suggestion that launches a scene) or from the space (a noise or a light). The definition of an offer is deliberately very broad and includes mistakes, accidents, errors and random events, as well as those offers consciously made by colleagues. This is deliberate. By being so inclusive the practice encourages improvisers to develop a relentless focus on using anything and everything, come what may.

Seeing a world full of offers feels very different from seeing a world full of problems. Problems are something you want to get rid of, whereas an offer is something you can take and use. When we staked out the foundations for our house, the excessive slope on the land was something we could have seen as a problem. If so, we would have sought to eliminate it rather than use it. This would have been possible, but it would have meant the time, expense and trouble of calling in a bulldozer. Moreover, had we done so, we would have missed the opportunity of hiding the garage away so we would have lost out twice.

Seeing everything as an offer is a simple idea which is quickly grasped and endlessly useful. This may seem like a small point but it creates a basic shift in how you interpret things and gives you something to do other than dwelling on the problem. This not only leads to different actions, it changes how you feel. If you see the rain that drives the builders into the basement as an offer, you stop feeling frustrated about what isn't happening. The builders feel differently, too. They are encouraged to volunteer more ideas, which makes their work more productive and enjoyable. Everyone feels the benefit.

Let's see if we can create an experience of how this shift can feel right now. Imagine I ask you to give me an original title for a story. Not an existing one like *Alice in Wonderland* or *The Godfather*, but a new title for a story that hasn't been told before.

Have you got one yet?

How easy did you find that? Does a title just pop into your mind or do you struggle, go blank and start to feel uneasy or tense? For most people, it's the latter, especially if I were asking you to say your title out loud in front of a group. There are two good reasons why. The first is the desire to do well. Normally we want to have "good" ideas so that we look "good." Unfortunately this delivers us into the hands of a scathing internal censor with a very particular idea of what "good" means (whether it's ingenious or grand or funny or moving). This gives you fewer ideas to choose from and starts to paralyze you with all kinds of premature judgments (an idea we will visit in more detail in Chapter 8). The result is you find it hard to respond quickly and fluently.

Second, you have no method for coming up with an original title. You are just trying to pull it out of thin air, so unsurprisingly, you flounder. The common image of creativity as a mysterious process that only a gifted few possess compounds this error. Quite often people will become completely locked up in a matter of seconds as the two difficulties combine in a powerful snap judgment along the lines of "I am useless at this kind of thing."

Let's try again and this time I will give you some direction based on the practice of seeing everything as an offer. As before, we are looking for an original title for a story. This time, before you do anything else, look around you and just start to reel off (or note) what you see, particularly anything you hadn't noticed before. Don't limit yourself to the names of objects—include textures, associations, anything. Open up to your other senses too, what do you hear, touch, feel, taste, smell? Include your inner sensations, too. It only takes a few seconds and allowing yourself to slow down, just a tiny bit, will enable you to respond all the faster. I am going to join in and do the same thing as I write. Here we go…

Couch, leaf, black, cement, house, cloudless, purple, soft, corduroy, square, handle, smooth, patchy, musical, grouchy, raffia, Japanese, roller skates, trunk, beauty.

There are some offers. As yet I don't know where these will lead me but I know they are offers. Now that they have been made visible dozens of potential titles are available, too, just by combining them. For example:

"The Japanese Roller Skates" or

"Patchy Black" or

"The Grouchy House" or

"Raffia and Cement" or

"Cloudless Beauty" or

"Couched in Purple." I could easily go on, but you get the point.

If you have seen *The Usual Suspects* this exercise might seem familiar. In that film, the protagonist (Roger "Verbal" Kint, a.k.a. Keyser Söze), played by Kevin Spacey, is interrogated. He tells a story so extraordinary and complex that his interrogators are convinced he couldn't possibly have made it up. They conclude he is innocent and let him go. As they are preparing to do so, a panned shot around the room shows us all the offers he was using to make up this incredibly intricate story. Photographs, business cards, posters and all the little details in the room where he was being questioned were the offers he used to spin a yarn to get himself out of trouble. It seemed impossible he could have invented all this and in one sense, he didn't. He just used the offers that were around him.

This is what seeing everything as an offer can do for you. As one workshop participant said, "You mean, there's free stuff everywhere." This is a nice way to put it. Looking for offers moves you into a mental space where everything has potential. The neat thing is that this attitude is self-supporting; if you look for offers you will find them. Whatever you are doing, whatever you need, thinking of everything around you as an offer will provide you with more material to work with.

This view of the world as an abundant place full of offers constitutes a significant shift because we are used to feeling that there isn't enough to go around. The idea of scarcity is etched deep in our minds, perhaps because for a large chunk of human history most things (food, for example) have been in short supply. Certainly the idea of scarcity has played a very important role in how we think about business and economics.

Something scarce is more valuable. It was the scarcity of spices that drove European exploration from the fifteenth century on. A shipload of pepper, nutmeg or mace landing in seventeenth-century London would have been worth a fortune.

But ideas aren't like spices. Ideas feed off each other; they combine and spark to create yet more ideas, so you don't want them to be scarce; you want them to be everywhere. As two-time Nobel Prize winner Linus Pauling said, "If you want to have good ideas, you have to have many ideas."[2] Thus if you are in a business where ideas count, which these days pretty much everyone is, it is better to live in a world of abundance, not one of scarcity. One sure way to do that is to regard everything as an offer.

To take full advantage of this practice it is important to understand that, just like on stage, the offers we have to work with aren't only the things that are explicitly given to us by colleagues, customers or clients. The improviser's definition of offers includes accidents, mistakes, unforeseen consequences and the things we normally ignore. A chance comment, some leftover beetroot, an unexpected phone call, the back of a paycheck, these are all offers, too. For example, someone at Orange (a telecommunications company) once had the presence of mind to see the back of the paycheck as an offer, so they printed something on it. "Thanks" to be precise. This demonstrated a thoughtfulness that people really appreciated. This was a small thing and very cheap to do, but given how important morale is (and how poorly most large companies fare on staff-satisfaction surveys), it wasn't trivial. If you are constantly on the lookout for offers, ideas like this crop up all over the place.

Failures can also be offers. The history of science is full of "accidental" discoveries (such as the famous story of Alexander Fleming and penicillin). The same is true in the arts. I once heard the Uruguayan singer-songwriter Jorge Drexler explain why he sang "Al otro lado del río," his Oscar-winning song from the film *The Motorcycle Diaries*, unaccompanied. In a previous concert the sound system had completely failed on him just as he was about to play the song, so he had no choice but to sing it a cappella. He

----

2   Francis Crick, as quoted in the lecture "The Impact of Linus Pauling on Molecular Biology" (1995).

liked it so much that a year or so later he was still performing it that way. The story did nothing but enhance the beauty of the song.

When something awkward occurs you can productively reframe it as an offer. Recently on the way to a workshop, Gary managed to lose his glasses. Without them the only way he could see anything was to screw up his face into what looked like an angry scowl—hardly the ideal expression with which to greet nervous participants. The thought "there must be an offer here somewhere" helped Gary stayed calm while he decided what to do. He explained what had happened and invited people to come really close, much closer than they normally would, so that he could see them better, which created a much more intimate atmosphere and a very different quality of energy in the room. And all because Gary lost his glasses.

Unpredicted difficulties, small or large, can be seen as offers. Imagine you are organizing an expedition to climb Everest and an unexpected storm hits. The team of climbers on the mountain can't even get out of their tents, let alone make a summit attempt. If you were to see this as an offer you might radio the climbers from base camp and instruct them to eat and sleep as much as possible, while you buy up supplies of food and oxygen from the teams who are retreating off the mountain because their plans didn't envisage a storm. That way, when the weather clears, you are in a great position to make a summit attempt. This was exactly what one of the teams did during the otherwise disastrous spring of 1996 and they succeeded in safely reaching the summit.[3]

Treating the awkward, difficult or unexpected as an offer means there is always something productive you can do. The practice can be woven into the tiniest of everyday occurrences. If a budget gets cut it's a chance to do something in a different way or to not do it at all (thereby giving you more time for other things). If your train breaks down it's a chance to make all those calls you have been meaning to make. If your train breaks down in a tunnel (where there is no coverage) it could be an offer to do

----

3   As ever, disaster generates interest. Much has been written about the events of that spring including filmmaker Matt Dickinson's book *The Death Zone* and Jon Krakauer's controversial account, *Into Thin Air*.

the opposite and take those few minutes to be still and quiet, as a conscious moment of meditation in a busy or stressful day and so on.

Anything can be used to further flow in one way or another. Just like Keyser Söze in *The Usual Suspects*, we live in a rich soup of offers, waiting to be discovered (whereas the improviser has only a spare black stage). Not only that, we have the luxury of time. We don't always have to respond in the moment. Often we can afford to take a few minutes, hours or days to look around for offers that we haven't previously seen.

Nonetheless it is important to understand that seeing everything as an offer is not about looking on the bright side. In Monty Python's *Life of Brian* people break into song as they are being crucified, happily intoning, "Always look on the bright side of life." This is not what I mean by seeing everything as an offer. Looking on the bright side is a kind of judgment and, as we will explore in Chapter 8, part of the improviser's practice is to stay out of judgment (i.e., to try and avoid premature decisions about what is good or bad).

Seeing everything as an offer does not require you to see the loss of your job, your dog or your grandfather's antique wristwatch as a good thing—it just asks you to look at the reality you face, ugly or otherwise, and ask yourself the question "What is here that I can use?" An offer is not nice or nasty, prickly or cuddly; someone falling asleep in your presentation, a pay raise or a broken leg are all offers in equal measure. The only question the practice leads to is "What do I want to do with this?"

This is not to say there is no place for positive thinking. Seeing good in things is useful when it corrects a tendency always to see the negative (a tendency to which many of us are prone) but this context is easily forgotten. Some proponents of positive thinking suggest that thinking positively is all that matters and that if it isn't working, it's because we aren't thinking positively enough. Even if this were true, it would require the constitution of a saint. When bad things happen, we feel bad. Trying to see them as good feels fake and creates conflict within us. Much better to concentrate on how you can constructively use whatever you have been given.

Improvisers sometimes express this practice as "use what you have." I find this change of emphasis can be useful when I am stymied. If the practice is "use what you have," then "what do I have?" is an obvious question you can attack immediately, which gives you a simple, easy way to get going.

For example, I was once asked to run a session for three thousand people. Since I am more accustomed to thirty than three thousand, I tried to adapt exercises designed for a few dozen, which really didn't work. I kept seeing the large numbers as a problem because it meant I couldn't do what I normally do. Yet when I started by asking myself "If what I have is three thousand people, how can I use them?," all kinds of inventive ideas started to occur—from the Mexican snake (a variation on the Mexican wave) to mob navigation (you had to be there).

Instead of trying to come up with something in a vacuum, this practice encourages you to go and look. Much like the exercise of searching for a story title, it reminds you to look outwards for inspiration. What have you got in the archives, who have you got on the team, what is there in the fridge? Do you have a little bacon, someone who was brought up in China or your predecessor's assessment of the situation you face? If you don't know how to get going, just ask yourself what you have and how you can use that. Film director Robert Rodriguez describes how he made his seven-thousand-dollar, career-launching movie *El Mariachi* by using what he had: "How do you make a cheap movie? Look around you and take stock in what you have. If your father owns a liquor store, make a movie about a liquor store. You have a dog, make a movie about your dog. Your Mom works in a nursing home, make a movie about a nursing home. When I did *El Mariachi* I had a turtle, a guitar case and a small town in Mexico. So I decided to make a movie around that."[4] Using what you have is beautifully economical. Look around you. What have you got? What is your turtle, guitar case, dog or nursing home?

- - - - - - - - - - - - - - - - - -

4   See the *Robert Rodriguez Ten Minute Film School*, a wonderful ten-minute documentary which not only explains but demonstrates what he learned making *El Mariachi*.

They say there are only two things you can be certain of—death and taxes.[5] I venture to suggest that this practice provides another one. Namely, that whatever happens, you can always find an offer to use somehow. When panic sets in this thought can keep you centered. It gives the mind somewhere to go other than into a spin. All you have to do is ask "What can I do with this?" and you immediately have something constructive to do. Moreover, the practice is self-fulfilling. If you relentlessly adopt the attitude that there is an offer in any situation, then there will be. This is indeed a creative act.

Not that offers are always pretty, or easy to see. I once got caught by a wildcat strike at London's Heathrow airport on my way to a course in California. While my bag made it to San Francisco, I was stuck in one of the ugliest, most over-crowded airports in the world with thousands of angry and frustrated people. The little voice in my head reminding me that "there must be an offer here somewhere" quickly started to become irritating. But through gritted teeth, it forced me to reflect and eventually I realized that the offer here might be for somebody else, so I called a friend in California and offered him my place on the course. This made me feel a whole lot better. As it turned out, he had a fabulous time and our relationship became stronger, creating a stream of new offers for me. But there was also an immediate, if somewhat subtle offer, available to me as well. My final destination had been a Zen retreat and what could be more Zen than an opportunity to work on staying calm amid such mayhem?

In any given situation there is more than one offer. Since the offer is in how you look at a thing, not in the thing itself, you can always push further and find another offer or offers, which helps create the feeling of abundance. That feeling makes it much easier to be confident, with all the attendant virtues that brings. For example, when I was a junior executive in an advertising agency, I was surprised to find that the most experienced copywriters and art directors were the most open and the least combative. One

- - - - - - - - - - - - - - - - - -

5 The market for cryonics—deep-freezing human remains so that when technology progresses, you can be brought back to life—suggests that some people question the certainty of death. Nonetheless if such technology were to become possible, it would no doubt be heavily taxed, so one certainty remains.

of them explained to me why that was: "When you've been in this business as long as I have, you know there's plenty more where that came from." The confidence that he would always be able to come up with another idea was what made him easy to work with. Realizing that everything is an offer can be a shortcut to that place of confidence. If one idea, suggestion or possibility gets knocked down, you know there is always another one waiting in the wings, that, who knows, might even flip the existing idea in a way that will salvage it or make it better.

Over time this leaves its mark. When you have found an offer in a strike, an aggressive comment (like "this is a stupid") or a personal weakness (e.g., being bad at remembering names) then it starts to add up. I may not know what is going to happen in a workshop but I do know that in the past people walking out, the language barrier, physical injuries, an unwillingness to participate, a fire alarm and technical breakdowns have all been offers I have found a way to use, which creates a certain feeling of trust both in yourself and in an open-ended, unfolding process. It helps you become more comfortable being uncomfortable.

It can also save you effort. For example, imagine you come home from work exhausted and there, teeming with energy, is a toddler, eager to play. You feel you have no energy left to be inventive, but how much do you really need? Adults often feel that they have to organize and structure everything but you don't have to invent a game from scratch. Why not just work with the offers the child gives you and let them do most of the work? The day I discovered this I played with my eldest son (who was then about two) for over half an hour with hardly any effort on my part. The offer he gave me was a ball, so I threw it. He brought it back, so I threw it somewhere else. From the expression on his face, I got the impression that he thought I was trying to fool him about where the throw was going, so I let that become the game, which evolved bit by bit into quite a complex one. He was very happy rushing around and I very happily sat still. All I did was respond to the offers he gave me. I did not need to initiate, plan or organize anything. Simply by using the offers you are given, you can let an idea or a game or a story emerge instead of trying hard to consciously invent it. There is sometimes less work to be done than we imagine.

Embedding this practice into your behavior can also help you avoid polarization and conflict. In business, conversation is often adversarial. Imagine you are discussing your workspace and someone says, "We are thinking of changing the office layout to an open plan." People quickly take positions—for or against—perhaps on the basis of an extraneous factor like who is proposing the idea. A debate ensues between two contrasting or opposing points of view. Such an approach, which is based on advocacy, has its uses—for example, in parliament and the courts—but for any creative process there are at least three problems with adversarial conversations.

First, only two possibilities are ever put on the table: yours and mine. In a conversation of this kind what I want is my idea to "win." With this kind of focus, there is little chance that a new, better, transforming idea will occur. Second, if two points of view meet in debate, one has to lose. So this kind of discourse inevitably produces winners and losers, which in turn creates division, even resentment or conflict—a high cost. Third, adversarial conversations are often decided on the basis of power: the most powerful people, not the best ideas, win. This cements the existing hierarchy, prevents a flow of new ideas and energy and reinforces the status quo.

If you see the original comment as an offer you will have a different kind of conversation, one that is additive not adversarial. First and foremost, you would ask yourself how you can use this idea. You would seek to be with it, to understand it, to explore it, develop it, extend it or add to it and the other ideas it leads to. You might find yourself asking a whole series of powerful questions like:

"What will an open-plan layout bring us?"

"Open plan is a big shift. What other changes would we need to make along with that?"

"Do you think there would be more or less real openness if we could all see each other?"

"What if we made the meeting rooms open plan, too, so that meetings could be overheard?"

"If the plan of the office is open, what else do we want to be open?"

The focus of the conversation would be "What can we make with the idea of an open plan?" instead of "Do we like an open plan or not?" Thus seeing things as offers leads to the kind of conversation which automatically generates new actions, ideas and energy. And think of the effect that this behavior has on people around you. Who would you rather work with, talk to or go on a journey with? Someone who is constantly judging and arguing or someone who consistently looks for ways to use whatever is happening?

If one part of this practice is seeing offers, the other is making them. Making offers is a basic component of creating relationships. Think of someone you like to work with (or be around). Do they make you a decent number of offers in the form of explicit questions, suggestions or ideas? Do a good number of these offers invite you to add something? Then try the opposite. Think of someone you find hard to work with (or hard to be around). Do you feel you always have to initiate everything, that they don't give you much to go on? Are they opaque and hard to read? I used to experience this sorely as a teenager when the girls I liked failed to return my calls. Nowadays it might be a potential client that doesn't return calls. Either way, if you don't get any offers back, it is a good sign that the relationship is going nowhere.

Of course, if everything can be seen as an offer, then you are making offers (of some kind or other), whether or not you mean to, but it makes a difference if you consciously pay attention to the kind of offers you give. I could argue that the silent brooding accompanying my black moods is an offer of sorts, but as an old officemate once said to me, "It's hard to know what to do with that." Moreover you can't *make* other people see things as offers. If you want to play catch, you would do well to throw me the ball.

Actively making offers has a number of benefits. At the most basic level it is an injection of energy. To use a plumbing metaphor, people who make lots of offers are "radiators," constantly contributing their energy. By contrast, people who don't make many offers are "drains," sapping what energy there is. If you have more radiators than drains in your team, you will get things done. If you have more drains than radiators, you end up with a vortex of negativity and ideas tend to disappear down the plughole.

Beyond the energy they contribute, making offers is a way to take a share of the responsibility and lighten the load on others. Imagine you and I are beginning to build a relationship (we might be collaborating professionally) and you come to visit me in Madrid. It will help me and our nascent relationship if you give me some explicit offers about what you would like to see and do. If you say, "I don't mind," that makes things much harder for me. Though it might seem accommodating, you aren't taking any responsibility at all. Much easier for me if you say, "I want to try sherry straight from the cask" or "Don't take me anywhere near a bullfight."

For my part, I can be helpful by making clear offers, too, offers that explain what I am interested in and qualified to show you, rather than leaving it all up to you. For example, I might suggest taking you to bars rather than showing you the Prado since my experience of tapas outweighs my knowledge of art by some distance. However, note that making the offers is what helps, not being attached to them—otherwise I will end up in the Café Gijón brooding over the olives as I await your return from the delights of Hieronymus Bosch, which won't do much for our relationship.

Making offers is different from agreeing. I can madden my wife by saying yes to everything and making no new offers back again. This may seem cooperative (after all I am not saying no), but in reality, I am making her do all the work. If you accede to every suggestion while making none of your own, you aren't really being very helpful. The practice of making offers obliges you to take a share of the responsibility.

My wife once observed that customer service in Spain is delivered by customers. The people who answer the phone often seem to have a script and the only things that are on it are "we'll make a note of it," "you need to speak to someone else" and "we'll get back to you." You, the customer, find yourself doing all the work because they rarely make any other offers. It need not be like this. For example, years ago, when the computer virus Melissa ran amok, I urgently needed to upgrade my antivirus program. I had bought my software in the U.S., I lived in Spain, I was talking to a U.K. help line and

I hadn't registered the product. Nonetheless, despite the fact that I wasn't on his database and couldn't produce any proof of purchase, the agent quickly made the offer of sending me a new CD. Melissa was thus vanquished and my satisfaction with MacAfee soared.

In this case, the agent I spoke to was able to make an appropriate offer (without needing approval from anyone else) and he did so within seconds, which did something more than solve my immediate problem. Some time after Melissa, I called MacAfee to buy an upgrade. I was told that the registration number (from the free CD) would give me this for nothing, but I volunteered to pay because I was still so pleased about my Melissa experience. At the time MacAfee was said to be one of the most profitable companies in the world and that didn't seem like coincidence to me.

Making offers also enables you to impart direction. In the absence of a script, it is the offers the improvisers make that influence how a story unfolds. You can direct or shape an interaction through the offers you make even though you can't control it. The same is true in an organization—you don't have to be able to control what is going on in order to be able to influence it through the offers you make. This doesn't mean you have to look for the right or best offer. Improvisers understand that there are always lots of offers you could make and that it doesn't help to agonize over your choice. Find something that gets you going in a direction that feels helpful or interesting, even if you don't know quite how or why and be prepared to go with it. Staying open like this allows other people to develop it, by adding their own offers, in ways you might not have anticipated. Over time, practicing this will develop your instinct or feel for what works.

It doesn't matter if the offer you make seems obvious. Indeed, performers say that if they feel a scene is getting stuck, they will try and make a new but obvious offer. If it is dark, start a scene in a cave. The audience will think this is fabulously clever, yet the improviser is simply using the obvious. Sometimes this is because what is obvious to you often isn't obvious to anyone else, but things which obviously fit are also immensely pleasing in themselves. You don't have to be constantly surprising your audience in order to delight them. In fact, too many surprises and they get disoriented.

Making obvious and explicit offers is necessary in a creative process. Anything new is really just a new combination of existing elements. But to come up with new combinations, you need something to combine. Improvisers are inventive because each of them makes offers and they weave these together into a connected whole that is original. It is rather like Lego. Each of us has some bricks of different shapes and colors and the more of them we can get out on the table, the more things we will be able to make. If we each keep our bricks to ourselves, we won't be able to build much.

The practice of seeing offers everywhere may have been codified by improvisers but creative people tend to behave this way naturally. For example, designer Paul Smith and the founder of IKEA, Ingvar Kamprad, are two people who instinctively look for offers. I don't mean they go bargain hunting in the supermarket; what I mean is that they are relentlessly focused on using whatever comes to hand as fuel for their own process.

Paul Smith wrote a book entitled *You Can Find Inspiration in Everything: And If You Can't, Look Again.* A more concise expression of this practice would be hard to find. Kamprad is famed for regarding everything as an opportunity. For example, there was a period in IKEA's early history when they found that people bought more than they had planned and couldn't get it all home. So IKEA started to rent people roof racks for their cars. If the customer returned the roof rack they got the money back and IKEA got them back into the store. If not, IKEA had found a way to make it easier for people to buy things they hadn't planned on, as well as providing a service and garnering a little more income.

The idea of seeing the customers themselves (and the labor they can supply) as an offer is at the core of IKEA's business. IKEA uses the customer's time and labor to enable them to sell things more cheaply. The resulting furniture is quite literally a cocreation with customer and store each doing their part. IKEA offers cheap home furnishings but only to those people willing to volunteer their own time and energy. Millions of people the world over may whine about building flat-pack furniture (or how long it takes to get around the store) but had IKEA not been able to see their customers as an offer, IKEA as we know it would not exist at all.

However, when it comes to seeing things as offers even IKEA can't hold a candle (or an ecological light bulb) to nature. In a natural system all waste is food. No scrap is too small, no morsel too disgusting to be used. Nothing is thrown away because there is no away. Everything is an offer to some creature or other, happy to ply a living where others are unable. For example, the remora (a small fish) sees no nicer spot to live than the mouth of a shark, where it lives off the morsels the large predator drops. Our soft spot for cute creatures may lead us to get upset at the wholesale slaughter of baby turtles as they make their deadly first journey to the water, but according to an ecologist I spoke to at the Tortuguero reserve in Costa Rica, they are merely "feeding the beach." The high-protein diet they offer to their predators makes a contribution to the ecosystem and thus indirectly to turtle welfare, bloody though it may seem. And what finer example is there of nature's ability to see everything as an offer than the dung beetle?

We have come quite a long way with a very simple idea—the offer. In the course of the last ten years I have seen how sticky a piece of language it is. People pick it up quickly and remember it easily. Since the improv practices all fold into each other, you could argue that you only need to remember one. If so, then this would be a great candidate. And here's why.

In Stevensville, Montana, there is a very unusual brewery. The WildWood Brewery is a zero-emissions plant. As well as producing high-quality organic lager and seasonal brews, such a plant can produce edible mushrooms, fish and crayfish, fungi for use in paper pulping, cleaning products, medicines, animal feed, methane gas (for sale or heating), electricity and any number of other products. The basic idea, as you may have guessed, is to take everything as an offer. Instead of conceiving of a brewery as a linear process where raw materials are transformed using energy to create a finished product plus waste, the designers of a zero-emissions plant regard every output from every stage of the process—whether it is materials, heat or water—as an offer and then ask themselves what they can do with it.

Thus spent grain from the brewery provides the base for growing mushrooms. Used mushroom substrate feeds worms. The worms themselves can be sold for composting or used as feed for fish or chickens and so on. This is a very different approach from the one we are used to. Such processes evolve and change according to local conditions and the passage of time. However, over time such systems achieve levels of productivity and efficiency that should make us salivate. A zero-emissions brewery or NASA's Apollo 13 mission demonstrate that seeing everything as an offer is a powerful springboard which can turn limitation into innovation.

Natural systems show what is possible if you take the idea that everything is an offer to the extreme—a diverse, rich, productive system that produces no waste, because it's all food for somebody else. If only we could do so much with so little, all six billion of us could live fabulously well without having to worry about the destruction and depletion of the living systems on which we depend. By contrast, our current "heat, beat and treat" industrial systems produce colossal amounts of waste (in terms of both materials and energy) along with the finished product. Nature can't afford that and neither, in the long run, can we.

The world is complex beyond our comprehension. It holds myriad threats and obstacles, the vast majority of which we have only a hazy notion of. No one knows what a sustainable future would look like, let alone how we might get there. I wouldn't want to suggest, even whimsically, that improvisational theater can save the world. Nonetheless, the simple idea that everything is an offer could be useful scaffolding—a piece of temporary structure that can hold things together while something new emerges. If we really take this idea to heart, it could help us to redesign our organizations and systems so that, like the zero-emissions brewery, they become more productive and less damaging. That would seem to be one hell of an offer.

5 🚗 Creating Adventures

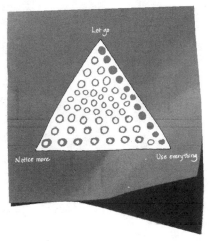

One day on his way home from work, Danny Wallace had an epiphany. As often happens in London there was a security problem on the Central Line, so everyone had to get off the tube and squeeze onto a bus. Wallace found himself sitting next to a bearded stranger who, out of the blue, offered him a piece of advice. "Say yes more," he suggested. Thus Danny Wallace became more than just a freelance radio producer. He became the Yes Man and, for a period, lived his entire life by a simple maxim: to "say yes where once he would have said no." He wrote himself a Yes Manifesto and swore that until the end of that year he would "say yes to every favor, request, suggestion and invitation." He made a solemn commitment to do this no matter what the circumstances.

Saying yes changed his life in big and small ways. It pulled him out of a downward spiral "of slouching, napping and channel hopping." He discovered that he liked to eat fish, got a job as a TV presenter, fell in love with his own city, won twenty-five thousand pounds (which he promptly lost again) and went to Australia. In the process he reconnected with old friends, made new ones, became popular at work and found his heart's desire. A "stupid boy project" became a way of life. It is an irreverent and funny story, told mostly at his own expense, but it also provides a real-life experiment with the improvisational practice of accepting offers.[1]

- - - - - - - - - - - - - - - - - - - -

1   He tells the story in the book *Yes Man*, which is well worth saying yes to.

There are essentially only two ways you can respond to an offer—you can accept it or you can block it. Accepting means recognizing an offer and using it or adding something to it. If I give you an apple you might eat it, cook with it or place it on your son's head as a target for your crossbow practice, but any of these involves acknowledging that you have an apple and using it for something. This is what it means to accept. By accepting you say yes to something, at least in spirit, and find a way to work with and take advantage of what you have. Thus by becoming the Yes Man, Danny Wallace forced himself to accept any and every explicit offer that came his way. For awhile he made accepting the guiding principle of his life.

As his story illustrates, accepting creates adventures. The adventure that is On Your Feet was created through a process of accepting offers that led from a T-shirt to a consulting business. There are many different ways to accept any particular offer and as we shall see, you can accept without agreeing or approving of something. Nonetheless it is a helpful starting point to equate accepting with yes. We will get to the refinements later.

If offers aren't accepted they are blocked. Blocking is the opposite of accepting. It means to contradict, deny or ignore what you are given. Saying no is the most obvious way to block. When the bank manager rejects your loan application or you refuse to let your kids watch more TV, those are blocks. Just like accepting, blocking appears in many different guises—I can block by ignoring your recommendations or ignoring you or doing the opposite of what you suggest, but one way or another a block is a push back or rejection of some sort. While there are subtleties here, too, in general blocking captures the spirit of no. Blocking does not build ideas or relationships—it closes down or eliminates possibilities and stops action.

On stage it is vital that improvisers accept offers. Since they have to create a story from nothing in the unforgiving glare of the footlights, they need to be able to get going instantly. It is by accepting offers that improvisers join one idea to another and create flow in their story. If they block offers, they cut flow (or prevent it from occurring) and disconnect ideas and people. This is a high cost to pay. Thus the counterpoint of accepting offers is to limit how much you block. The two practices are joined at the hip. You can't think about one without thinking about the other—if you accept more offers you will block fewer and vice versa.

The practiced improviser will therefore accept an offer unless there is a good reason to block it. As several rather honest executives have confessed to me, this is the inverse of the behavior one often observes in business, particularly among those in positions of power and authority. Managers will frequently block an offer unless there is a very good reason to accept it. This matters. In that small distinction lies a good part of the difference between a creative, responsive, agile and flexible environment—such as that of the improvisational ensemble—and a laborious, difficult or fearful climate, which can prevail in business organizations.

This does not mean that accepting is good and blocking is bad. You need both, but in different measures and at different moments. The skill is to know how to use accepting and blocking to your advantage; not by using them equally, but by understanding the consequences of each so you know which serves your purpose.

That is what we will explore in this chapter and the following one. First we will examine the benefits of accepting and the costs of blocking, which are considerable from the improvisational point of view. However, in order to get to a balanced picture, the following chapter will spell out the difficulties, dangers and risks attached to accepting and how, in certain circumstances, blocking can be constructive.

Accepting is a creative force. On stage this practice is fundamental to the creation of a story. Imagine you start a scene by returning a rotten apple to the grocer. It will help our cause enormously if I accept the offer to be the grocer that sold it to you. I could be a sycophantic, rude or flatulent grocer, but I am a grocer, not an alien or a mutant ninja turtle. Accepting gives us a clear, simple beginning to a story.

The same is true, whether your particular story is a friendship, journey, customer relationship or organizational culture. Whenever you want to create something new or grow, develop or learn, it will help to practice accepting offers. Whatever the context, accepting offers will build and create new ideas, enable you to make more with less, generate momentum quickly and build relationships. We can summarize the value of accepting like this:

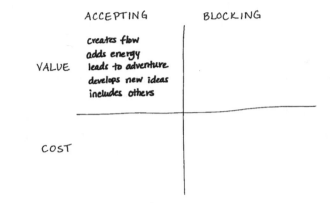

I used to work with a snack food company called Derwent Valley Foods, creators of the brand Phileas Fogg. At the time they were a small, energetic and rather eccentric company. One day, in a brainstorming meeting, I made a whimsical suggestion: "Why don't we make tortilla chips that are to ordinary tortilla chips what Carlsberg Special Brew is to ordinary lager?" Carlsberg Special Brew is a very strong lager famous for being much loved by English down-and-outs, so it was the kind of comment that would normally be ignored in a meeting. Yet in this one it wasn't. The idea was wholeheartedly and immediately embraced and lead to a torrent of other offers and a product quickly started to take shape. The recipe was developed with a chili so hot that health and safety officials considered slapping a health warning on it and the pack design showed Phileas with sweat on his brow. Consumer research was conducted not to test the idea, but to see how far it could be pushed. Suitably offbeat advertising was developed and all of this happened so quickly that within six months (an eye blink in the world of consumer goods) the product was on the supermarket shelves. Within a year or so it became the biggest selling Phileas Fogg variety. Such rapid progress was driven by the climate of accepting that reigned throughout the company at the time, a climate capable of turning an idle comment into a fully fledged product in no time. It also made Derwent Valley Foods a joy to work with.

A climate of accepting goes hand in hand with a sense of fun—they are intimately related. To be accepting is to be open, willing to see things differently, to take things lightly. This not only makes life more pleasant but has the practical advantage of inviting new and different ideas.

Recent history provides some prodigious examples of what accepting offers can lead to. The open-source movement, for instance, is evidence of what is possible when you allow offers to be accepted from anywhere. The open-source operating system Linux has become a credible alternative to the leviathan Microsoft—something that no corporation has managed. Linux draws on a huge pool of talent and ideas because it is built around the idea of accepting contributions from any programmer on the planet. Those offers get incorporated, a new version is put out as an offer to the open-source community, other offers are made and accepted and so on. This demonstrates that a willingness to accept ideas can make up for a lack of resources. Indeed, in a sense, accepting creates more resources; by bringing more ideas into play (instead of sidelining them or ignoring them) there is more to work with.

Accepting offers from all quarters also makes an organization (or an organism) more flexible and adaptable. If you have a more diverse pool of possibilities to draw from, it is easier to find an effective response when the market or the environment changes. Thus accepting offers helps you to evolve more quickly. A piece of open-source software and a strain of bacteria have this in common.

When a bug occurs in a piece of software a wide variety of people with a wide variety of experience, knowledge and skills can suggest solutions, making it more likely that the bug is eliminated or overcome quickly. With real live bugs (i.e., bacteria) a very similar phenomenon occurs, albeit to their advantage not ours. Bacteria are very accepting of their genes. Instead of keeping them locked away in the walled nucleus of a cell (like we do), they allow them to float freely in a long necklace within their cells. This makes it very simple for different bacteria to accept genes from each other—they can swap, exchange or copy them very easily—allowing for rapid evolution. This is what makes it difficult for scientists to keep up with mutating plagues and diseases like crop pests or strains of flu.[2]

This ability to grow and adapt quickly is extremely valuable. Nonetheless there is another effect of accepting offers which is arguably even more important for organizations—how it makes people feel. Accepting connects you and your ideas to me and mine. It thus enables us to have a conversation, pursue a common purpose or cocreate something. Since we are fundamentally social beings, the degree of connection we are able to create is fundamental to our emotional (as well as our economic) well being. As Nobel Prize-winning biologist Francisco Varela put it, "When a biological system comes under pressure, the way to make it more healthy is to connect more of it to itself."[3] Accepting offers creates such connections.

As I mentioned above, Derwent Valley Foods were fabulous fun to work with. The fact that my ideas might be taken and run with was a big part of this—it encouraged me to keep coming up with them and made me feel that my input was worthwhile. An atmosphere of accepting feels great to everyone involved. In the open-source movement people will work for nothing. The chance of having an offer accepted and of benefiting from the offers that others have contributed creates a virtuous circle of collaborative interest that is enough to make the whole thing work. To borrow an idea (or accept an offer) from Stephen Covey, you could say that accepting makes deposits in the emotional bank account, whereas blocking makes withdrawals.

The motivational aspect of this practice makes accepting of particular interest for people in positions of leadership. When he served as Captain of the USS Benfold,

- - - - - - - - - - - - - - - - - - - -

2   See *The Beak of the Finch*, a fascinating book about how evolution can really be observed, by Jonathan Wiener.

3   Quoted by Fritjof Capra in his Web of Life course (Schumacher College, Devon, England. June 1998).

Commander Mike Abrashoff demonstrated he was particularly good at accepting. One of his crew complained that they wasted far too much time and effort repainting the ship and suggested they use stainless steel fasteners which didn't rust. Abrashoff accepted this idea and acted on it, even though it meant he had to go and buy the fasteners in a hardware store on the ship's credit card (bizarrely, at the time the U.S. Navy supply system couldn't provide them).

Such a willingness to use the ideas of the crew did much more than save time (and paint). It was a simple way to generate the esprit de corps that Abrashoff wanted. That spirit infused the ship and created a climate where a myriad of new ideas and initiatives poured forth, which in turn led to higher battle-readiness scores compared with any equivalent ship. The title of Abrashoff's book, *It's Your Ship*, reflects this inclusiveness; he stands in stark contrast to the traditional captain who always thinks of and refers to the vessel under his command in the possessive "*my* ship."

In workshops people sometimes push back against the idea of accepting offers because they think it sounds "fluffy." They make comments like, "Look, my job is to make tough decisions so accepting isn't really relevant to me." Such comments reveal an assumption that accepting is a weak or passive position. It isn't. Accepting is not submission.

Imagine that Reggie walks into his boss's office at Sunshine Desserts and says, "I want a pay rise." CJ can accept without rolling over and giving Reggie what he wants. For example, CJ might respond by saying, "I didn't get where I am today by giving employees what they ask for. Tell me, Reggie, what have you done to deserve a pay rise?"

This might not be very friendly, but look carefully, and you will see that CJ is accepting—he acknowledges Reggie's point and makes an offer back, thus sustaining the flow. He has given Reggie a chance to justify himself, but without submitting to his request. CJ accepts Reggie's offer *and* remains firmly in charge.

To accept, you don't have to submit to or even agree with someone else. What you have to accept is the reality that they perceive, which is different from your own. If I say

"I'm hungry," then that is my reality. You can accept and express a different point of view at the same time by saying, "That's surprising, given that you have just eaten six ham sandwiches," but that is very different from telling me that I am *not* hungry. Denying someone's reality is an attempt to control them and does not help build ideas or relationships. You don't have to accept what other people want, you just have to accept that they want it.

This is a subtle point so perhaps it isn't surprising that I first became aware of it during a talk by a Buddhist priest. I was on a cooking and meditation course where I met Edward Espe Brown, a Zen master, cook and cookbook author. One day Ed was discussing the importance of accepting in the Buddhist tradition and one of the participants, a girl called Angela, couldn't contain herself. "This is absurd," she snapped. "When people do stupid things, I get angry about it. I can't just accept it. That would be stupid." There was a pause. "Maybe you should accept that you get angry," said Ed quietly.

The same happens on stage. When you bring the apple back to the grocer, I don't necessarily have to accept the apple—I can refuse it and argue vehemently that you don't have proof of purchase, but in so doing I accept the offer that I am a grocer.

This difference between accepting and submitting is important and can be visualized like this:

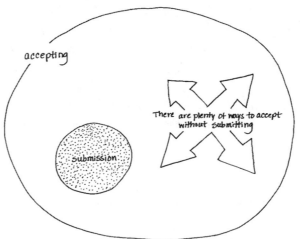

The skill is to find ways to accept the reality of others and make new offers of your own (which is represented in the diagram by the area within the accepting oval, but outside the dot of submission). One sure way to do this is to use "yes, and…" A few years back, after one of our workshops, Haley Rushing decided to adopt what she called a "yes, and…" attitude to everything. Rather like Danny Wallace, she made a rule for herself that whatever she was given, she would take it and add something to it. She didn't tell anyone at the advertising agency where she worked about this, she just did it. Within two weeks people were commenting on what a joy she was to work with. Her commitment to accepting made a noticeable difference to her work, her reputation and her relationships in a surprisingly short space of time. People may not have known what she was doing, but they noticed the difference it made.

Sometimes we resist accepting offers because we feel we are moving plenty fast enough already. In Chapter 3 I mentioned the term "steerage way"—the idea that you can only steer a boat if it is moving forward through the water. Sometimes it feels like we are on a whitewater raft heading down the rapids rather than a tranquil rowing boat but, even so, the same principle applies. The strong current means you are already moving fast, but if you want to be able to steer, you still need to paddle because only when the raft is moving faster than the water will you be able to direct it. Similarly, if you want to avoid being carried along willy nilly on a current of events, you may need to keep accepting offers even when it feels counterintuitive to do so.

Occasionally this discussion of the virtues of accepting leads people to believe I am recommending you should say yes to every offer. I am not. It is impossible to accept every offer, and if you try, you will quickly end up feeling confused, overburdened or exploited. Accepting too many offers can bring its own difficulties, as we shall see in the next chapter. What is most important, whether you block or accept, is to do so consciously rather than simply being driven by habit and circumstance.

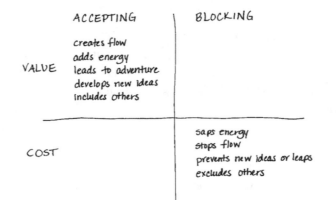

	ACCEPTING	BLOCKING
VALUE	creates flow adds energy leads to adventure develops new ideas includes others	
COST		saps energy stops flow prevents new ideas or leaps excludes others

If accepting is the motor that drives ideas and relationships forwards, then blocking is the brake. It stops flow, cuts things out, eliminates, jettisons and discards. Blocking alone will not create anything—be it an enchanting conversation, a new product or market share. To be safe and maneuverable, any vehicle needs brakes, but if you apply the brakes too firmly (or too often), you never get going. And it would be perverse to drive with the brakes on.

Similarly, if you block too often or too enthusiastically, everything becomes hard work, so blocking needs to be used more carefully than accepting. They are not of equal weight. Blocking has a high price for improvisers because it cuts the flow and disconnects the different actors even as they try to cocreate something. If you bring the apple back and I say, "This isn't a grocery store, it is the throne room of Queen Zog," that makes things difficult for both of us. We now have no shared understanding of what is going on and neither does the audience. It is hard to know what to do next.

Blocks are a natural reaction to the unknown. Novice improvisers block to avoid the unknown and to stop things happening. It feels safer to stay with what you know and blocking stops things from changing. There are two problems with this. First, it prevents you from creating action. You might be scared to progress, but staying where you are also has risks. Second, a single, clumsy block can destroy a lot of work. Imagine we start telling a story in a group, each person adding one beat and accepting the offers that have come before by using the words "yes, and…." We might get a story that goes something like this:

"Pete woke up…"

"Yes, and…the first thing he did was pick up his guitar…"

"Yes and…he started to play a piece by Bach…"

"Yes and…his wife shouted up to him from the kitchen…"

"Yes and…she said, 'Stop that classical crap and play something decent…'"

"Yes and…Pete riffed seamlessly into *Stairway to Heaven*…"

"Yes and…as he hit the highest note, a string broke…"

There's a certain head of steam here. Even though offers are being accepted we have bits of tension and conflict—Pete's wife hating Bach, for example—and the story has momentum; people feel involved and connected in the cocreative process. So imagine that the next person says:

"No, it didn't."

This stops the story dead in its tracks. Confusion reigns. The person who made the preceding offer (the string breaking) is mortified and usually believes they have done something dreadfully wrong. The rest of the group is irritated by the person who blocked. No one knows what to do. We will often use such a demonstration in a workshop. It can be great fun for us to be the blocker because we get to wield so much power—the power to wreck things. This is the power that blocks have.

Though the example given is just a game, people recognize the feeling because they have experienced it before. Imagine, for example, that we are part of a team working on a new mission for our organization. We have done our research and are in the process of developing our ideas. We then learn that the CEO has suddenly announced what the mission is going to be. This is the equivalent of the "no, it didn't" in the "yes, and…" story and would have the same effect—the block wrecks our ideas and makes us resent the CEO. Even if some explanation is given (e.g., "The board and the shareholders were pushing the CEO to act and McBane and company came up with some brilliant ideas.") a block is still a block. It does damage however you try to spin it.

In everyday life blocks have much the same costs as they do in an improv scene—they disconnect people and ideas. If Gary had blocked my questions about how improvisation works when we met to discuss a T-shirt, On Your Feet wouldn't exist at all. Blocking creates a negative spiral. New ideas don't occur so problems are harder to solve. People become suspicious and wary of each other because they are worried they will be blocked, so energy is sapped and momentum is lost. You have to work a lot harder and results are more difficult to achieve. Look carefully at a relationship you find difficult, whether professional or personal, and you will find there is a lot of blocking going on.

The effect of blocks can be insidious. Since a block prevents change, it feels nice and safe to say no to things, then it becomes a habit. Since it continues to give you something (safety), you continue to block until it is so normal that you no longer notice it. Before his epiphany, Danny Wallace had been blocking everything without realizing it. He says: "I'd been laboring under the impression that everything in my life was fine. I was a single man in his mid-twenties living in one of the most exciting cities in the world. Turns out I was a single man, in his pants, sitting in his flat."

If one block causes problems, two can be lethal. When block meets block, you clash or crash. It's like a Christmas pantomime, where, "Oh yes he does," is met with the equal and opposite response, "Oh no he doesn't."[4] You can't keep that up for long, even in a panto. In everyday life when you get into such a loop it quickly becomes frustrating. Time and energy are squandered. If both parties keep blocking there is intractable and painful conflict. It isn't a good place to be. Just ask someone in the kitchen of a soon-to-be divorced couple.

The inherently destructive nature of blocking is exacerbated by the fact that we have a blind spot when it comes to blocks. Let's illustrate that now. Think of a block from your own experience. It doesn't matter if it is big or small, from home or work, just try

- - - - - - - - - - - - - - - - - - -

4   Pantomime is a form of children's theater, normally based on a fairy tale, performed at Christmas time. It has a very long tradition and, whatever the panto, there is always a dumb villain who engages in an argument with the audience at some point.

and identify an occasion when a block occurred. Blocks are so common this should only take a nanosecond or two. Got one?

The chances are that the occasion you have thought of is one where someone else is blocking you. Is that so? For example, I might think of a friend who never comes to visit me in Spain, blocking all my invitations. This would be typical. If you have chosen a situation where you are the one doing the blocking, you are unusual. Only about five percent of people do that. The reason is that blocks are asymmetric. The emotional force of a block is directed at the person receiving, which means that when you are blocked, you feel it sorely, whereas when you block someone else, you might not even notice. Thus we tend to remember the blocks we receive, not the ones we give, which creates a blind spot.

Often, because of this blind spot, we mistakenly conclude that the problem is the other person. Yet that is only because we don't notice the blocks we dish out. A little earlier I mentioned that if you think of a relationship you find difficult, whether professional or personal, you will find there is a lot of blocking going on. I should add that some of those blocks involved will be yours.

Companies can block their own consumers at every turn without realizing that they are doing so—they fail to answer the phone, refuse to mend something broken, send you things you didn't ask for or deliver the service that suits them, not you. Unsurprisingly this makes people unenthusiastic or cynical about corporations. If a company were really serious about developing relationships with their customers, one thing they could do would be to look at their own behavior and audit all the occasions when they are blocking so they could start to remove some of them. Just getting rid of a few could make a big difference.

It may seem strange to devote time and space to a practice you want to avoid, so let me offer a parallel. When I was learning Spanish the best book I had was called *1001 Common Mistakes in Spanish*. Written specifically for English speakers, it operated on the principle that identifying and eliminating common mistakes is a shortcut to speaking Spanish well. A similar principle applies here—if you become conversant with the kinds of blocks we commonly use, it will be easier to cut them out or cut down on unconscious or habitual blocking. It is therefore important to understand that not all blocks are obvious. There are a number of more sophisticated (or devious) ways in which they can occur that are not signaled by a full-blooded no.

One familiar variety of the block is the "yes, but…." Couples are good at this one, often with the addition of sweeteners such as "darling" or "honey," which do nothing to alter the fact that it is a block. "Yes, but…" also makes a large number of appearances in business meetings. Saying yes makes the phrase seem positive and operates as a mask for the insidious "but…" that is the prelude to a block. People often say it without thinking. Indeed, in workshops we see people substitute the words "yes, and…" with "yes, but…" and fail to even notice they have done so. "Yes, but…" can become second nature.

Softer than the "yes, but…" but still a form of blocking is "yes, anyway…." This is more subtle and can be harder to spot. The phrase "yes, anyway…," or its many equivalents (such as "you know, that reminds me"), seems to connect two points, but in fact skates rapidly from one to the next, leaving the previous offer stranded and undealt with—effectively blocking it. People who are enthusiastic (like me) are particularly prone to this one. For example, imagine we are colleagues in conversation and you raise the issue of paternity leave. I seem to hear what you say but I reply, "Yes, very interesting, a difficult issue, so…anyway, I have been thinking it's time we reviewed our graduate trainee selection process." I have effectively blocked the conversation about paternity leave. This is not as direct a block as saying no, but it sweeps the offer you made under the carpet, ignoring it and moving swiftly on. If you really want to have the conversation about paternity leave, you will have to force the issue. One familiar example of this is when organizations commission new research rather than act on the findings of the previous report. It looks like action but is in fact a block.

Funnily enough, "yes, anyway" can be a particular problem with people who have learned to spot "yes, but…." Aware that "yes, but…" is a problem, they just substitute it with "yes, anyway…" (or the equivalent) and think they have solved the problem. Yet it isn't enough to simply change the words you use, you have to be willing to change the substance of what you say. I have come across people who employ the phrase "let me build on that…" as a kind of "yes, anyway…." They simply use it as a stepping stone to leap to another idea they are more interested in and do no actual building at all.

Blocking isn't just about the words you say. Like offers, blocks can be physical as well as verbal. Your tone of voice, body language, posture, position or movement can all create blocks—from obvious ones (like leaving) to more subtle ones (like facial expression). These "body blocks" can be very powerful. Gary maintains, from years of selling T-shirts in market stalls, that he can tell from the way a person's feet are positioned whether or not they will buy something (i.e., accept) more accurately than from anything they say. We had one client with whom a similar thing happened. While she seemed at first glance to accept a lot of offers, we found the relationship with her was difficult. After awhile we realized that she would block with her body language even while mouthing encouraging words. Like Gary's market customers, we found the physical blocks to be a far more reliable indicator of what she really meant than what she said. The implication is that if you want to become more aware of how and where you block, it isn't enough to pay attention to your words. You have to look at how you might be blocking physically, too.

One final block to mention is inaction. Doing nothing can be a thumping great block. If I never return your calls, I prevent any kind of flow whatsoever between us, as accounts payable departments of large companies seem to understand only too well.

♡

It would be easy to stop here and conclude quite simply that accepting is good and blocking is bad and there was a time, years ago, when I used to do something like that. Plenty of other people have reached exactly this conclusion—remember the performer whose three-word summary was "Just say yes"?

Yet in my experience this is a misleading oversimplification. In workshops people would describe real situations they faced where it clearly wasn't helpful to accept an offer. So my colleagues and I went back to the lab and scrutinized what happens on the improv stage. What we saw was that though improvisers might say yes more than most, they certainly don't say yes to everything. If they did they would never get clear direction to a story, let alone bring it to a conclusion. If you say yes to everything, before you know it, you will have a herd of cows, a slaughterhouse, a power cut, a local witch, the fire brigade, Charles Dickens, a shipwreck, a Harley Davidson made of ivory and Johnny's toothache, all in the same story. Try making sense of that. Along the way, and particularly toward the end, you see improvisers blocking the ideas that they don't think help their story.

Thus even on the improv stage, where creating flow quickly is absolutely vital, accepting is no panacea. While it would be wonderfully neat to be categorical, context always matters. What you want, where you are, and who you are with will all have an effect on what you should say yes to. Accepting may have more obvious virtues than blocking, but as I have emphasized, they each have value and shortcomings. The art is to know how to use both to best advantage, which means we are only halfway through the story of accepting and blocking.

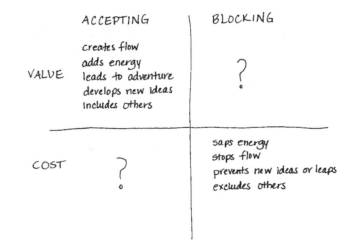

To complete it, the next chapter will look at the costs of accepting and the benefits of blocking. "Yes" may be a noble and generous sentiment and a valid tactic to correct an exaggerated tendency to block, but as Danny Wallace, the Yes Man, discovered in the red light district of Amsterdam, an inflexible adherence to accepting can be awkward, embarrassing or even downright dangerous…

6 🐰 Safekeeping

Imagine you make an impromptu trip to Amsterdam and someone you just met offers to show you around. You accept. Your new acquaintance suggests a visit to a leather bar in the gay neighborhood. You say yes again. Once inside you also say yes to a few beers and before very long one of the exceedingly friendly locals offers you some psychotropic drugs. Do you say yes again?

A few weeks into his experiment as the Yes Man, this was the situation in which Danny Wallace found himself. His faithful commitment to the Yes Manifesto had not only made him an ordained minister and owner of a penis patch, but put him into this decidedly tricky situation. He escaped with nothing worse than a hangover and an expertly crafted charcoal portrait of himself with a small dog, but it could have been a lot worse.

Yes has power, but that power can be perilous. Personally I don't want to say yes to endless spam or to shoehorning the content of a three-day workshop into one. Whatever the benefits of accepting, "just say yes" has downsides that are real and important. An excessive enthusiasm for yes and the demonization of no (which often accompanies it) are both oversimplifications. Blocking skillfully can be a defining force. For example, the actor Tom Hanks attributes his success to precisely this ability: "I think I've been able to say no to the wrong things...[and] that requires a degree of discipline and no small amount of understanding of the work you want to do. I think that's the only way we really get to define ourselves, not so much by what we say yes to, as to what we say no."[1]

Though this might seem like a storm in an improvisational teacup, I think it matters. It may be logical to react to an excess of blocking by advocating that you should always accept, but the trouble is that this leaves you lurching from one extreme to the other and does nothing to help you develop a sensitive or sensible practice. By contrast, Keith Johnstone, one of the original thinkers in this field, offers a more balanced view of the relative merits of accepting and blocking in his book *Impro*: "There are two kinds of people in this world: those who prefer to say yes, and those who prefer to say no. Those who say yes are rewarded by the adventures they have, and those that say no are rewarded by the safety they attain. There are far more no sayers around than yes sayers."

This is beautifully nuanced. Given the prevalence of no sayers and the high costs of blocking, it is unsurprising that most of us, like Danny Wallace, would benefit from redressing the balance a little in the direction of accepting. Yet that's not the whole story. To complete our understanding it is important to understand the flip side of these two practices.

I recently asked Gary what he thought the main downsides of accepting were. "Death," he replied cheerfully. Although he was exaggerating for effect, there is more than a grain of truth in what he said. For example, it is autumn here and among the pines and oaks that cloak the hillsides around my house, the mushrooms are mushrooming (as they do). Were I to go for an early morning stroll and accept any fungi I might find as an offer for my breakfast, it might not kill me, but it might make me sick.

Say yes to everything and you can get hurt. Caution and prudence are biologically programmed to protect us, and thank goodness. Accepting takes you on adventures but adventurers often get hurt. You might die of boredom if you never have any adventures, but nonetheless it is important to recognize that you can pay a price for accepting.

----

1   Interview, *The Guardian*, January 12, 2001.

	ACCEPTING	BLOCKING
VALUE	creates flow adds energy leads to adventure develops new ideas includes others	
COST	requires effort forced to let go can feel weak takes you far, fast	saps energy stops flow prevents new ideas or leaps excludes others

Danger isn't the only problem. Accept indiscriminately and you will be rudderless. If all offers are accepted, you exercise no choice over the direction in which you go, and you take no responsibility for the direction in which your story develops. This may be appropriate on the odd occasion (for example, early in a process when you need to get going fast) but in general it will leave you floundering. Never has the paralyzing effect of trying to accept too many offers been clearer to me than in the writing of this book. After more than a decade working with improv I have thousands of scraps of material. If I tried to include them all I would get completely stuck, buried under the mass of all those little nuggets. I can only dig myself out by blocking many of the offers that are suggesting themselves to my beleaguered attention.

You can't literally accept every offer anyway—you need to accept enough to keep you moving and take you in the direction you want to go, while you close down or block those that take you in another direction instead. If you don't, it can drive you mad—perhaps literally. Some kinds of schizophrenia seem to involve an inability to edit or prioritize incoming stimuli, so to try to accept every single offer that comes your way could be psychotic.

The very fact that accepting offers moves you forward can at times itself be a problem. Accepting is a powerful engine—it can very quickly drive you a long way in a direction that you might not want. Like all powerful engines, you need to know how to handle it—the fastest cars have the most powerful brakes for obvious reasons. Do you really need another new product launch or investigative committee? Is it really wise to take up the dinner invitation of an old flame who contacted you through friendsreunited.com? If you accept too readily, one thing can all too easily lead to another (as the tabloid newspapers are fond of putting it), with all the complications implied.

Sometimes accepting might just take too much energy. It requires you to be attentive and willing to be changed and that doesn't come without effort. Try to accept too many offers and you can easily become exhausted and stressed. I have heard a number of people extol the value of taking a different route to work each day, the idea being that this will help you to see things differently and get you out of a rut. I can see value in this, but what if you're exhausted? On the way to work and more particularly on the way home, you might just want to use the minimum of energy and follow a routine that requires the minimum effort.

Accept too much and your attention is spread very thin. If the phone rings while I am getting the kids ready for school and I take the call, I am unlikely to be at my most coherent while I discuss an off-site meeting in Florida, yet I will also get a rocket from the teacher for arriving late (again). To achieve what I want—happy teacher, happy client—I need (temporarily, at least) to block one of them. In a time when ADD (Attention Deficit Disorder) is commonplace and we are constantly bombarded with distracting stimuli, it is important not to accept all of it if you want to retain your sanity and get things done.[2]

Just as accepting has costs, so blocking has benefits. As Keith Johnstone puts it, blocking brings us security and there are plenty of occasions when safety is what matters most. Standing at the top of Les Couloirs Belges (off the south face of Saulire in the ski

----

[2] Doesn't it strike you as ironic that to refer to Attention Deficit Disorder people often use an acronym?

	ACCEPTING	BLOCKING
VALUE	creates flow adds energy leads to adventure develops new ideas includes others	stops unwelcome advance retains or attains security avoids risk or change cuts off sidetracking creates drama
COST	requires effort forced to let go can feel weak takes you far, fast	saps energy stops flow prevents new ideas or leaps excludes others

resort of Courcheval 1850 in France), it would be a boon for me, my companions and the emergency services if I remember that my skiing is not what it used to be, block the offer of the mogul-ridden black run that presents itself and turn off down the gentle blue one instead.

In an organization like On Your Feet where people tend to have short attention spans and value learning more than growth, we have to remind ourselves of the value of blocking, particularly when we run repeat programs for large clients. They want the consistency that comes with a design honed through experience, which you get to by blocking new offers.

Blocking is thus a practice we can use to protect ourselves from change. Different people (and different cultures) are comfortable with different levels of safety, but at some level it is something that we all genuinely want and need. Blocking can even be a business opportunity. Virgin Mobile in Australia (a cell phone operator) recognized that sometimes we need protection from ourselves. Their data showed that when drunk, people tend to call ex-partners, bosses and colleagues and say things they later regret. So they offered a "dialing under the influence" (or DUI) service where they will blacklist (i.e., block) certain numbers before you go out, ensuring that you can't call them before 6AM the next morning.[3]

Blocking isn't only about staying safe though. By eliminating possibilities, blocks impart direction. On stage improvisers give direction to their story through the offers they choose to block. To create a good story they will need to block something, be it the slaughterhouse, the shipwreck or the Harley Davidson made of ivory. Much like Tom Hanks's career, what they reject does as much to shape the identity of what they are creating as what they accept.

Blocks can save you time and energy by cutting off redundant sidetracks. I once saw a CEO deliver a very explicit block to one of her directors. It was during a retreat dedicated to company strategy and this particular director kept bringing the conversation back to issues that concerned his own department. After he had done this a number of times, the CEO said, "John, please do not raise this subject again, it is not what we are here to discuss." John squirmed in his seat but the CEO judged—rightly, in my view—that losing some goodwill from this errant director was worthwhile if it meant the important business got done.

If you feel you are being pushed around, a block can force someone else to sit up and take notice of you. We had one client who kept changing the dates for a session without taking us into account. In such circumstances a short, sharp block can work wonders, so we politely told him we would not be able to do any more development work until the dates were fixed and an advance was paid. This got his attention without having an angry confrontation. Deliberately and consciously blocking in this way feels very different from having a hissy fit.

There are also times when you absolutely don't want any flow. When I first started working with improvisational techniques I was somewhat in thrall to the idea of accepting, so the idea that blocking deliberately could be useful was something of a revelation. It finally came home to me very early one morning, in a minicab on my way to

- - - - - - - - - - - - - - - - - - -
3   Note that this innovative idea came from seeing "bad" customer behavior as an offer.

Heathrow airport. A minicab is not one of the famous black London taxis, but an altogether murkier breed. At that time of day the last thing I wanted to do was talk, particularly since it quickly became apparent that the driver's views were racist. I didn't have the energy to protest, yet I couldn't stand the thought that I was giving his obnoxious ideas some kind of credence by not arguing back, so I consciously decided to block. First, I blocked by not saying anything. I found I had to work hard at this; it felt rude to maintain silence in the face of someone who was demanding a response. I concentrated on not making any nonverbal offers either, no nodding of the head or quiet tutting. Once I started to enjoy the effect, I really committed to my block and pretended to fall asleep and the driver lapsed into a broody, malevolent silence.

What was new to me here was the idea that I could choose to block. By doing so I could cut off a conversation I didn't want to have. It was simply unthinking habit that made me feel I ought to talk to him. Had he been a colleague, the stakes would have been higher because I would have to consider the cost of a block in the context of a relationship but, like the CEO in the strategy meeting, I could still have chosen to block if I thought the gain was worth it. You always have a choice. When you exercise this choice you can measure it—you can block gently but firmly. Whereas when you block unconsciously, you not only block more often than you need, but you frequently do so in a brusque, irritable or insensitive way, so the situation can easily escalate into a row.

Thus accepting and blocking both have benefits and costs, and which one you choose to do in any particular moment depends upon what you want to achieve. A definitive answer (such as "just say yes") is very seductive, but life tends not to submit to such tidy laws. It may be true that most of us block too much—for example, parents may tend to block their children's requests more often than they really need to—but that doesn't mean that accepting little Johnnie's offer to shove crayons up his sister's nose is a good idea.

This forces you constantly to reflect on what you really want, which is a good discipline. It is easy to neglect this and be carried along by inertia, as I was at first in the minicab, going

	ACCEPTING	BLOCKING
VALUE	creates flow adds energy leads to adventure develops new ideas includes others	stops unwelcome advance retains or attains security avoids risk or change cuts off sidetracking creates drama
COST	requires effort forced to let go can feel weak takes you far, fast	saps energy stops flow prevents new ideas or leaps excludes others

along with habit or what other people want for us—whether its our parents, our peers or society in general—rather than working it through for ourselves. As Tom Hanks puts it, you need to have "no small amount of understanding of the work you want to do."

It follows that I can't tell you when you should accept or block, but I can illustrate using my own experience. Workshops are full of all kinds of different offers, most of which I can't possibly anticipate. First, I need to have a clear grasp of what the overall goal is. For example, let's say I am running a short opening session for a week-long leadership course. My aim is to get a diverse and nervous bunch of strangers relaxed and working together quickly so they can learn from each other as well as from the lecturers. I don't want to expound a theory but help them get to know each other and enjoy themselves. This becomes my point of reference.

If one of the participants asks what my theory of leadership is, it is tempting to answer because I get to look clever. But the risk is that we get into a distracting debate so in this case I will happily block such an offer, perhaps by suggesting we talk about that later. If, on the other hand, someone makes an observation about the experience itself (e.g., "I noticed that I couldn't control what was going on there and I didn't enjoy that.") I would ask them to say more, thereby accepting the offer. I know that this could promote a richer conversation about the experience itself, which is what I want to focus on.

Improvisers choose to accept offers that help their story and block the offers that detract from it. In a scene on a desert island, crabs, messages in bottles and rafts would be offers that more obviously feed the story than dental floss or unfinished novels. (However, you can't be too rigid about this because a desert island story might become more interesting if one or two offers that don't obviously fit are accepted—for example, the castaway might be a novelist who is delighted to be cast away so that he can finally finish his novel.)

The skill of knowing which offers to accept or block is intuitive and visceral, not mental, but that doesn't mean it can't be learned. Developing a feel for which offers will help your story, whether it's a workshop or a conversation, is something you cultivate through experience and practice. The learning is in the doing—there are no clever shortcuts. You have to have the patience to keep noticing what happens as a result of the offers you accept or block. You have to learn to rely on instinct rather than argument.

❀

Finally, I would like to address one specific question that we frequently get asked about accepting and blocking: what do you do when someone else blocks you? It's a good question because it happens to all of us. It also gets to the very core of this practice.

In essence, the answer is to treat the block as an offer. You might be wondering how a block can simultaneously be an offer, so let me explain via a story. I was once running some focus groups for The Discovery Channel. The idea was to understand what people felt and thought about the idea of "discovery" in general, so I got people to talk at some length about what discovery meant to them. We discussed when and how discoveries happened, what it felt like when you make a personal discovery and so on. In one group seven of the eight participants were engaged by the conversation. The eighth was sitting straight-backed, with his arms firmly folded and a scowl on his face, saying nothing. He clearly wanted nothing to do with the conversation—a clear block. Yet whatever was intended there was nothing to stop me treating this posture as an offer and using it, so I did.

"Peter, you don't seem very interested in this," I said, stating an obvious fact. "Frankly, I think it's stupid," he replied, using negative judgment to deliver another block.

Undeterred I decided to take that as an offer too. "Why does this conversation feel stupid?" I asked. "Well, I am a soldier, and I just came back from a peacekeeping mission in Bosnia and this all seems so silly in comparison," he said. Rather than trying to convince him otherwise, I accepted that offer too, even though it seemed to take us off the subject: "I can see that it might. Tell us, what was it like in Bosnia?"

At this point his body language softened and we were back in flow, heading in a different direction, but in flow nonetheless. "Well, it's very different from what you expect, you do your training and learn your drills, but when you arrive and go on patrol in the villages what you discover is…," and on he went, creating an unintended but seamless connection to the conversation about personal discoveries. He had enough presence of mind to notice this and enough humility to laugh at himself so he carried on uniting his little tributary of flow with the main stream. In this case, treating a block as an offer allowed me to reengage someone who did not want to participate. It also brought something new to the conversation.

This story makes visible some subtleties of accepting and blocking. Peter thinks the conversation is stupid and blocks. It is difficult for him to physically leave (which would be the ultimate block), so he does the next best thing and blocks via his body language. I noticed this, but instead of interpreting it in the way he intended, I used it as an offer to draw him into the conversation. Even when he blocked again, I continued to take his blocks as offers until he himself, quite unintentionally, created a connection that allowed him to accept the offer of joining a conversation about discovery. The crucial point here is that whatever someone's intention, you can decide whether to take something as an offer or a block. With practice, even the most obstructive behavior can be regarded as an offer.

There are plenty of improv games that work on just this principle—one player is instructed to block by giving a storyteller a word that has nothing to do with the story but which has to be used. What you find is that when you are forced to treat something as an offer, it becomes one. The same thing can happen in everyday life. I heard of one manager who was very successful at getting innovative projects through a deeply conservative corporate culture. When asked how he did it, he said, "I just interpret no as a request for more information," thus turning intended blocks into offers.

When people ask what to do about a block, I suspect that what they *really* want to ask is, "How do I stop those idiots who don't see that I am right from blocking me?" Such an attitude is fruitless. Even Peter's commanding officer can't order him to be willing or interested—you can tell someone what to do, but you can't tell them what to feel or think.[4]

The way you influence other people's behavior is by altering your own. When faced with a block, don't fall into the temptation of thinking that it's the other person who needs to change. Instead, focus on yourself and ask how you can use something intended as a block, thus turning it into an offer. This is an incredibly empowering thing to do. Get good at it and it can help you feel almost immune to attempts to obstruct or sabotage your work.

The alternative is to meet a block with a block. I could have ignored Peter, effectively blocking him back, and in the short term that may have seemed like a safer option, but it would have cut off any chance of flow with him, leaving him out of the conversation completely. This would have been a failure on my part since moderators are meant to be able to ensure everyone is included. That failure would have come back to haunt me—damaging either my reputation (if the client had pointed out my failure) or my self-esteem (if only I had noticed).

There are some occasions when ending the conversation can be productive or even elegant. For example, I recall one eight-second telephone call from someone at Orange that I would argue was a great success for both parties. I had responded to a promotion and the girl who answered said, "We are offering a new handset if you move from pay-as-you-go to a contract—would you like to do that?" "No," I said, whereupon she immediately replied, "OK, thanks anyway, goodbye." She respected my block and blocked back with such good grace that it left me a very satisfied customer. I often tell the story as an example of good customer service, so there are occasions when cutting the flow will work, but it isn't the norm.

- - - - - - - - - - - - - - - - - -

4   As Fountains of Wayne put it in the lyrics of a lovely little song entitled "Hey Julie": "Working all day for a mean little guy, With a bad toupee and a soup-stained tie, He's got me running round the office like a gerbil on a wheel, He can tell me what to do but he can't tell me what to feel."

You can represent these simple options in a schematic diagram like this:

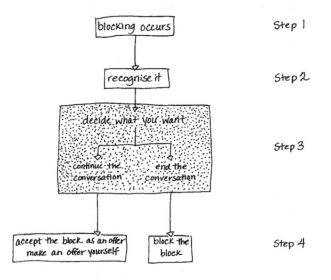

The story about Peter and discovery also illustrates the connection of accepting and blocking to the core of this practice. I have to notice more—if I am too wrapped up in the conversation to notice Peter's body language, he will sink irretrievably into the background. If I take Peter's block as an offer using everything (even that which doesn't seem promising), I can ensure that flow is maintained, but I can't control the direction it takes us in, so I have to let go of my agenda and of any snap judgments I might make like, "This guy is a pain in the neck."

In these two chapters I have endeavored to be even-handed, giving space to the advantages and disadvantages of both accepting and blocking. Nonetheless I want to reiterate that this does not mean accepting and blocking should be used in equal measure.

You will have noticed that I held back the costs of accepting and the benefits of blocking until the second of these two chapters. I did so for a reason. I have noticed that if you present the four-box grid in a balanced way from the outset, explaining the costs and benefits of both accepting and blocking, people immediately leap to the benefits of blocking. They tend to latch on to the arguments I have given in this chapter to justify why they block so much. They easily forget or ignore the considerable negative emotional force of blocking (and the immense generative power of accepting). In other words, they tend to block the very offers that would force them to change or learn. With that in mind, I only introduced the upsides of blocking once we had considered the downsides.

My considered view is that most of us, most of the time, would do well to accept more offers and block fewer. Certainly if you are serious about innovation, collaboration or creativity, like Norman of Big Technology Inc. (the CEO we met in Chapter 1), creating adventures is more important than keeping safe and that means accepting more offers. I also believe it is important to be vigilant about the conserving instinct. Not only is blocking a more destructive force that should be used more sparingly, but the habit of "safety first" can creep insidiously into every nook and cranny of your life. An excess of caution is not so different from living in a state of perpetual fear. I grew up with this—at least when it came to vehicles. My father was an aeronautical engineer so his professional context was one of "double fail-safe" and "class-A locking" which makes sense when an airplane can fall out of the sky. But it also meant that he would force me to give my motorbike the equivalent of an annual service before going on a twenty-mile ride. I could never explain to him how what seemed merely prudent to him took away a lot of the joy, fun and wildness that I was seeking.

One senior executive had a very perceptive way of summing up the balance between accepting and blocking. In the immediate aftermath of a workshop he said, "I have realized that I block about 95 percent of the time." Gary and I asked him what conclusion he drew from this, and he said, "Blocking seems to be an essential part of my role, so I think I probably *should* be blocking about 70 percent of the time, but I realize now that often I just block out of habit, ignorance, or fear. I am going to work hard to cut out the 25 percent that I block unnecessarily because that is where the future of my company lies."

7   A Rare Combination of Serenity and Adrenalin

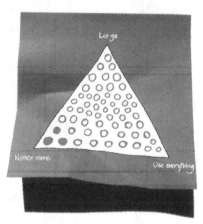

Filmmakers have a saying: "Everyone is the hero of their own movie." A few years ago I learned, somewhat painfully, that you can also be the villain. I was facilitating a two-day meeting for a multinational company at one of the stately home-turned-posh conference centers that are implausibly common around Heathrow airport. No sooner were the pleasantries over than the creative climate I had been hired to engender evaporated in a withering exchange of internal politics. People took sides, literally—headquarters on one side of the table and country managers on the other, with me sitting rather uncomfortably at the end. I was caught in the middle of a conflict I was unable to prevent.

As the afternoon wore on, the two sides grew further apart. They aired more grievances and resolved none. It felt like the table was getting wider and wider, like something out of *Alice in Wonderland*. I soldiered on as if everything were completely fine, but eventually I had to call a stop because it was time for dinner. Inwardly I was reeling, quite at a loss as to what to do. Everyone was polite, but with that particular kind of poisonous courtesy that the English reserve for moments of high tension. It was obvious that we had not only failed to reach a resolution, but that we hadn't even turned a corner toward one. I didn't enjoy my food much that evening.

Nor did I sleep very well despite being exhausted. I was sure that everyone thought I was useless and stupid and that they would blame me for what was obviously a debacle. What's more, I was convinced they were right, that I was useless and stupid. The yawning gloom of a sleepless night settled on me, and I felt that the disaster had indeed been my fault—nothing had worked as planned and I had been incapable of doing anything to stop people attacking each other. I finally gave up trying to sleep at about 5AM and went for a walk around the grounds.

It was extraordinarily quiet and though the sun had yet to rise, it was beginning to get light. The stunning beauty of the formal gardens, the ancient house and the distant meadows stilled my mind, and for the first time, I noticed that I was worrying, almost exclusively, about myself. I was concerned about what people thought of *me*, how *I* was doing, the agenda *I* had designed and so on. Even the feeling it was *my* fault was self-centered, as if I were the sole cause of everything that had happened. Embarrassing though it is to admit, it was only at this point that I tumbled to the fact that it wasn't all about me. With this simple realization the gloom dissipated, and I finally felt able to concentrate on what could be done.

In any event the conflict was resolved in twenty minutes. Once I stopped obsessing about myself it became easy to see that the two sides were so deeply entrenched in their own points of view that they simply couldn't hear each other. I mapped out what I had heard from each of them as a kind of diagram, literally making it visible. I summed up using language that was as neutral as possible and concluded by making a few simple suggestions for next steps, which I asked people to raise their hands to volunteer for.

People readily offered to sign up for the next steps, there was a huge outpouring of emotion, and to my astonishment, the group gave me a standing ovation. All it had taken was me using my independent position to help each side hear the other, but the previous day my self-absorption had blinded me from seeing it (as it had them from hearing each other). I had been thinking hard but, as an improviser would put it, I wasn't present. I didn't notice anything except myself. This may have been understandable (after all, my reputation and my livelihood were at stake), but it didn't help me or the group. What helped was shifting my attention away from myself and my own preoccupations, which in the end helped me too. In the bar that evening, the most important of the clients was unstinting in his praise. "One day you might not be entirely bad at this," he mumbled. The experience is one I still go back to—it was a powerful lesson in the importance of being present.

Being really, truly present is a fabulous feeling. It is a rare combination of serenity and adrenalin. You feel serene because you are living right here, right now. All your senses are focused on the question or the ball or the snow or whatever it is. There is no fragmentation of your attention. Preoccupations about what has happened in the past or what might happen in the future recede. It feels as though time expands or slows down and you don't have to think. Your body and mind are one. Worries evaporate, decisions are easily made and everything flows through you. The boundaries between yourself and others seem to disappear or thin; there is a seamless understanding. At the same time, such moments are shot through with adrenalin because you don't know how they will unfold. There is a charge, a thrill of seeing how this moment will change things. The word is said, the ball is hit, the turn is made and you are carried along with it, you know not where. It's a rush.

These are the kinds of sensations that tell you when you're present. Whether you are in a meeting, on the squash court or riding a motorcycle, the feeling is much the same. Being present is about cultivating an exquisite quality of attention. That quality of attention, simultaneously open and focused, is powerful. It gives you options, choices and abilities you might not otherwise realize you have. Moreover it is deeply satisfying, not only to yourself, but to others as well because we love to be around people who are really present. It is an enthralling quality when you encounter it in someone else, which is why we often comment upon leaders or performers who have "great presence."

Nonetheless it is an elusive quality. It is about *really* watching, listening, sensing and feeling what is going on in the moment. It implies staying with your senses for a few moments longer than your normally might, rather than speeding off into the land of abstract thought, of plans, lists and categories. It entails noticing whatever it is that actually turns up—irrespective of what you hoped for, wanted or predicted. Being present is thus intimately connected to noticing more. Obvious though this may sound, it is remarkably easy to neglect. I remember one embarrassing occasion when three people turned up at a session Gary and I had designed for twenty. What was embarrassing was not the small numbers but the fact that it was a few minutes before we properly noticed. Even though there were only three people in the room, we spoke as if we were addressing a group of twenty. We were stuck on what we had decided in advance, and we were not being present to what was actually happening.

Being present matters because important information always lies in the moment. A good outcome may depend upon noticing a fleeting expression of doubt or surprise on someone's face or the space on the right side of the field. There is no substitute for presence. External guides (like recipe books) won't tell if you if your sauce is thickening too slowly, you have to notice that for yourself. This takes effort and persistence to cultivate. It is one of the more difficult practices to get your head around, perhaps because it requires more than your head, as we shall see.

At first glance, it would seem that there isn't much to this—either you're there or you're not. But as is often the case, things aren't quite that simple. Many of us perfected the art of being physically present but otherwise absent at school. I could easily answer "present" to the roll call while slaughtering an opponent in an imaginary game of marbles. The habit is alive and kicking later in life at home and at work. As a manager once remarked to me, "Most of our meetings suck because we decide not to be there." We all have moments when, despite being physically there, we are, in another sense, absent.

Being present is more than merely showing up. It is a choice we make. You have to actively "lean forward" into your senses so that you notice more. It implies constantly bringing your awareness to what is happening right now and giving the present priority, which means suspending or pushing aside other kinds of mental activity, like judgment, evaluation or planning. It is hard to be present when you're worrying about whether you look cool or sound stupid.

The practice of being present is fundamental to improvisation. In order to perform well, good improvisers do not focus on themselves. They know that if they try to be the hero, they may end up as the villain. Instead, they direct their attention outwards. This is the bedrock of their practice. It helps them become comfortable with not knowing what is coming. They focus on the moment and let go of egotistical worries or desires to push the process in a particular direction. This allows new ideas to emerge and lets everyone make a contribution. By being present they make themselves available to their colleagues. If you are present, you are quite literally "there" for someone. This makes it a generous position, in stark contrast to someone stuck in their own head, pursuing their own agenda.

There is an improv game (popular on the TV show *Whose Line is it Anyway?*) that illustrates the improviser's ability to get ideas from being present. The actors are given a prop to use in as many original ways as possible. The only rule is that you can't use the object for its intended purpose. Played well, it looks like the actors are plucking ideas out of nowhere—a pair of garden shears becomes a ferocious monster or an X marking the buried pirate treasure. In fact, ideas come from being present and aware of the qualities of the object (and letting go of the preconceived labels). It is better to notice that it is strong, square or squashy, than that it is a bolt, a book or a banjo. By being present to the qualities of the thing, you can see how to use it differently (the NASA engineers I mentioned in Chapter 4 were, in effect, playing a version of this game for deadly stakes).

For me, being present is vital when leading workshops. However much preparation I may have done, I have to let go of that and notice what actually happens so that I can see what is needed. At the beginning of a workshop (and the same goes for any meeting or get-together), a group might need to complain or laugh or reflect. No one can forewarn you which it will be because they won't even know themselves until the moment arrives. The only way to deal with this is to be present once you can see "the whites of their eyes." Being present allows you to pick up the clues that enable you to choose the path to take through the territory you have prepared.

Being present can be vital in a tense moment. I remember an occasion when I had invited a group to share observations on an improv exercise they had just done. Several people made thoughtful observations before Nigel, the Brit in the group, piped up. "I thought it was a stupid waste of time; there must be a better way of doing it." Ouch. The session could easily have begun to unravel at that point and everyone looked at me to see how I would react to an aggressive comment. However, on this particular day I was really present, which kept me close to the question itself; I found myself genuinely curious to see if there could be a better way, so I suggested that we try it again and that Nigel help me lead to see what we could learn.

"No, it's ok. I didn't mean it like *that*," he replied awkwardly. It turned out that I was more interested in Nigel's comment than he was, and whatever his intention, it looked to everyone else as though he was being deliberately obstructive. The threat diffused, we moved on, and for the rest of the session and afterwards, Nigel became enthusiastic rather than skeptical. By simply being present to his question I was able to stay out of judgment about him, myself or the exercise and find a way to defuse a difficult situation.

It is easy to get caught up in ourselves, but the trouble is that if you aren't present, other people will check out too. I once organized a course called Sit Stretch Eat Play that was a blend of Zen, yoga, cooking and improvisation. One of the participants was an executive who arrived straight from a meeting in London. By way of greeting, Ed Brown (the Zen and cooking teacher) and I had tea with him. Alan, the executive, was a whirlwind. For twenty minutes or so he talked nonstop, at extraordinary speed, of people and events that Ed and I knew nothing of. Though he had arrived physically, he wasn't present to us or anything around him—mentally he still inhabited the space he had left. Instead of allowing what the moment had to offer, he continued to be agitated and distracted. It was like watching someone jousting with ghosts.

While the executive ranted, the Zen master fell asleep, sitting cross-legged in half lotus on the sofa. Ed's reaction made literal something that often happens metaphorically—we check out. Thus begins a circle of cause and effect that is more tedious than vicious, but which is important nonetheless. After all, not much of a relationship is possible if we are both dozing.

The same can happen in reverse—instead of getting left behind, you can get ahead of yourself. Gary admits he is prone to this. He often catches himself using each moment to prepare for the next one, microplanning what to say or how to react without ever stopping to actually be there for the moment in question. This is ironic—the desire not to be caught unaware is what makes you unaware, which is rather like trying to shop your way out of debt with a credit card.

Many successful businesspeople recognize the danger of executive suites and palatial corner offices which disconnect you from what is really going on and invite absence more than presence. Ingvar Kamprad, the founder of IKEA, prefers to spend time in the loading bay rather than in the offices of managers. Senior executives at British retail giant Tesco periodically spend time working at the cash registers. Being physically present in this way is necessary, but you also have to make the mental effort to really pay attention once you are there. If you do, you acquire a different kind of information than you get in reports and studies. Try designing a questionnaire to capture the timbre of a customer's voice.

Being present is fundamental in negotiations, difficult conversations or media interviews. You can prepare meticulously for what you think might happen, but what you think might happen normally doesn't, so you risk getting lost as soon as you come off the narrow path you rehearsed. While you desperately try to remember your killer points, the conversation has moved on. By all means prepare, but also make an effort to be present. Indeed, make that part of your preparation. If you are present, you will inevitably find neat little hooks that connect what is actually happening with what you want to say or achieve. This is extremely satisfying for everyone involved and creates a kind of conversational Velcro.

Beyond whatever business advantages it may bring, being present affects the quality of your personal relationships in a profound way. How many parents end up with regrets like those voiced by *Newsweek* journalist Anna Quindlen (in an online article): "I wish I had not been in such a hurry to get on to the next thing: dinner, bath, book, bed. I wish I had treasured the doing a little more and the getting it done a little less."

The practice of being present is one way to "treasure the doing." As a wise old friend of mine puts it, "I try to have a good day, every day."

Yet how many of us really practice being present? When you get home, is part of you still musing on work, reluctant to leave? And when you are at work, are you wishing you were elsewhere—playing with the kids or walking in the park? How often do we kid ourselves that we are multitasking when, in reality, we aren't paying proper attention to anything? Being present is not the kind of behavior that gets noticed or valued much in organizations. Meetings and conversations easily become vehicles to advance particular agendas, cement reputations, impress someone or mark territory. How much time and energy do we spend trying to be seen as clever or informed or powerful or funny?

I have no doubt that being present is harder than it used to be. If you work on the land you have to be extremely attentive to the subtle and shifting patterns of nature, so the being-present muscle is well exercised on a daily basis. Yet few of us spend much time in nature these days. I have one neighbor, Vicente, whose livelihood depends entirely on the cherries, olives, chestnuts and figs he grows, but he is extremely unusual nowadays, even in the rural community in which I live. In a city, you are almost completely disconnected from such subtle stimuli. Moreover, the abrasive reality of the metropolis is such that you don't really want to be too closely present to it. In most western cities there are very few scents that you want to smell at all, thus we abandon our most evocative sense almost entirely.

Technology doesn't help. It constantly provides new and addictive ways to distance or absent yourself in the form of mobile phone calls, text messages and e-mails (hence the "Crackberry"). Though such devices can enable you to stay in touch, they don't help you become present. I love technology and would not be able to live the life I do without it, but it is obvious that the quality of attention you can give to someone on e-mail or on a phone is not the same as it is when you are with them. Something important is lost.

This matters in two ways. First, it means that more and more of the time we are using narrower and narrower channels. We lose the habit of being present with people so that even when we are with them, we don't pay full attention. Second, the technological devices themselves act as literal distractions, interrupting meetings and conversations and often taking precedence over the person you are physically with, which in turn sends a strong signal that being present with others is not important.

In some companies interruption is institutionalized—it is policy that you should answer the phone to a customer no matter who you are with or what you are doing. However important customer service is, is this really wise? When a conversation gets interrupted repeatedly in the course of a few minutes, attention is so fragmented that the quality of conversation and thus the quality of ideas or proposals that can be produced inevitably suffers. In the end this won't help the client either, even if their calls are always answered, not to mention what it does to the self-esteem of the staff, who are literally at the beck and call of their customers.

As well as being a constant source of interruption, technology can also act as a veil or barrier. People inside companies can easily become woefully disconnected from the reality their customers experience. Very few executives experience how irritating their own computerized telephone answering systems can be. These technological fixes might save a bundle in wages and training, but how much do they really cost in terms of frustrated customers and lost opportunity? Being present with customers not only helps them, it helps you, since they are constantly giving you precious information about what works, what's interesting, and what isn't—the kind of information that helps you innovate and improve. A menu-driven computer can't do that.

What can you do then, to practice being present? A yoga student once asked an illustrious teacher if a particular series of exercises, practiced regularly, would be enough to open the shoulders. "Yes," she replied, only to hastily correct herself. "I mean no. There is something else. You have to want to."

A similar logic applies here. The first step is to *want* to be present. It might not seem like you have much choice, but as the manager whose meetings "sucked" pointed out, we *decide* not be there. We have the opportunity to make a different, more conscious decision, rather than just be carried along by habit and routine. You might think that developing the quality of your attention is beyond you, but the people I have met who have great presence weren't born with a special inner stillness; they have actively worked on it.

Let's try something now—keep your eyes on the page while I ask a question: if you look up, how many different reds do you think will you see? Have a guess, then look up and see. Take your time, look carefully left, right, up, down, near, far and count the number of reds.

I got eleven, how about you? People normally guess low because there are plenty of reds we don't notice. We select what we see. There is so much information available to us that we simply can't take it all in, so our senses have to abbreviate. If I step out into the garden on a summer's evening I will notice the scent of jasmine but sit there for twenty minutes and the sensation will disappear. The scent hasn't gone, I just don't notice it any more. Things can also appear as well as disappear. If you are thinking of buying a Mini you suddenly see them everywhere. They were there before but you simply weren't primed to notice them.

The senses are not scientific instruments that pick up data objectively; they are exquisitely tuned to the choices we make. This means we have the opportunity to alter what we perceive. You can indeed choose to be more present, and if you do, different information will become available to you that can change the ideas or the relationships you have. Look for the reds you were previously ignoring and they will leap out at you.

When you feel stuck or exposed or confused, don't retreat into your head in search of a good idea or a clever comment. Look out, toward your surroundings and the other people you are with. Often an appropriate idea or response will quickly suggest itself to you.

This shift of focus may be a little counterintuitive at first, but it is easy enough once you get the hang of it. This can be quite a big change—most of us normally spend an inordinate amount of time and energy worrying about ourselves. So when that knot in your stomach tightens up and you feel panic beginning to rise, push your attention out instead of letting it flee (or sink) inwards. Don't think you have to come up with an answer or a clever response. Look around you, notice what other people are doing or saying, pay close attention to their expressions, their body language, their energy. If you do, just like the improviser, you will find that, almost invariably, something suggests itself. We often work harder than we need in order to try and look good, and we can save ourselves a lot of effort simply by being present. As I found in that hotel near Heathrow, the added irony is that worrying less about yourself is often the most effective way, by far, to help yourself as well.

Another thing to do is to notice and say obvious things. This helps because the pursuit of the obvious draws you forward into what is happening, rather than taking you away and toward your own preconceived agenda (to be smart or funny, perhaps?). By obvious, I mean observations or comments on what is happening, unembellished by interpretations. For example, "John didn't move" would be an obvious statement about someone's behavior during a game whereas "John refused to play" would be an interpretation.

There is a hidden advantage here because what is obvious to you is not necessarily what is obvious to me. Ask a friend who sat through the same meal, movie or meeting as you what was most obvious to them and you will see what I mean. Since we all notice different things, you don't have to be clever to be original, which means that being creative is easier than you might think. A great deal of invention occurs just by connecting obvious things in a new way. If you don't voice what is obvious, there is no possibility of this occurring.

Here is one way to check how present people are in your organization: take a stopwatch into a meeting and measure how much time there is when no one is speaking. This might seem like an odd thing to do but when people are present, they take a little time (even if its only a few seconds) to be with what has been said. They don't fill silence with talk for the sake of it, so there are often moments when no one is speaking.

If your experience is anything like mine you won't be getting a callus on your stopwatch finger. A minute's silence in the meetings I attend is unheard of. A few seconds is pretty rare—business tends to promote the survival of the loudest. Yet is what we say really so worthless as to be unworthy of even a few moments to reflect or simply be with it?

Why not challenge this? Why not introduce the idea of a few seconds of silent reflection here and there. Who knows, you might even start the meeting with a whole minute of it (if you have the time to spare, that is). Thus you might encourage people to notice how quickly they leap to conclusions. A little silence could allow people's ideas just a tiny bit of space in which to be experienced and understood properly.[1]

In modern life we tend to treat our bodies as containers for our minds, rather than as an integral part of them. As Sir Ken Robinson put it in a speech at the 2006 Technology, Entertainment, Design (TED) conference, "We regard our bodies as a means of transport to get our brains from one meeting to another," but the body is not secondary; it a primary influence on our thoughts and behavior. You don't think the same thoughts while walking that you do while sitting at a desk.

This means that your body is a good place to start when it comes to being present. Unlike your mind, your body can't get stuck in past judgments or get ahead of itself making busy little microplans. Your body is always, in a very literal sense, quite present and you can use that to anchor your mind as well. At specific moments in the day, try bringing your attention to your body. Is one shoulder raised, are you slouching, where is your tongue? Notice how it feels as well as how it is positioned—do you feel tension or excitement or calm? You don't necessarily have to do anything about this, just notice it, use your body to ground you.

If you get stuck, try changing your physical position. This will shift your point of view. We quickly adapt to and screen out stimuli that don't change (which is why the smell of jasmine disappears if you sit still). Changing your physical position gives you

- - - - - - - - - - - - - - - - - - -

1   The Finnish are very fond of silence. They designate whole areas of land "quiet" zones where any activity that might produce noise is highly restricted. Somehow I can't imagine that happening in Spain.

new stimuli and can therefore help you to be present (it also helps you engage your emotions, which is why we talk of being moved by something). This is one of the most common pieces of direction we give people in workshops—move. It is remarkable how many people will try to find inspiration from inside their heads while they sit still. Instead of letting your attention retreat into your head, encourage it to advance, outward into your body and the space around you. You'll be surprised what you can find there.

Improvisers use a couple of techniques that can help. The first is to really commit to whatever you are doing, which on stage normally means to commit oneself physically. Don't just brush your teeth, *just* brush your teeth. When you do this, through some curious alchemical process, new ideas and actions magically emerge.

Improvisers also concentrate on adopting a physical attitude they call "fit and well," which is the opposite of "sick and feeble." It consists of being open, balanced and upright. This physical attitude is in itself a creative force and will often induce or allow new ideas to come forth. Confidence can create competence, as well as the other way around.

There is nothing mystical about this. Recent developments in science have started to uncover the biochemical underpinnings of thought and feeling, and it turns out that the neurotransmitters that mediate how we think and feel are produced as much in the body as in the brain. Your bodily state literally affects what you think. It is not a metaphor. Move your body and you will change your personal biochemistry in a tangible way.

You can make techniques like these part of a regular routine, or you could use a specific trigger to help you remember the practice, like every time you get in the car. This is a great place to be really present—it could save your life (or someone else's). Adopting a reflective practice acts as a counterweight to the pressures of modern life that make it hard to be present. There are plenty to choose from. Yoga, tai chi or aikido all work with your attention. The practice of mindfulness is beginning to be applied in the realm of business. Meditation is another obvious one. If meditation sounds too strange for you, try the relaxation response. Described by Herbert Benson of Harvard Medical School in his book *The Relaxation Response*, this method bears a striking resemblance to meditation but is couched in familiar, scientific language.[2] Practicing it will not only help you be present, it is good for your health. Dr. Benson and his colleagues at the Benson-Henry Institute for Mind Body Medicine at Massachusetts General Hospital have treated thousands of patients and published dozens of studies identifying medical conditions which can be relieved or altogether eliminated with the help of the relaxation response (including cardiac arrhythmias and duodenal ulcers, as well as more common complaints such as insomnia, premenstrual tension or anxiety).

Some people take up something practical like weaving, knitting or drawing for the same reason and to great effect. Anything regular which encourages you to focus on the moment will help you with being present, not to mention the fact that most of these things are enjoyable in themselves.

It would be unrealistic to suggest that you can perpetually be absolutely present (or that you would want to be). Nonetheless through practice you can raise your baseline. Moreover, you can also choose when it is particularly important to be present and devote your efforts to occasions when it really matters. An American acquaintance of mine who worked in a large financial company found herself perpetually sitting in meetings. Convinced this was unnecessary, she announced that she would no longer attend any meeting just to show her face. Instead, she would only go to those which she judged required a more significant form of presence. After a few months she had cut the amount of time she spent in meetings in half. Asked what effect her absence from these meetings had had she replied, "Absolutely none—apart from giving me a lot more time to get on with my real job. The fact is I wasn't really there in the first place." If you can't always be present, do the opposite and take a leave of absence.

Being present doesn't sound ingenious or new because it isn't. It is an ancient notion, so it won't provide the kind of knowledge you can use to impress people. Developing the habit can be a question of finding a specific context where it is particularly

- - - - - - - - - - - - - - - - - -

2   Benson describes the relaxation response as the opposite to the adrenalin (or fight, flight, fright) response which coincidentally was discovered by a predecessor of his at Harvard, in exactly the same room!

important to you. For example, a senior manager in a consulting firm explained to me how being present helped her give people bad performance appraisals. That was where it took root for her. Instead of trying to plan in advance how she would break the news, she decided to make a real effort to be present, shifting her attention to the other person in the interview itself. Once she did, the natural openings would occur, or sometimes the person themselves would lead the conversation toward the bad news, with only gentle nudges from her. Had she been concentrating on her script these would have passed her by, making her task all the more uncomfortable and the announcement of bad news all the more abrupt. This didn't mean she gave up her goal; indeed, quite the opposite. By being really present she was able to achieve it much more elegantly.

It helps to identify an anchor experience in your own life, where being present has really worked, which can then become a touchstone. The episode I began the chapter with is one of mine. I wish I could say that such an episode hasn't reoccurred, but it isn't something you can learn once and for all, which is why this is a practice. Don't be disheartened if you find yourself having to learn the same lesson time and again; it is in the nature of this work. It reminds me of a story about a Zen student who once asked his teacher if it was enough simply to show up. "Yes," replied the master, "but maybe showing up isn't quite so easy."

8 The Chief Psychological Chore of the 21ˢᵗ Century

The first time I ever tried to ride a unicycle I concluded that staying upright on such a ludicrously unstable contraption would require a temporary suspension of some of the laws of physics. It seemed impossible not to fall and I felt like a bit of a clown for even trying. Nonetheless I persevered and three bruising weeks later, I suddenly found myself wiggling along more or less upright for about thirty feet. Just before I crashed I realized how right I had been: it is *indeed* impossible not to fall from a unicycle. You ride one by constantly allowing yourself to fall and pedaling like mad to catch up. You are, in fact, *always* falling, but with application you can learn how to fall elegantly in whichever direction you choose: forwards, sideways, even backwards. You can't defy the force of gravity but you can harness it.

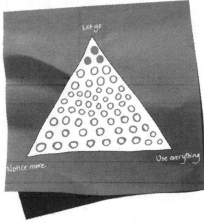

However, in order to do so you have to allow yourself to fall, which means letting go mentally as well as physically. You have to give up the idea of finding a single, stable point and then you allow yourself to begin to fall bodily while you pedal to catch up. Only once you are able to let go in both senses will you be able to balance. If you cling on instead you will stop falling elegantly and crash. Letting go establishes a state of dynamic equilibrium. This is why getting off is just as hard as getting on—at that point the flow that keeps you steady has to be interrupted.

Thus letting go means a lot more than having a few beers in the bar after work. Kevin Kelly, editor-at-large of *Wired* magazine (his official title is Senior Maverick), described "letting go with dignity" as "the chief psychological chore of the twenty-first century." The improviser's practice can give us some insight into how to go about that chore. For a coherent story to emerge, improvisers have to be constantly willing to let go. If they cling to ideas instead, they block the forward movement of the story. Imagine you and I are on stage together and I start a scene by saying, "It looks like you'll need a filling in that molar." This is the first indication you have that I am playing a dentist. Having had no chance to consult me, you had a completely different starting point in mind. However, if, as soon as I make the offer about the filling, you let go of your idea (whatever it was) and become the dentist's patient, the fact that you had a different idea will not register with the audience, and it will look as if we planned a scene in the dentist's office. Thus we start to connect and cocreate seamlessly.

The same is true off stage. On Gary's first trip to London, he, Lizzie and I were in conversation with a potential client when the client suddenly stopped us in mid-flow and said, "I have to say, there is great chemistry between the three of you, you must work together a lot." We burst out laughing and explained that, in fact, this was the first time that the three of us had ever been in a meeting together. The four of us then explored what had happened. What our potential client had noticed was that we were very responsive to each other. Lizzie might say something like, "Gary, why don't you explain how you have used the idea of blocking to help salespeople," and Gary would readily jettison whatever he had been about to say and accept her offer. The sense of rapport and connection that the client remarked upon was caused by this willingness to let go of our own particular agendas. It created a fluid and easy conversation and gave an impression of great confidence, which, given the circumstances, was quite surprising. The chemistry that makes groups of people perform well lies in these tiny details of connective tissue.

The obverse is also true. If I persist with my idea and you with yours, however smart or interesting those ideas are and however diplomatic we may be, we won't work well together. This matters. Ideas don't grow or build unless somebody is willing to let go. Nokia, the mobile phone company, started life as a wood-pulp business. Can you imagine how much people had to be prepared to let go of for it to get from those origins to where it is today? The important question then becomes "What should you let go of?" Improvisational practice offers a few specific suggestions, namely judgment, shadow stories and routines. Let's examine each of these in turn.

Improvisers mean something particular by the term judgment. They use it to refer to the snap evaluations and categorizations that we constantly make without even noticing. For example, we often decide before someone opens their mouth that what they are going to say is boring or brilliant. We walk into a room, pick up a book or hear a single bar of music and start to label and pigeonhole what we see or hear before we have really experienced it. Such judgments smack of certainty. This marks them out from intuition, which by its very nature is a vague, diffuse sense that is hard to justify or explain. You might call this prejudgment but I wouldn't call it prejudice because it isn't systematic.

To a certain extent this tendency is hard wired. Our nervous system is designed to take short cuts, fill in gaps and act on the basis of partial information. However, at the same time there is also a cultural habit that tips us into a process of constant evaluation which goes beyond trying to make sense of incomplete data. The constant barrage of commentary from the media entrenches the importance given to having a point of view. Technology provides ever more opportunities (like blogs) to express those views. The instant the film credits roll, we turn to the person next to us and say, "Did you like it?" It's uncool to have no opinion.

The improvisational practice is to recognize this kind of judgment and let go of it. Businesspeople can get quite upset about this. "I am paid to exercise my judgment" was the spiky response of one participant who felt affronted by this suggestion. Yet there is plenty of opportunity to exercise measured, skillful judgment without rushing into it. It is inane to kill an idea before it is allowed to develop. This is what snap judgments do.

By letting go of these prejudgments, improvisers keep more ideas in play and focus on feeding the flow. This allows ideas to grow and evolve. Ideas that may be weak to start with can be transformed, through connection or combination with other offers, into something of value. If they can't they will fall by the wayside and be superseded by new ones. In other words, improvisers evaluate ideas by working with them to see if they are useful, rather than by assessing them in an abstract sense. They are perpetually prototyping, which helps make the improvisational process energetic and rapid.

By contrast, the evaluative frame of mind tends to close down anything that is new or different, or could become new or different. This cuts off possibility rather than creating it. For example, someone might say (or think) "I hate all this silly stuff" before they have even arrived at one of our workshops. A person with this mindset is likely only to notice or attend to whatever they perceive as silly. This might make them feel right (as in, "You see, I knew this would be silly.") but it removes the possibility of any discovery, learning or growth. Do this and you dismiss possibilities you have yet to explore.

As well as preventing you from realizing the potential of ideas, getting stuck on judgment can land you in trouble. Imagine you are a parachutist coming to land in a large, flat field with only one obstacle (a tree, for example). If you focus on the tree, the chances are you will end up in its branches. Parachutists call this "target fixation," and it is an illustration of how judgment can suck you in. For example, thoughts such as "I am no good at strategy" can become self-fulfilling prophecies. Just like the parachutist, your behavior shifts in tiny, invisible ways to make your judgment come true. You do better by letting go of the judgment—parachutists are trained to focus on the flat bit of the field where they want to end up, not the tree they wish to avoid.

If you are quick to judge it can also stop your learning. For example, early in the Second World War, a German Messerschmitt Me 109 fighter was captured intact and taken to Boscombe Down on Salisbury Plain in southern England—one of the Royal Air Force's testing bases. This was one of the first opportunities the British had to assess the enemy aircraft's strong and weak points, to inform the tactics of the Hurricanes and Spitfires defending Britain against the Luftwaffe. The British reports on the Me 109 stated that, "[I]n general flying qualities the airplane is inferior to both the Spitfire and the Hurricane at all speeds and in all conditions of flight. It does not possess the control which allows of good quality flying and this is particularly noticeable in aerobatics."

However, during the Battle of Britain the Me 109 was to prove superior to the Hurricane and evenly matched with the Spitfire I. In the straitened circumstances of war, the British engineers desperately wanted to find the Messerschmitt lacking, which limited the usefulness of their report. Curiously enough, the Germans did much the same. Around the same time the Luftwaffe evaluated a captured Spitfire, and the test pilot, Hauptmann Werner Mölders, concluded that, "as a fighting aircraft, it is miserable."[1]

It is important to consciously practice letting go because judgments of this kind affect us more than we realize. If you don't let go of prior judgments, good or bad, the chances are you'll design your research to confirm what you believe and miss learning something of value.

More than anything, we tend to judge people quickly, particularly ourselves. We often have a running commentary in the back of our minds, which is none too complimentary. "That's a stupid thing to say," "nobody here likes you," "you're an impostor; you don't know anything about that" are the kind of comments that typically rattle around in the back of our minds. This isn't modesty but the insidious whispers of self-judgment.

Thus it takes only nanoseconds to turn a tiny incident into a personal crisis. I remember a session I was running where someone fell asleep. There, in the front row of the audience, a young man with glasses had nodded off. In a fraction of a second I concluded that he was asleep because he was bored, that everyone in the audience must be equally bored, that I was boring him (as I always bore people) and therefore I must be an incompetent, worthless individual who would never find work again. It is amazing how quickly I can do this. In fact, it almost certainly had nothing to do with me at all. There was a good chance he was jet-lagged, and it was after lunch so a "food coma" had probably set in.

It is important to recognize that we can't help but make such judgments. Even before consciousness enters the game, our senses make active discriminations about what

- - - - - - - - - - - - - - - - - - -

1   Brian Johnson and Terry Heffernan, *A Most Secret Place: Boscombe Down 1939–1945*, (London: Jane's, 1982).

information to pass up the line. But there are still choices we can make. The point is to keep letting go, moment by moment, so that you can remain open to new information. Don't try to have no judgment, but do try not to hold on to any particular one. Constantly letting go turns out to be the crucial ingredient in the relaxation response (a kind of western meditation that I mentioned in the previous chapter). The health benefits it delivers did not require people to sit still or be quiet; all that was required was to constantly let go of worries and preoccupations.

Clinging to judgment can keep you stuck in the past. However, you can also get stuck in the future. Or, to be strictly accurate, you can get stuck in what you think will be the future. All day long we generate projections about the way a story, conversation or process is going to go. Improvisers call these shadow stories. Imagine a long shadow stretching out in front of you when the sun is low. In a similar way shadow stories stretch out in front of you. Like your own shadow, they are the result of something real (the story so far), but just like shadows, they tend to be distorted. As soon as I write, "Once upon a time there was a…" you will imagine a child, wizard, troll or some other kind of fairytale creature (rather than a foreign minister or a nuclear physicist). Whereas if I say, "Today the Bank of England raised…" you will expect me to say "interest rates," not "the flag of St. George" or "the ceiling in it's Threadneedle Street building." We fill in the blanks before waiting for the thing to end. Shadow stories can crop up before you even start a conversation. You might be familiar with a kind of inner dialogue that goes something like this: "Then I will say, 'No, it was a year's work,' and they'll say 'It was only six months,' and I'll say, 'But it really started in March,' and they'll say, 'That was preparation,' and I'll say, 'But it still cost us money,' and they'll say…"

In reality, "they" will probably say nothing of the sort, so this imagined game of mental ping pong can derail you. Similarly, if you attend a week-long leadership course but can't let go of the shadow story you came with, you will miss the chance to learn all kinds of things you didn't expect or anticipate as the week unfolds.

Since there is nothing you can do to stop shadow stories coming, the practice is to let go of them, or at least, not to become attached to them. When you let go of one shadow story another one will soon spring up unbidden, which you can also let go of. This means there are plenty of opportunities to practice.

One specific way of working on this is to make sure that you don't finish other people's sentences. Let them say what they want, rather than filling in with your own shadow story. If you let them finish, you might find that what they say is more interesting than you had imagined. Even if it isn't, they will thank you for respecting them.

Another specific thing you can do is make your shadow stories visible. At the beginning of a workshop I might say something like, "You might be wondering what improvisation has to do with you." This is my own shadow story, and by making it visible, I invite people to tell me I am wrong or confirm I am right. Whichever it is, I get better information. I also remind myself to deal with what is in the room, not with what I think might be in the room. Getting ahead of yourself often creates more pressure and worry than it saves.

Letting go of judgments and shadow stories is intimately connected to being present. You can think of this in terms of past, present and future. Judgment takes you out of the moment by pulling you back toward the past—you make a judgment based on previous experience. Shadow stories do the opposite, they pull you out of the moment by taking you into the future—a future which may or may not come to pass. Thus, letting go of both is important if you want to stay in the present.

In addition to judgment and shadow stories, improvisers also practice letting go of routines. On stage a routine is a repeated or stable pattern of behavior. Two people talking at a bus stop would be a routine in an improv scene. When a routine is broken, action occurs. A routine can be broken in many ways. The routine of talking at the bus stop might be interrupted by the bus arriving or by someone else joining the line or by bird poop landing on someone's head.

Everyday life is full of these repeated patterns on all levels. You have personal routines (checking e-mail), collective routines (how and when you hold meetings), even industry routines (a new model or product cycle). Clinging to routines feels familiar and safe, but it is hard to make an interesting story or develop new ideas if you aren't willing to let go of some routines.

There are plenty of routines you could choose to break. For example, this morning at breakfast my children were reading the ingredients and copy on the back of the cereal box for the umpteenth time, just as I did forty years ago. The routine of cereal box design is decades old. Imagine that a cereal manufacturer chose to interrupt this routine by printing a story on the box instead of promotional guff. Once the story becomes the new routine you can interrupt that and change the story. You could then interrupt that new routine by inviting children to write the stories instead of copywriters, and you could make books of the best ones.

Thus breaking, challenging, disrupting or otherwise letting go of routines is a simple way to move toward the twenty-first-century holy grail—innovation. When you break a routine you inevitably get to new ideas and opportunities. The nice thing about this is that you can start small. There are thousands of routines you can break. You can start immediately and can do it on any scale (i.e., you can break personal routines, team routines, company routines, industry routines). If you always meet in the office, why not break that routine by meeting at a coffee shop (resuscitating a common seventeenth-century routine). If you habitually dress up for work, then dress down (or vice versa), whether it is Friday or not. If you always advertise on TV at Christmas, spend the money on something else instead. And so on.

This doesn't mean eradicating all routines. Routines create a pattern that is useful when you want to ensure you don't miss anything (like a pilot's preflight check), when you want to conserve energy (your morning routine) or if you want your product or idea to mesh seamlessly with a common standard (e.g., protocols). On-stage routines also have value. Without any routines you will have a pretty chaotic story.

However, there are plenty of routines, like the cereal box, that we have become very used to but which aren't remotely necessary. I am reminded of an Argentinean friend who once asked her mother why their family always cut the head off a fish before baking it when none of her friends did. "It's because your grandmother used to have such small oven," she said. "It was the only way we could fit it in." There are plenty of routines whose original reason for being no longer applies, which are just begging to be broken.

Over time what you are looking for is a kind of "punctuated equilibrium"[2] with an ebb and flow created by first establishing and then breaking routines. This ebb and flow has a rhythm that you can become sensitive to. You can also be quite deliberate about it. Here's how.

Step 1—List the Routines.

Take some project or process that feels stuck and list all the routines you can find. Include anything that is a repeated piece of behavior, like "we use TV advertising," "we sit in the same place at the table" or "our recommended retail price is always something and ninety-nine cents." You want to be as comprehensive as you can. Don't worry if the routines sound obvious or dull.

This step alone can be illuminating. Is the list long or short? Were routines easy or hard to find? Are they your own particular routines or are they industry or category ones? Can you spot any redundant conventions (like the headless fish)?

Step 2—Choose Some Routines to Break.

The second step is to choose a few of these to break (you only need a few). Look for the ones that might be limiting you, or that might just be fun to play around with.

Step 3—Brainstorm Ways to Break These Routines.

Then brainstorm ways in which you could break them. Don't hold back here. This is a chance to let a little bit of nonsense into the process, and nonsensical thoughts often lead you toward new ideas.

- - - - - - - - - - - - - - - - - - -

2   This is a term popularized by paleontologist Stephen Jay Gould which suggests that in evolution there are long periods of relative stasis, interrupted by explosions of variety. Both its proponents and their opponents seem fond of using the shorthand phrase "punk eek," probably for different reasons.

Step 4—Choose Which Idea to Use to Break the Routine.

> From the long list of ideas, choose one to adopt. This is the point where you get practical, so you might need to tone down or adapt some of the wilder ideas to fit your circumstances.

Let's imagine that you have to give a presentation to a committee which is hearing presentations all day. To make yours stand out you decide to break a routine. It is easy to list the routines surrounding presentations:

The audience is seated;

The presenter stands at the front of the room;

Slides are used with text arranged in bullet points;

The presenter speaks in a measured voice, neither whispering nor shouting;

The presenter talks in uninterrupted fashion.

You quickly decide that the routine of showing bullet-pointed slides is a good one to attack, so you start to come up with ways you could break that routine. You don't worry yet about how practical the suggestions are, so you soon have quite a list of things you could do, like this:

Use no words at all, only pictures;

Find movie clips;

Draw your slides by hand;

Use a mind map to present from, instead of a deck of charts;

Use objects or props instead of slides;

Learn your speech by heart;

Write the presentation in verse;

Use actors or colleagues to act stuff out.

With all these ideas on the table you can sift through them (Step 4) with a more pragmatic eye and look for those you might use. Some ideas you might be able to literally take and use, or you might take one of the more extreme ideas and adapt it in some suitable way. For example, you might not be able to do a whole presentation in verse (which after all, would quickly become another routine, albeit a rather unusual one) but you could use a rhyming couplet to make each key point memorable, like this: "Routines that you break, action will make."

The practice of letting go enables improvisers to develop an unusual attitude toward change. By attitude, I mean more than just an opinion about something. When aeronautical engineers talk about the attitude of an aircraft, they mean the angle it adopts relative to the airflow around it. I mean attitude in this almost physical sense. The attitude you adopt governs how you interpret and respond to the circumstances approaching you and what happens as a result—just as the attitude of the aircraft to the air determines whether it flies or falls out of the sky.

This attitude is to be willing to be change. Rather than flee from change or deny it or try and pass the responsibility for change onto someone else, improvisers embrace change, personally. They seek it out. Within each scene or story, improvisers look to accept the offers that oblige them to change because they know this is how the characters and relationships in the story grow and develop. Without change there is no action. Offers that force them to change thus become attractive rather than scary, and uncertainty becomes something that they warm to rather than worry about. Improvisers don't know what's coming any more than you or I, but they understand the power of not knowing and appreciate that the short-term safety of staying unchanged is illusory: the scene will stagnate and the audience will lose interest.

Improvisers thus distinguish between action and activity. If someone is changed by what happens they call it action. If not, it is activity. Let me illustrate using movies. Think of a Bond film (*any* Bond film). The chase (whether it's in a car, a boat or on skis) starts with 007 ahead of the bad guys and ends with 007 ahead of the bad guys. A lot happens but nothing has really changed. Expensive special effects notwithstanding, an improviser would call this activity, not action. Action should not be confused with simply rushing around.

Contrast the Bond movie with a scene from the end of the Oscar-winning film *American Beauty*. The protagonist, Lester Burnham (played by Kevin Spacey), is working out in his garage when he is approached by his neo-Nazi neighbor, Colonel Frank Fitts. Burnham makes some ambiguous comments about his marriage and Fitts tries to kiss him, much to Burnham's consternation. Thus we learn that Colonel Fitts is a repressed homosexual, and this knowledge completely changes our understanding of the character. All we see is a small movement, but this is action because of what we have learned. It turns out that action, learning and change are intimately connected. If you want to create action or you want to learn (who doesn't want both of these?), you have to cultivate the practice of being willing to be changed.

This might sound obvious, but to an improviser looking at a business organization for the first time (as Gary did, some ten years ago), it is striking how little people are willing to be changed. From his perspective it remains baffling how much time, energy and attention people in business devote to activity. Much of what people do in the office every day may help them feel busy or important or safe, but it doesn't create what an improviser would call action. Funnily enough, business language seems to confirm this. For example, marketing plans are made up of "marketing activity," and in the improviser's sense, that's just what it is—activity. Very little of it effects enough change to pass muster as a piece of action.

The value of action over activity is illustrated if you think about how much the *American Beauty* scene and the Bond sequence must each have cost to shoot. Two actors in a garage, or a massive crew, exotic location and a bundle of special effects. Where there is no real action you have to spend a lot of cash to make it interesting. Not only that but you have to spend ever-increasing amounts of money as the bar is raised every time. Creating action through some kind of emotional change is a much more cost-effective way to engage an audience of any kind—whether it is in a cinema or the conference room.

Embracing change in this intensely personal way is not an attitude many people habitually adopt. Yet how can an organization learn, or create action, if the people in it don't? As I mentioned earlier, businesspeople often talk about "managing" change, as if by preparing well enough, you can make sure you are not caught unawares. Even if this were possible, and it would require a degree of clairvoyance that isn't commonly available, to an improviser such an attitude seems counterproductive. It's a bit like saying, "If we could just switch on the light then I won't be afraid of the dark." If you just have the patience to stay in the dark, after awhile you'll find you can see better than you thought possible. If you switch on the light, your eye never adapts.[3]

There is one last piece of improvisational vocabulary that relates to letting go and being willing to be changed: platform and tilt. A platform is the place, setting or world in which a story takes place. In a movie it is normally established in the opening sequence; in business, it would be a description of the category, technology or way of doing business. A platform could be two rival families, at loggerheads over power in a medieval Italian city. Or it could be telephone companies charging for calls in terms of distance and time.

Action is unleashed when that platform is tilted (filmmakers call this the "inciting incident"). A tilt changes something central to the platform so that everything starts to shift, often gathering speed as it does so. When a young man from one powerful family falls in love with a girl from the rival family, you have the tilt that launches the action of Shakespeare's *Romeo and Juliet*. Similarly the appearance of Skype and other voice-over-internet protocol operators tilts the existing platform of telecommunications. In business terms tilts might happen when a new competitor enters a market, a new technology appears or a takeover bid is launched.

Improvisers use the idea of platforms and tilts to help guide their action. First they need to establish a platform, otherwise they don't have anything worth tilting. In other

---

3 Understanding this can help if you are ever out in the wilds at night. When you switch on your flashlight to look at the map, close one eye (always the same one). The eye that is closed will remain adapted to the dark, since it will not be exposed to the light, improving your night vision tremendously. Apparently this is a technique commandos use for nighttime operations.

words, you don't start with a tilt. But once the platform is established, you have to look for an opportunity to tilt it. This unleashes a torrent of action that is normally resolved in a new platform. Depending how long a story is, you may go through this sequence several times. Once again, this encourages you to let go (of the existing platform) and be changed (by the tilt). The construct also helps improvisers navigate through confusing circumstances. It gives them a piece of structure to think about where they are in a story or process—constructing a platform, tilting it or resolving it into a new platform—which helps them decide what to do next.

The same way of thinking can be a useful way for businesspeople to frame what is happening. Are you in a phase of platform building (which might suggest collaborating with competitors, building and agreeing to protocols and so on) or is there a tilt happening? If so, what kind of tilt is it, where is it coming from, and how can you embrace it? If not, might it be helpful to precipitate a tilt so you are in a better position to take advantage of it?

Most companies don't do this, they fight tooth and nail against the tilt. For example, during the 1990s I was personally involved with the launch of the EV1, GM's electric vehicle. At the time there were rumors (given some credence in the documentary film *Who Killed The Electric Car?*) that GM was spending as much on the legal fees fighting California's zero-emissions legislation as they were on marketing the car. Whether that was literally true or not, I have no doubt that GM resisted the change. Some fifteen years later the Toyota Prius is a huge success and GM has nothing to rival it. Had GM embraced the tilt, it might have been quite a different story.

♡

On the morning of Friday, September 14, 2001, On Your Feet was due to present at a human resources conference at the Washington Athletic Club in Seattle. Like many other events in that fateful week, it came close to being cancelled but, in the end, went ahead. Halfway through the morning the organizers must have felt they had made a monumental mistake. One of the speakers (a stand-up comedian) had persisted with his normal act, which included gags about terrorists and blowing up buildings. It is hard to fathom why anyone would do such a thing, but my surmise is that it had a lot to do with the inability to let go or be changed. Stand-up comedians have meticulously prepared material which takes a huge amount of work to develop. This comedian may have felt he either had to deliver his normal act or not perform at all. Whatever his reasoning, the results of clinging to the old material were disastrous.

My colleagues arrived to find the conference in uproar. The comedian had just finished his act. Some of the audience were in tears and others were furious. This posed an awkward dilemma because the consequences of canceling or carrying on seemed equally grave. After a quick huddle Gary and the team recommended that they go on, and the organizers somewhat reluctantly agreed.

I later asked Gary how they arrived at that decision. "It didn't seem right to do what we had planned, and though it was a risk to change everything at zero notice, doing nothing would have left a horrible apologetic emptiness." In his introduction Gary acknowledged the strangeness of the situation (thus using it as an offer) and explained how improvisation is based on a way of working where you create connections in difficult and changing circumstances. This beginning reframed the piece, moved it away from comedy, and made it relevant to what was happening in the room at the time. People still laughed, for the familiar reason that they saw seemingly unrelated things being brought together in a story. This was enormously cathartic, even if it was the kind of laughter which is only a hair's breadth away from tears.

While being changed often feels uncomfortable and risky, it is important to recognize that it isn't the only risk. The willingness of On Your Feet to be changed by the circumstances was much less of a risk than carrying on unchanged as if nothing was wrong (which was what the comedian had done). That would have done absolutely nothing to turn a desperate situation around. It was a risk worth taking and it paid off, not just for Gary and the team, but for the organizers and for the audience. As someone put it afterwards, "I realized today that the shortest distance between two people is laughter."[4]

- - - - - - - - - - - - - - - - - - -
4   I believe this saying is attributed to Stan Laurel.

People sometimes confuse stand-up comedy and improvisation. That is understandable since they are both forms of comedic theater, yet in fact they are quite different. The comedian wasn't able or willing to let go, but to the improvisers it was second nature. The differences between these two apparently similar forms of comedy are revealing. Stand-up comedians lay great store by their material: content really matters. They spend time researching and observing and then they work it into routines and gags, with particular delivery and timing. Each comedian, whether it's Tommy Cooper or Jerry Seinfeld, has a distinctive personality through which the gags are delivered that becomes as much a part of the act as the material itself.

There is a parallel here. Traditionally companies focus on the material product. They spend a lot of time and energy making something that works well, which can be efficiently (and consistently) produced at a low price and sold in great volume. Similarly, manufacturers (and later, service companies) developed the model of a simple, consistent personality or brand which is managed and controlled as if it were a tangible asset. This personality wraps the material product and represents or amplifies its differences or superiorities.[5] In both cases there is a well-defined offering that is put before an audience in a highly finished state.

Improvisers, by contrast, constantly generate innovative material. They have the skills to adapt, change and create as they go, and they navigate their way through adventures that they could not have imagined in advance. In business too, we are beginning to see that great command of your material is no longer enough. Technology means that the material differences between one product and another are tiny and short lived anyway. The explosion and fragmentation of the media (leading to and driven by the Internet) means that it is increasingly hard to find a mass audience to whom you can deliver your carefully crafted message—let alone persuade them to hear what you want to say. And since they are very sophisticated, even if they hear it, there is no guarantee

- - - - - - - - - - - - - - - - - - -

5   Lately some brand marketers have come to believe that personality alone is enough, without any material differences. In my view, that seems about as sustainable as a comedian with no original jokes.

they will do what you want. As a comedian might put it, they are a tough audience. This could serve as a very apt metaphor for how business is changing. If the twentieth century was an era of "stand-up" business, then this new century is ushering in an era that could aptly be described as "improv" business.

9 🐦 Get Bad at Poker

Wander through Union Square in New York City and there is a chance you will come across a street entertainer of a most unusual kind. Normally, you watch or listen to a performer's act. They might play the banjo, juggle or pose like a statue, but one way or another they provide the entertainment and you provide the audience. You not only give them money, but a little of your time and attention. Not so with this particular gentleman. Give him a dollar or two and you get to talk (or shout) at him for thirty seconds. *He* is the one that listens. This isn't a trick to lure you into his act, listening *is* the act. The joke is that people in fast-talking New York City need to pay someone to listen to them. Like many good jokes it makes a serious point: that being heard is of value to us (though we don't normally expect to pay cash for it).

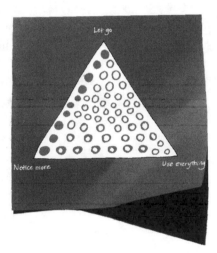

We all need to be heard. Being heard validates us and connects us to other people. On a scale of basic needs it isn't quite on the level of food, drink or air, but it doesn't lag far behind. Listening is the glue of human relationships. You and I might sit in a room and take turns to talk but unless we listen to each other, there is no conversation, just alternating monologues. Unless we listen, we do not relate to each other, frustration and disappointment set in and it becomes almost impossible to make anything together.

The improv stage brings the importance of listening home with a vengeance. Improvisers have to listen incredibly well; otherwise they quickly become isolated and exposed. It is only through good listening that they can exchange information, learn from each other, build ideas and create action. The quality of an improviser's listening is put under the microscope because the gaps or jumps that occur when they don't listen are unmistakable in the glare of the footlights—to colleagues and particularly to the audience. These gaps are costly. When performers fail to listen they destroy the very connective tissue they are working so hard to create. Instead of one coherent story, you get disjointed fragments about a German shepherd dog, a spaceman or a wedding dress. It becomes hard to weave these together, so as a result of bad listening you not only get an inferior product but you have to work much harder. You also forfeit the goodwill of the audience because people automatically cool toward someone who does not listen, whereas they warm to someone who does.

Scrutinize any normal interaction and you will find the same gaps and jumps occur. However, the damage is not immediately obvious because people do not give the explicit, uncensored feedback that an audience gives you in a theater. Nonetheless the failure to listen comes home to roost. Even though the effects may be disguised or delayed, the consequences are much the same in everyday life as they are for improvisers. When people don't listen well, time and energy are wasted, misunderstandings are deeper and more common, it becomes harder to develop new ideas and trust is weakened. When other people don't listen to us we feel diminished and unappreciated. When we don't listen to others we lock ourselves away in our own little world.

If asked, most people would agree that listening is important, yet that doesn't necessarily translate into action. Take European politicians as an example. They often talk about how important listening is, but in June 2005, after the French and Dutch had roundly voted against the new European Constitution, the president of Luxembourg declared that "the French and Dutch people didn't say no to the constitution." This is puzzling—what did they say then? My conclusion is not about Dutch or French voters at all—what it tells me is that the president of Luxembourg had no inclination to listen whatsoever.

Yet to be fair to the president of Luxembourg, politicians aren't alone in this weakness. Over a decade of workshops I have had the opportunity to observe thousands of people and how they perform in improvisational exercises that require you to listen.

The pattern I see is that few people consistently listen well and even fewer listen as well as they think they do. Does that fit your experience? Do you feel that your family, friends or colleagues consistently listen well? The polite answer is often, "Not as well as I would like." And what about you? Let me ask an indiscreet question (after all, there's nobody else listening). Are you a good listener? Even if you wouldn't publicly make that claim, just between you and me, what do you think?

Imagine I told you that you weren't. How would you feel? In my experience people are easily offended if you suggest they don't listen well. While it isn't quite on a par with saying that democracy is a bad idea or that there are times when you can't stand your kids, it's close. We feel morally obligated to listen and listen well, and it becomes taboo to admit that we don't. As a result, we look the other way and avoid mentioning it altogether. When everyone does the same, the result is a conspiracy of politeness that is very comfortable but prevents us from doing anything to improve our listening.

With improvisational exercises this isn't possible. In workshops poor listening is sometimes so obvious it can be a little embarrassing, particularly because the bosses often seem to be worse than anyone else. Mortified participants will frequently make solemn commitments to "listen better." Laudable though this may be, it isn't very helpful either. It amounts to no more than saying "try harder," and how helpful is that? It doesn't help you understand what gets in the way of listening, nor does it give you anything practical or specific to do.

If you really want to work on the practice of listening, it is helpful to acknowledge that it is not just important, but hard. It isn't remotely surprising that we find it hard to listen for there are plenty of things that get in the way. It is worth making a little effort to understand what those barriers are. Then, rather than simply trying to listen better, we can look for specific pieces of action that will give us something concrete to work on.

In the same way that mobile phones and BlackBerrys don't help us be present, the physical environment doesn't help us listen. In cities (which will soon hold the majority of the world's population) people are subject to an unceasing barrage of sound, which we mostly don't want to hear, so being the highly adaptable creatures that we are, we become good at shutting it out. Instead of actively working to hear as much as possible (which must have been more common when finding food or avoiding danger depended upon it), we have become very good at filtering. So when you do want to listen, you have to swim upstream against the current of a deeply ingrained habit.

The social environment accentuates this difficulty. We have what you might call an "oratorical fixation." People are generally admired and rewarded (both socially and financially) for speaking well. People who sound smart get the plaudits and the promotions. The higher up you get, the more severe this gets as business tends to encourage behaviors which are more forceful than sensitive. Executives often only pay lip service to "soft" skills that are regarded as weak or wimpy. Thus there are few models of excellent listening to emulate.

Formal training follows the same pattern. Almost everyone will have been on some kind of course to help them to speak better (normally in the form of presentation skills), but who has ever been on a course to help them practice better listening? The very idea of such a thing seems a little odd. This works against good listening in two different ways. Not only do we lack the training, but we are given to understand that talking matters more than listening. Look at your own day—how much time and effort do you devote to listening, and how much to speaking? If you have to give a presentation or make a speech, I expect you prepare meticulously, but does anyone ever prepare to listen? Can you even imagine what preparation for listening would consist of?

Our fondness for control also affects our ability to listen. This is a fundamental theme we will return to later (in Chapter 14) but for now I want to consider it simply in relation to listening. Imagine you and I sit down to have a conversation. I won't let you choose what we talk about, and however our chat meanders, I always bring it back to the subject that interests me. I dictate the structure of the conversation, with specific rules about how you answer my questions and what you can ask of me. Some other people are also listening to our conversation, but from behind a mirror (where they are also chatting with each other, nibbling sandwiches or answering e-mails). Would you enjoy such a conversation? Would you really feel heard? What quality of listening is really going on in such circumstances?

Yet in market research, a business function where listening to customers is the raison d'etre, this would be considered normal. Indeed, what I have described here is the most open, flexible style of research (i.e., qualitative). Yet if you insist on controlling the conversation to this degree, I would contend that you are listening in a very limited way. I spent many years doing market research, and I didn't meet many businesspeople who were really willing or able to listen openly to what their customers actually *wanted* to say. There are normally far too many agendas in play. The irony was that, on the rare occasions when they were really willing to listen deeply, the discoveries they made were far more valuable.

It isn't just the physical and cultural environment that makes listening hard. Our own internal environment exacerbates the difficulty. The desire to listen has to compete with lots of other desires. We have a number of different characters within us, each with different (sometimes conflicting) interests, vying for ascendancy. In improv games these characters become highly visible. One of the strongest is the peacock, the character whose only desire is to be the center of attention. He thus wants to be listened to, rather than listen, and consequently tends to pay little attention to anything he hasn't said himself.

Another powerful character is the rooster, who wants to be right, whatever the cost. Since he has already made up his mind, convincing other people comes much higher on his agenda than listening to others, and if necessary, he will ignore them to prove he was right, even if it jeopardizes the flow.

Then there is also the ostrich. This is the fearful one who, frightened of what they might hear, would rather not listen. Even the good citizen can be a problem. Keen to ensure he is making a contribution, he looks for opportunities to speak up, even when it's redundant. This gently but insidiously erodes the quality of listening as each good citizen tries to work the conversation round so they can make their point, making conversations unnecessarily long, dull and rambling (this is particularly obvious in conference calls).

Each of us will have these (or other) inner voices in different blends. The point is not to set up a pat typology but to notice that these competing desires are real and strong, which is why simply trying harder to listen better won't work. There is some unlearning to be done here, and rather than mental arguments which merely lead to a battle of wits, what is required is real experience. It is the only way to demonstrate that the advantages of listening outweigh the fears. There is no substitute for practice.

Many different terms have been coined to identify different kinds or qualities of listening. Distinctions are made between downloading, objective or attentive listening and empathic or generative listening. What improvisation adds to these concepts is one simple, powerful idea, grounded in action.

Improv directors and teachers discovered awhile ago that "be changed by what you hear" is a much better piece of direction for an actor than "listen better." This is logical—you can only know I have heard you if there is some kind of observable response, otherwise you are merely broadcasting. In a nutshell, their advice would be to get bad at poker—it is the opposite of the poker face that gives nothing away—you need to show, demonstrate or signal that you have heard.

Thus, although listening is obviously connected to noticing more, the particular practice of being changed by what you hear shows that it is also connected to letting go. Being changed by what you hear is a particularly important example of being changed in general. The demonstration of listening matters to the people around you—it is how you relay the fact that you have, in some way, been affected by what they say; that is, you have listened. What's important here is the shift induced in the person listening. If you know you have demonstrated that you heard them, you are obliged to listen because unless you do, you have no idea what to do as a result. If I tell you I got a pay rise and you say nothing while I am clearly delighted, it is pretty obvious you haven't heard me. To demonstrate you have listened you can't just respond randomly either, you have to slap me on the back or say something appropriate like, "Maybe you could lend me some cash then." Holding on to the simple idea that you need to be changed by what you hear obliges you to listen.

It is this practice that can make improvisers seem psychic. They are so readily changed that it seems like they must have known what was coming. If you force yourself to be affected by what others say, you cannot just stick to the ideas you began with; you have to include, respond to, connect with and build on other people's contributions. This kind of listening acts as a centripetal force that brings things together and creates a single, shared, coherent story.

This principle applies on a multimillion-dollar warship as much as it does on the improv stage. Remember Captain Mike Abrashoff of the U.S. Navy? The first thing he did when he joined the ship was to interview every member of the crew. This alone seems like quite an effective exercise in listening and certainly required the dedication of a large amount of time. Abrashoff however, decided it wasn't enough. He knew that cynicism ran deep among the sailors, but he also realized that the whole process could be seen as an elaborate and costly public relations exercise meant to woo the crew without making one jot of real difference.

Some organizations, particularly big ones, seem to get stuck at this point. As with Abrashoff, their instinct or their research tells them that their public (be they crew or customers) thinks they don't listen. They know this isn't good and want to correct it, so they make it a priority. So far, so good, but the next step can be a false one. Armed with conviction and purpose, they go out and talk about how well they listen—hence advertising campaigns with taglines like "the listening bank" or "everything we do is driven by you" (for a car manufacturer). This is exactly the kind of response you would expect from someone who doesn't listen, because they try and talk their way out of it instead of demonstrating their listening. It is akin to the person at a party who, after talking about themselves for some time, finally turns to you and says, "But that's enough about me. What do you think about me?"

By contrast, Abrashoff acted in line with our improvisational practice. He allowed himself (and the whole ship's company) to be changed. When he heard a good idea from a crew member that was within his power to implement, he would announce it over the ship's intercom, even while the crew member was still sitting in his cabin (which lead to his nickname of "Megaphone Mike"). If someone suggested that small-arms target practice be done at sea in order to save precious time on shore, he would take them up on it and announce it instantly. This demonstrated that he was really listening to the crew and taking their ideas seriously. Any remaining cynicism evaporated—this was clearly not a public relations exercise. The knock on effect was that crew members yet to be interviewed started to really think seriously about what they wanted to say.

In workshops I see the same pattern. It can be really helpful to look actively for an opportunity to be changed by something I have heard early on. For example, I might visibly change in response to a comment. Imagine someone asks, "What would happen if we stood in a circle, instead of a line?" Rather than simply acquiesce, I might say something like, "I wasn't planning to do that, but why don't we try it?" That clearly signals that I have changed and therefore that I have heard them. Into the bargain I get to try something new (and who knows, doing the game in a circle might be a stroke of genius).

This attitude—of looking for an opportunity to be changed by the group—isn't automatic. I have had to learn through experience that demonstrating listening is worth much more than the security of sticking with my plan. Though it feels safer to stay with what you know, you generate far more trust and get the group working effectively faster if you demonstrate listening. It's only natural. If you feel I am trotting out a script that doesn't take you into account, why should you be interested?

Being changed by what you hear doesn't mean you have to be as loud as a ship's intercom, it just needs to be noticeable. You don't necessarily have to talk at all. The change can be an emotional one: a gesture, an expression, a movement. Though these might appear quite small, the charge they carry can be great.

You can also demonstrate you have been changed (and thus that you have listened) in what you write. A couple of years ago, I got an e-mail out of the blue from someone in Belgium I had never heard of—the kind of e-mail that normally gets deleted automatically, if not by the software, than by me. The sender, Kristin Verellen, was wise enough to play back, in the very first line of her e-mail, a phrase of my own (one I had used in a chapter of the book *Brand New Thinking*). I remember that I warmed to her instantly, even though I didn't know why. I simply couldn't help but feel engaged, even in an unpromising medium like e-mail. Only later did I work out why I felt this way. Kristin's e-mail demonstrated that she had been changed by reading what I wrote, and because I felt heard, I was open to having a conversation with her.

The value of being changed by what you hear becomes apparent when it is absent. Children often won't show they have heard (just one of the reasons they drive their parents nuts). If I ask one of my sons to put his shoes on and he continues with his head buried in a comic, seemingly oblivious to what I have said, there will come a point, after perhaps three or four requests that I lose my patience and shout. The inevitable sarcastic response, along the lines of "All right, I heard you," feels so unfair because he gave me absolutely no indication whatsoever that he had heard at all. How on earth was I to know?

There are occasions when you don't want to be changed. At the Battle of Copenhagen in 1801, the British hero Admiral Nelson held a telescope to his blind eye, uttered the famous words "I see no signal" and proceeded to ignore the change to his orders issued by Admiral Hyde and slug out a victory, which I suspect was just as well. Had the battle not gone his way, I think his failure to listen would have been seen as less than heroic, even for Nelson.

One of the most striking demonstrations of the power of listening has taken place over the last ten years in South Africa. The Truth and Reconciliation Commission has been an extraordinary way to bring about healing through hearing. A space was created where the horrors that had been perpetrated could be heard, not judged. People of every color and class were encouraged to come forward and speak about what had happened to them or what they had done. These were not legal hearings. This was an expression of humanity, not an exercise in advocacy. Nor was this a one-off piece of grandstanding. For years after the abolition of apartheid the commission quietly continued its work, in town-hall meetings and public gatherings throughout the country, and the results have been impressive. When I visited South Africa in 1985 a state of emergency had been declared and the common view was that full-scale civil war was inevitable. Whatever other problems it might face, the possibility of civil war in South Africa is now remote. The Truth and Reconciliation Commission is a large-scale example of a movement which has become known as "restorative justice"—an approach which focuses on the restoration of relationships and to which listening is central.

Listening does seem to call forth the best in people. However, that doesn't mean it is a disinterested behavior appropriate only for unselfish or altruistic ends. Quite the opposite in fact—it is a fundamental practice for anyone, particularly those in a position of leadership, and is vital to their chances of achieving their goals. Nonetheless it works because of the effect it has on others.

For example, if people feel heard they will volunteer their ideas. Commander Abrashoff's crew were always making suggestions that saved time, money or effort. Toyota's famous production system ceaselessly encourages suggestions from all their workers and a very high proportion are put into action, which is the most effective proof that these comments are heard. In both cases the act of listening yields a double benefit. First, there is an unending source of ideas for improvement coming from the people best placed to make them—the people who are closest to the work itself. Second, people feel valued because they know their voices are heard, which keeps them motivated and starts to create a self-reinforcing, virtuous spiral of positive energy. This is not a small thing. Toyota is the only major car manufacturer to be consistently profitable over the last forty years, and the USS Benfold would regularly outscore its sister ships on the crucial measure of battle readiness.

Given the motivational power of listening it is ironic that we talk about motivational speakers. The best of them are masterful performers and can be paid vast sums to whip up a storm at company conferences, but expecting a celebrity speech to motivate people in a lasting way is optimistic. The effects of such speeches are short lived. Many famous examples are "eve of battle" speeches (for example, Henry V's famous speech just before the battle of Agincourt). In such circumstances the immediate effect is all that matters. However, if you aren't about to strap on your armor, once the frenzied enthusiasm has died down, what is left? Most likely you are still metaphorically doing small-arms practice on shore.

In the long run listening to people is far more motivating than speaking to them, and nothing motivates you like seeing your own words have an effect. Boston Philharmonic conductor (and leadership consultant) Benjamin Zander tells the story of a violinist who pointed out to him that he was missing an important crescendo. The next time they played the piece, Zander included it. The violinist collared him afterwards and said, "You did *my* crescendo." He was thrilled that he had been heard, and Zander was thrilled that the time and energy he had put into listening to his performers had paid off.

That kind of motivation is invaluable, and, by stark contrast with motivational speakers, it costs nothing, which is a thumping big offer. Next time you have the annual conference or company meeting, why not invert the normal convention and instead of getting an outside speaker, turn it into an Abrashoff-style exercise in listening that demonstrates a real willingness to be changed? Or design it to elicit suggestions and ideas and then use the podium to announce those ideas that you can put into action immediately. If it feels risky to turn a conference into a listening exercise, just imagine for a moment the risk you are taking with yet more blah blah blah.

Good listening can even help people express themselves better. I spend much of my day speaking a second language, and even after fifteen years I find there are certain people with whom I speak well and others with whom I tend to fumble. The difference is the quality of their listening—the good listeners have a kind of momentary patience that the others lack. This quality relaxes me and brings out the best in my Spanish. Psychologists call this "hearing into speech." It suggests that you have the power to make people around you more eloquent. You don't have to recruit new people or send your staff on a training course. You don't even have to tell them about it, all you have to do is listen.

I recently had personal experience of this phenomenon. A very senior client in a very large organization recently asked me what I thought of his company. He emphasized that he wanted to hear what I really thought and asked me to take my time to reply. The sincerity of his question, which displayed a genuine willingness to listen, had an interesting effect on me. It cut off any cynical, sycophantic or self-serving comments I might have been tempted to make (and there were plenty that sprang to mind). I felt obliged to give a thoughtful answer because I knew it would be heard. Thus the quality of the attention you give will affect quality of the information you get.

I once attended a beginners' art class at Flatford Mill in Suffolk (the site of John Constable's famous painting, *The Hay Wain*). The teacher began by asking us, "How many of you can draw?" A few hands were tentatively raised. "How many of you can sign a check?" he asked and we all raised our hands. I assumed this was a gentle rebuke to those people who had yet to pay. In fact, it was nothing of the kind. "If you can sign a check, you can draw. You just need to believe it." He was right, as the results over the next few days proved. There are many skills like this where self-belief is a critical part of the ability itself. However, listening is *not* one of them. Indeed, the opposite is true: the more you believe you are a good listener, the greater the risk that you don't practice it. Listening is not a fixed attribute that you possess like height; it is an active process. It doesn't happen automatically, and it doesn't derive from self-belief.

So here is one final recommendation for anyone interested in improving their listening: assume you are failing. There aren't many occasions when regarding yourself as a failure is productive, but this is one of them. If your listening isn't quite what it might be (and as we have seen, a lot of us fall into this camp), this is obviously a wise thing to do. Recognizing it gives you the chance to do something about it.

Even if you are a good listener, I would argue it is better to believe you aren't. If you hold the belief you are a good listener too close there is a chance that you will rest on your laurels and your listening might begin to falter. Since listening cannot be accumulated or stored, but must constantly be demonstrated, it is more productive to believe something that is wrong. This will keep you working at it and thus sustain the ability.

This is what improvisers tend to do. In addition to any other practice they adopt, they constantly remind themselves that they can always listen better.

You can amp this up by explaining to others that you are aiming to improve your listening and then enrolling them to help by asking for feedback. A similar logic applies here, too. Imagine that they have experienced you as a hopeless drone, immune to their suggestions, ideas and advice; they believe that an overhaul of your listening skills is long overdue. If so, they will be mightily relieved that you have finally realized it. If, on the other hand, they have no issue with your listening, they will be impressed by the high standards you set for yourself, and perhaps even start to raise their own. If they have no point of view whatsoever, then you are putting listening on their radar and signaling that it is an important issue for you.

Furthermore, asking for feedback is in itself an act of listening for which you get credit. On Your Feet once asked an independent researcher to get feedback from our clients. Regardless of what they thought about us, they were all impressed that we were asking. We discovered quite unintentionally that the very act of listening moved us up a notch or two in our clients' minds.

With listening you are never done—you can't be too good at it and it is never a waste to practice. Giving your attention to other people is an act of generosity, to which people invariably respond, yet such generosity also works in your own favor. It's hard, so focusing on being changed by what you hear can be more effective than simply trying to listen better. And whatever happens, it pays to have a modest assessment of this particular ability so that you keep on practicing. Who knows? With enough practice a whole new career on the streets of New York City might beckon.

10   Plug and Play

If you attend a course on how to complete a tax return, it is very clear when and where to apply what you learned. Once a year it will come in very handy; the rest of the time you wouldn't even think about it. The opposite is true here. There isn't one particular context, like the end of the tax year, in which to apply these practices. This sometimes confuses people since they are looking for a specific signal or situation that tells them when to use them. When nothing neatly labeled "improvisational moment" explicitly presents itself, they conclude that they haven't had an opportunity to apply the practices. However, the truth is there are too many situations where you could potentially use them, not too few.

If your car breaks down or you want to strike up a conversation with a stranger or repair something without the proper tools or engage a reluctant audience or make the most of a journey or invent a game for your kids or stay calm in the face of provocation or find your own way in a strange city or bear hardship with good grace, then these practices will help you to get more from the situation than you otherwise might.

This is possible because while improvisational practice may be a highly effective tool for generating new ideas, it is not just a brainstorming technique. As my friend Adam Morgan (author of *Eating the Big Fish*) pointed out when we first introduced him to these ideas, "What you are working with here are the basic building blocks of communication and relationships. What you call practices are like the fundamental grammar."

Because improvisational practice gives you a way to work with these basic building blocks, it can help you unravel conflict, create action, or connect with people. Also, it can help you become more creative. The simplicity of the ideas makes them easy to recall and use, especially when you are under emotional pressure. Nonetheless it is true that the sheer number of opportunities to use this practice can prevent you from seeing any particular one, so in this chapter I want to illustrate how the practices can be brought to bear in everyday life.

A good place to start is to imagine an ordinary day and look for opportunities to plug in the practice. In the end that is all you have at your disposal anyway—one day after another to make of what you will, that adds up to be your life. As French Tibetan Buddhist monk Matthieu Ricard put it at the 2006 TED conference, "Training your mind is not a luxury or a vitamin for the soul but something which determines the quality of every moment of your life."

For me the opportunity to practice starts as soon as I wake up. I am apt to start planning the day ahead even before I am properly awake by making lists, plunging myself back into worries and preoccupations and generally wrapping myself in shadow stories of what might come. If so, I am already anticipating events rather than experiencing them, and I can feel the pressure and anxiety begin to rise. Before events rush upon me, I have the chance to just be with myself and see how I am. All it requires is a little moment of noticing.

What could a moment of presence first thing in the morning bring you? If you live with someone it could be a precious moment of connection with them (after all, one day they might not be there). A few seconds of presence with your partner or with the kids—a gentle look, a demonstration of listening—could help dispel the tension of the morning rush before it happens.

Let's imagine an early bit of difficulty or disappointment. Coffee is an important part of my morning routine, so let's say that bleary-eyed and in eager anticipation of some Ethiopian Yergacheff, I go downstairs to make coffee only to find there isn't any. Here's a great opportunity to practice seeing everything as an offer. The lack of coffee may leave me feeling cantankerous, but remember, seeing things as offers doesn't mean regarding them as good. I don't have to be happy about it. That would be to fall into judgment, just as much as it would be judgment to blame my wife for not buying enough or the friends I had to dinner last night for finishing the last packet.

Instead of griping I can ask myself where the offer is in the interruption of a routine pleasure, which in my case happens to be morning coffee, but could be taking the dog for a walk (interrupted by him getting ill) or the radio breaking. I am not looking for a single right answer, but for a shift in attitude that enables me to see new possibilities. For example, I might:

> Use it as an opportunity to see what life without coffee might be like and weaken the hold the coffee monster has over me;
>
> Take it as a sign I should try the morning fruit smoothie that one of my friends is always recommending;
>
> Allow myself to really feel the raging fire of torment that the lack of coffee brings and use it to forge a cast-iron resolution to never, ever run out again;
>
> Notice and celebrate (through its absence) the extraordinary satisfaction one can get from simple things, like a cup of coffee;
>
> Get on the web and find emergencycoffeedeliveries.com (thus discovering a new resource);
>
> Go next door, substituting coffee for the customary bowl of sugar, and ask my neighbor for some, which could create a new connection with them.

And so on. If the coffee (or its equivalent) isn't available, ask yourself what is. Notice that the practice doesn't prescribe which one of these offers I should take. That's up to me. All it does is introduce a guiding discipline to make me think about what I could use in any particular situation, which shifts me into a constructive frame of mind. The practice will neither coerce you into any particular course of action nor relieve you of responsibility for your own behavior. What it will do is help you become more aware of the choices available to you and the consequences they bring.

Let's say you get stuck in a traffic jam on the way to the office. You can easily imagine the offers here—you could use it as a moment to laugh at the stupidity of much of modern life. If that's a little too sanctimonious for you, how about the opposite? Why not take the chance to engage in a little primal-scream therapy, venting your anger from the safety of your steel cage? Or take the opportunity to play music at a volume you don't dare to at home. But this is all rather familiar, so let's push a bit further.

Imagine that being late bothers you because being punctual is part of your identity. You see yourself as an efficient, ordered kind of person, so on this day you might feel that you have let things slip a bit, that you have "failed." There is a higher order of offer available here. Why not see that slip as a change instead of a failing? Why not embrace the change and see how it feels to be the kind of person who arrives late? Maybe no one else will even notice and you will feel great. Whatever happens, you stand to learn something.

Even before you get to your desk there are plenty of opportunities to apply this practice. Once you get there, they keep on coming. The phone rings. Try listening instead of checking your e-mail as you take the call. You have a meeting—how about working on actually being present? This can be as simple as breaking your stride and pausing, for a matter of a few seconds, before you enter the room (can anyone seriously claim they don't have time for that?). How about letting go of all those prejudgments about the guy from IT (or accounts or marketing or engineering)? You may have a strong shadow story about what a nerd (or bore or flake or squarehead) he is, but does that mean you have nothing to learn from him?

If the engineers say they can't mend a pump properly in a day, why not let go of your own agenda (Is your attachment to it really about keeping the plant running smoothly, or is it about making yourself look good?) and ask them how long it would take them to mend the pumps to their own satisfaction so that they could guarantee no more breakdowns? If the engineers say three days, think about the implications of accepting or blocking that offer. If you accept, imagine what that would do for your relationship with them. If you block, what do you suppose will happen next time you need help from the engineers?

And so it goes on. There are plenty of opportunities to weave the practices into everyday life. They can happily be applied in prototheatrical settings (like formal presentations) and often to great effect, but since they pertain to the underlying dynamics of how flow is created in any conversation, process or relationship, they can be applied all over the map. Since we human beings spend most of our time communicating or building relationships (or at least, trying to), we create a large playing field for these practices. An organization, even a big one like a multinational corporation, is no more than the sum of a complex set of interwoven relationships between staff, customers, regulators, suppliers, competitors and collaborators. Arguably the economy itself is just a rich web of relationships.

The application of these ideas isn't limited to the interpersonal realm. You can also use the practice to guide decisions and actions on a larger scale. If the local market is in crisis and your premium whisky brands suddenly look vulnerable, ask yourself, "What's the offer here?" Could you, for example, launch a low-price brand? This may fly in the face of the conventional wisdom (that Scotch is expensive), but surely when times are tough people will *really* need a good drink—they just won't be able to pay as much for it. A friend of mine took this attitude in a Latin American market that was in free fall and built a brand to over 20 percent market share from scratch in about eighteen months, which was a highly productive response to a crisis.

I often think that people who run new-product development projects ought to have a crash course in improvisation. Whether it's a drinks company ponderously researching pack copy variations or a software company wedded to the idea of an annual release, so much of what goes on in big organizations under the heading of innovation is slow and cumbersome. If they took the improv lessons to heart they would behave rather differently.

First you would think of the challenge as a story rather than a scientific experiment. Instead of trying to create a rigorously controlled process, you would concentrate on finding an interesting place to start and move into action without trying to define the end in advance. Why get bogged down in a comprehensive competitive analysis when you don't even know who the competitors are going to be for the thing you have yet to invent?

There is plenty to get you started. Look around and pay attention to the offers that you have at your disposal. This includes people and experience so thinking about these offers might affect who you get on the team. Do you have people who know what is happening in research and development, in Singapore or at the depot? Alternatively you might see that the sales force already has tons of ideas, born out of experience with real customers that you could take, adapt, flesh out and put into the market very quickly, so you start with that department. You would look at materials and technologies as offers, too, to see where you might find new possibilities. What do you already have that isn't being used, or could be used in a different way? What's your guitar case, who has a turtle, where can you borrow the equipment you need? You would include everything as a potential offer, including things otherwise regarded as problems or deficiencies. If your customers in Africa don't have Web access, could you set up a text-based order system using mobile-phone technology?

Your research would focus on getting information back quickly (rather than on evaluation) so that you can act on it and go around the loop again. You would look to create a flowing, iterative process where you could change your ideas, incorporate more learning and make a new offer (on a small scale) quickly so your product development might look more like micromarketing or prototyping than testing. You might make a beta version of your mousetrap and stick it in three shops where you volunteer to work as a salesman so that you quickly find out what works and what doesn't. If you are on the spot you will spot more things. You might discover that your mousetrap is better suited to catching cockroaches than mice, and what an opportunity that would be.

If bicycle manufacturers had been this close to customers they might have more quickly realized the potential of the "clunkers" that a bunch of enthusiasts were making in Marin County, California, in the late 1970s. These clunkers became mountain bikes, which now account for over half the sales of bicycles in the U.S. (with sales of over fifty billion dollars), and they were the result of a passionate group of people tinkering in an improvised and cocreative way, not an organized innovation process or a brilliant lone inventor.

This focus on trying things out, rather than trying to anticipate what will happen, is an important part of improvisational practice. Sometimes the very simplicity of these ideas can work against them. People can dismiss them as simplistic without putting them into action. Yet as I mentioned, one of the most important ideas in complexity science is that complex patterns do not necessarily have complex causes. These practices may be simple but they are capable of generating a sumptuous series of new possibilities if you are willing to play around with them. But you won't discover that if you simply talk about them or only try them once.

Unfortunately we are out of practice at practice. Quick fixes, overnight remedies and instant gratification have invaded every nook and cranny of our society, so in general, people have extraordinarily little patience. If ashtanga yoga didn't work for you, try Pilates instead, or the Warrior Diet.[1] We search for the killer application instead of applying ourselves. We look for someone else to provide an answer rather than trusting and developing our own abilities. Management theory itself is a fashion market and its designer labels are Harvard Business School and the rest (not that Harvard, et al., are to blame for this—our addiction to new stuff is what fuels the fads).

I have noticed this when teaching people to juggle. Juggling is a complex motor skill and yet people often give up in less than ten minutes. I know this because I have timed it. Imagine concluding that learning a difficult skill is beyond you in less than the time it takes to buy and eat a hamburger. Giving people feedback about how much time they have actually dedicated to the task helps, but without that help their resolve is weak—impatience sets in quickly.

We should have more faith in our own abilities. One of the great things about my job is that I regularly get to see people doing things they didn't think they could do. Watching an accountant discover that he can improvise a story that makes an audience laugh is a wonderful thing. If you want to discover what you are capable of, my advice

- - - - - - - - - - - - - - - - - -

1   I love this one. As it has been explained to me, it consists of eating nothing at all before five o'clock and whatever you like after that. Apparently this is meant to work because that's how it was in the "natural" days before twenty-four-hour supermarkets.

would be to be patient and start small. There is a lot to be said for under-promising and over-delivering, especially when you are making promises to yourself. Aim to do a little, and commit to that little. I started meditating when I took a business school course called The Reflective Practitioner. This course was an unusual combination of business acumen and spiritual practice taught at Portland State University by an academic and a Buddhist relationship counselor. Between classes we were invited to try meditation for one minute a day. Even ten might have been beyond me, but one? If you aim that low then you are bound to succeed and as the saying goes, "nothing succeeds like success." The single minute grew to half an hour and over a decade later I am still practicing.

If you find something small that works for you, in whatever way, a positive reinforcing loop quickly kicks in, and it is easy to make it bigger. Stretch goals may be great for inspiring long-range accomplishments, but when the aim is not to reach a particular end state but to cultivate recurrent or repeated actions and behaviors, a modest practice is more appropriate.

Don't feel that you have to set about changing anything immediately, you can start smaller than that. Try noticing first. Awareness has hidden powers. Take the example of juggling again. I learned some time back that it is much more effective to ask people simply to notice what they are doing than to try and correct it. Imagine we are working together on a basic three-ball exchange (the fundamental unit of juggling in which each ball swaps place). I see that the throws from your right hand regularly fall too far forward—out of reach of the left. Rather than give you detailed corrective instructions, I simply ask you to notice what is happening to the throws from your right hand. As your awareness kicks in, there is a very strong tendency to autocorrect and the throws from your right hand start to land in a better place on their own. Experience shows this works better than telling you what corrections to make.

The same is true with the improvisational practice. Try not to issue corrective instructions like "I must block less." Instead, if blocking were the area you wanted to work on, set yourself the goal of noticing when and how you block. Write it down in a journal or diary. See if you notice any obvious patterns but don't try too hard to analyze it. Stay with noticing. Often, that effort alone will induce a constructive change. If you keep noticing you will also be aware of the change that results, which can be delightful—being a witness to something new unfolding in yourself rather than feeling you have to push everything can be a liberation. If nothing changes, try something different—maybe you are already doing just fine in that regard.

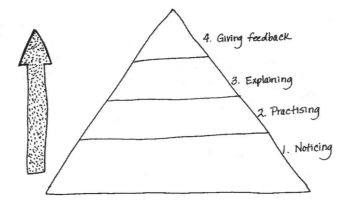

Once you feel you have gleaned some benefit or insight through noticing, then you might raise the stakes a little and try to actively practice something. But even so, keep it constrained. There is nothing like a limit to act as a springboard to creative change, so to continue with the same example, instead of saying "I must block less," be more specific and set yourself the target of blocking less at dinnertime, or blocking Maria less. It could be a person, a time, a place, or a context—it doesn't really matter. Staying small and specific like this also helps you see how you are doing.

Even a small change can have a big effect. In complex systems like you, me or the organizations we form, a tiny shift in the start point will dramatically affect what happens.[2] It is like golf—a small change in your grip can have a large effect on where the ball goes.

- - - - - - - - - - - - - - - - - - - -

2   In rather charming technical language, complex systems have high "sensitivity to initial conditions," which means that a small alteration in the start point can easily tip you from one "attractor basin" into another.

You can take your time about this. Because improv theater is naturally spontaneous, people often assume that the practices have to be used in an instantaneous way. This is ambitious, to put it mildly. It is the equivalent of picking up a bit of French grammar and expecting to be able to hold your own at a Parisian dinner party the very next day. The trouble with such high expectations is that you tend to be disappointed and give up quickly. This would be a shame. It is perfectly possible to use the practices quite deliberately, consciously or slowly, and this is the best way to start. To borrow a technological metaphor, you can work offline. Sit quietly at your desk and contemplate what the offer might be in a difficult situation you are facing. You might spend a few minutes doing this. Or a few hours. Or even a few days, returning to the question at different moments and allowing your unconscious to muse on it while you clean your office or bury yourself in research reports.

What is important is that you start with yourself. That might seem patently obvious, but I mention it because I have noticed that the first thing people often do after a workshop is rush off to tell other people what they have learned (or worse, what those other people should do). Doing this may give you the impression that you have put the learning into action, but in fact it means nothing of the sort. "Well, I told Bob all about his blocking problem" you say to yourself proudly, passing all responsibility over to him and cleverly washing your hands of any change on your own part. I am exaggerating, of course, but only a bit—people are very ingenious at resisting change, and one way to do this is to go into "telling" mode.

People sometimes feel that they have to tell others about the practice before they can use it. This is a common response and deserves a little consideration. It is true that there can be tremendous value for an organization in new shared language. For example, when a group cottons on to the idea that everything is an offer they start to see new things and behave in a new way. This is not to be underestimated; however, it is by no means necessary.

"I can't do anything until they do" is, in fact, a kind of block. Whatever you choose to do, you have to work on your own behavior, but you don't have to publicly label what you are doing. I can see an offer without saying so, work on being present without publicly going all "new age-y" or practice being changed by what I hear without having to broadcast the fact. Remember Haley Rushing? She made the resolution to accept through using "yes and…" wherever she could and her colleagues noticed the difference even though she never announced what she was doing.

If you accept the idea that you should start small and start on yourself, you may ask what you should start with first. This is a good question with a simple answer: start anywhere. You could choose blocking or offers or being present or being changed or using what you have or letting go of judgment. Begin anywhere you like, but begin.

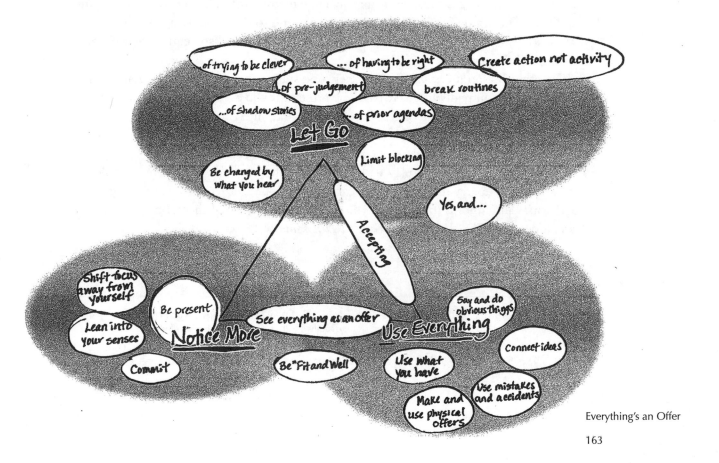

Everything's an Offer

163

The place to start will be the place that interests you. This might be a place of strength or weakness. It might be a piece of language or an idea that appeals to you for some idiosyncratic reason. On the diagram below I have mapped the possible start points and some of the connections between them. It is more comprehensive than the simple triangle I have been using as we've gone along and consequently messier, but at this stage I think its worth including a bit more detail, even it means sacrificing some simplicity.

If there isn't anything here you find interesting, I would recommend you put this book down now and go and do something that you do find interesting instead.[3] It might seem perverse to suggest this, but ironically enough, this would be another way of putting the practice into action since improvisers commit to the offers which most immediately appeal to them. It may not serve my book, but it would serve my larger purpose (to promote these ideas).

The other reason it doesn't matter where you start is the interconnected nature of the practice. If you really listen, you *will* be present. If you accept offers, you will be changed and so on. The practices collapse (or expand) into each other. While there is a structure it is a flexible, malleable one for you to play with rather than a dangerous machine that I should give you careful operating instructions for.

I would encourage you to play with this stuff in the way kids play with technology. Pick something up, try it, see what you can discover, put it down, pick something else up. If you want a motto to live by as you do so, try one or all of these, borrowed from Nike, Iddeo and *The Hitchhiker's Guide to the Galaxy*, respectively:

Just Do It

Fail early, fail often

Don't Panic.[4]

- - - - - - - - - - - - - - - - - -

3   When I was growing up there was a kids' TV program called *Why Don't You Just Switch Off Your Television Set and Go Out and Do Something Less Boring Instead?* I always thought that was both funny and wise.

4   This idea is twice borrowed. Jon Foster-Pedley of the Graduate School of Business at Cape Town University borrowed them from their original owners and put them together to make a point on his Creatergy course. And I borrowed them from him, to make a rather different point here.

If you prefer a little more structure, here are five simple steps to building an improv practice:

Choose somewhere to start—anywhere will do

Do something with what you have chosen (noticing it is enough)

Pay attention to what happens

Do it some more or adjust what you are doing

Repeat sequence

It really is that simple. The important thing is to get going. Insights and learning arise from the process of creation itself, not from trying to anticipate what will happen.

With that in mind, let me invite you to try something now. Would you fold your arms? As I have mentioned the physical bit of the practice is important (action always requires us to use our bodies in some way), so if this is going to work, you'll need to do it for real and not just imagine it, which probably means putting the book down.

Now fold them the other way (this might take a few seconds).

How did you get on? People normally find the second instruction harder than the first. Many people laugh. Some people fold them the same way without noticing. Others take a while to work out how to fold their arms the "other" way. (I am glad to say that no one has yet failed entirely when given a little time.) Even if none of those things happened to you, when I first suggested folding your arms you didn't have to ask "Which way?" No one ever does. We all have these deeply ingrained habits, and when we start to shift them, it can feel strange or uncomfortable.

Embracing these ideas may feel just like that. They will oblige you to let go of some cherished and deeply held notions, at least temporarily. Deliberately encouraging yourself into a space of not-knowing can be daunting. The first movements you make when learning new skills tend to be clumsy. However, in my view, it is worth the effort. We are already well versed at analyzing, dissecting and manipulating that which can be contained or constrained. There is much to be gained by learning to find ways to work with that which cannot.

PART 3

Shaping Stories

11   Color-Advance

The ability to respond fluently and creatively is an impressive skill when everything is changing and shifting around you. However, being able to shape what emerges as you go along, so that it forms a meaningful whole, can be even more impressive. Improvisers are able to do just that. They create stories with a beginning, middle and end, making it seem as if they had been scripted in advance even while they are still in the thick of the creative process. The foundational practices we explored in Part 2 are what generate the flow of a story, but improvisers also need to be able to shape that flow. They need to be able to orient themselves, keep the audience constantly engaged, and bring a story to a satisfying conclusion. The three chapters in Part 3 will give you some insight into how to manage the rhythm and cadence of a process you are involved with as it unfolds.

We have learned a lot about this from the curiosity and ingenuity of the people we have worked with. In this chapter we will explore the idea of color and advance—a tool that helps you understand and direct any kind of narrative flow. This was just an improv game until one of our clients took it and applied it in a way we had not imagined. It happened like this.

Liz had been on maternity leave from her job in marketing at Orange (a mobile phone company), and when she came back her team was faced with a problem. How do you cram six crazy months into the couple of hours they had for an update meeting? While Liz had been away the team had done a workshop with us, so they decided to use and adapt the ideas in the game Color Advance to help them.

Any story contains offers that add "color" and offers that "advance" the action. Color means texture, richness or detail. That includes blue, green, magenta, mother of pearl and the rest, but goes beyond literal colors to include metaphorical color (or detail). For example, "It was a cold, foggy morning" or "Nigel has a fine analytical mind." By contrast, offers that advance move the story forward. Quite simply an advance is an offer that makes something new happen. For example, "Fernando crashed his car" or "Nigel was hired as Finance director."

First the team played the game to teach Liz the terms. Then they invited her, as the audience, to ask for what she wanted to hear as they went through the story of the preceding six months: "color" where she needed more detail or "advance" where she wanted to move on. This provided a simple mechanism for her to give feedback and direction as they went, which not only demonstrated confidence and imagination on their part, but allowed her to feel involved. Liz herself now bore some of the responsibility for getting what she wanted which took pressure off the people presenting.

The distinction between color and advance can be applied to any narrative flow, whether it is a presentation, a conversation or a relationship. You might use it explicitly as a mechanism to get structured feedback and allow an audience to participate (as happened here) or implicitly to frame your own thinking about the story you are telling. One way or another the tool enables you to create a more engaging story. As people played around with this framework, the game found all sorts of new uses and applications.

Any story needs both color and advance. In television sports commentary the roles are split along these lines; there is normally one commentator who describes the advancing action and another who goes into more detail about specific points or plays (the color). You can also think of this in terms of cinema. In general, French films are full of intricate, luscious detail, but they tend to be short on car chases and explosions and sometimes they can get a bit dull. By contrast, while American films are typically action packed, they can also be eminently forgettable—without sufficient color we won't really be engaged emotionally, and we end up merely titillated by special effects, chases or fights.

Neither color nor advance is intrinsically good or bad. What is important to understand is that the ebb and flow between them keeps an audience interested. You can illustrate that visually, like this:

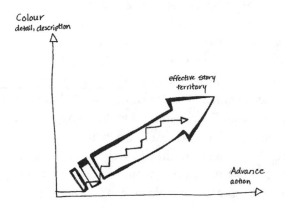

Engaging stories lie on the diagonal and zigzag between color and advance. At the beginning you need a little color to establish the context. Then you need to advance—something needs to happen until you get to something the audience wants to hear more about and then you add color. If I tell you our quarterly results are poor, you will quite naturally want to know why. What you discover (through the addition of color) will lead to an advance in the story. If it turns out that the bad results are because my team has failed to sell anything, you will want to change something—in this case, probably me. This to and fro between color and advance leads you into the territory where engaging stories lie.

There are rare occasions when you want only one or the other. For example, when dealing with an immigration officer, all you want is to advance (quite literally) into the country. Extraneous details (color) can be a liability which can lead you into a conversation you don't want to have. Hence the advice of a U.S. immigration lawyer who once told me to answer questions with "a maximum of two words, one of which should be 'sir.'" If, on the other hand, you happened to be in the vicinity when a crime was committed, the police will be interested in every single detail you can possibly recall even if you didn't see anything happen—the tiniest piece of color might provide a vital clue.

However, stories, conversations, meetings, journeys or business processes normally need a balance of both. If you have too much color, you can easily get bogged down in sidetracks and digressions. On the other hand, if you are always rushing on, you might miss the nuance or detail that is most important. Too much emphasis on advance can also stop you from really committing to an action. In the improv context, this was why the direction "color" was invented. An actor might say "It's hot" and then feel that was enough to establish it in the audience's mind. Thinking they were done with it being "hot," they would move on before the idea had a chance to add anything to the scene, so it became just filler. Observing this, director Keith Johnstone started to direct improvisers to add color. Adding description would force them to give that idea weight, helping to engage the audience. Color is also where the emotion tends to lie, and since you cannot engage an audience without emotion (thoughts are not enough), it is a vital quality when you want to connect with people.

Color-advance is unusual because it is a tool that the audience can wield, and yet the speaker or performer feels the benefit. It can help you avoid that horrible moment, in the bar the evening after the meeting, when you discover you should have gone into more detail about the R&D and spent much less time on the logistics. It helps you find that out before it's too late and gives you a very succinct way to get input from your audience as you go. As we saw, involving the audience also gives them some responsibility. In the storytelling version of this game, people are often surprised by how easy it is to tell an original story if the audience tells you when to move on or when to dwell on something.

When I tell people the story of the team at Orange they sometimes say "We couldn't do that here, it would feel forced." I wonder. That may be so, but it might also be a block from someone unwilling to be changed. People are often nervous about opening up to their audience because it means relinquishing control and that makes them feel vulnerable. The fear is that they might take you off-script or ask you awkward questions or take you in a direction you don't want to go. But what is the value in controlling what you say, if the audience doesn't get what they want? The safety of not being interrupted or directed by your audience is an illusion if you aren't connecting with what's important to them. The point is not to get through your stuff, but to get your stuff through. There is a big difference. Accepting offers from your audience does not mean you are submitting to them—there are plenty of ways to accept offers while keeping your own hand on the tiller.

Asking for either color or advance is a way of doing just that. By giving the audience these specific instructions, you can cut off other rambling or disruptive interruptions. When you understand that both are needed, it doesn't feel like criticism. If you don't interpret it as judgment, a request for advance does not mean "I am bored, get on with it" and a request for color doesn't necessarily mean "there is no depth to this." It simply helps connect what you are saying to what the audience wants to hear. If this particular language doesn't work for you, you can always use an equivalent that feels acceptable in your culture. In any case, you frequently find that the audience does not intervene very often so the risk may not be as great as you think. The benefit of making the offer, of including them and seeing them is always there, whether the audience acts on it or not, and it is much harder for an audience that has been offered the chance to give feedback to be cynical afterwards.

You can also use the tool to get direction on written material. When space is short, I have asked editors what balance of color or advance they want in the article. (If they know the terms, I might use them explicitly; if not, I can still use the idea.) This helps me decide whether to cover a small amount in some detail or write a sweeping overview. It also helps ensure that the editor and I have the same expectations.

Even if you completely reject the idea of using this language explicitly with other people, you can always use it on yourself, inside your own head, to help you shape what you say. Thinking in these terms will help you clarify what kind of information you need to give, and when.

Color-advance is a listening tool, too. It helps you to know what you are listening to or listening for. The terms work as signposts to help structure what you hear. As a conversation unfolds, these labels can help you to recognize whether you are diverting into a little tributary or progressing along the main stream. Over time Gary and I have learned to use this on the phone. There is a nine-hour time difference between Pacific time and Central European time, which means that whenever we speak, at least one of us is tired. In the long and rambling conversations we are apt to have, color-advance is a useful navigational tool. Nonetheless, if you were to eavesdrop on one of these calls, you would rarely hear either of us say these words out loud; we use them (in our own minds) to track the conversation.

For example, I may call Gary to discuss the new Web site design, but fresh off a plane from a conference in Wisconsin, he starts to tell me what happened there. Inwardly I label this as color and rather than immediately force Gary back to the main theme, I let him carry on for awhile, knowing that this is a useful way for me to upload collateral information but not the main point. Often something will come from that color which helps us with the main topic—he may have been given some feedback at the conference which helps us unravel an issue we are struggling with on the Web site. And even if it doesn't, I know what I am listening to and at an appropriate point I will inwardly press the advance button.

Tracking the conversation in these terms helps you assign priorities to what you are hearing and can give you a way to make sense of a lot of information. Being conscious of this framework adds a new layer of awareness that helps you to see and understand what is going on even while it is still unfolding.

Though it might seem that color-advance is limited to face-to-face interaction, over the years we have been playing around with it, we have discovered that the applications of color-advance don't stop there. Any activity can be seen as a narrative: your conversations, meetings, research programs, even your whole organization. Just like any story, there are different characters and interests involved, a goal or aim and barriers or obstacles which the protagonists have to overcome. This means that a narrative tool, like color-advance, can help you understand any story, even a merger between leviathan organizations.

For example, when Proctor & Gamble buys Gillette, or France Telecom buys Orange, is that color or advance? Posing this question is a very simple way to look for the logic of such a deal. If Gillette adds yet more color to the part of the Portfolio where P&G already has a lot, you might question the sense of it. Or if the creative culture of Orange seemed like too big an advance for a public utility like France Telecom, you might also have doubts. In a carefully considered merger or acquisition there would be a balance of advance into new territory with enough color in common to make the thing gel. Few of us are in a position to influence such events, but it can be a helpful way to understand them.

The concept can be used to frame new product development. For example, when Apple launched the iPod (and iTunes), this was clearly an advance; it created a whole new way of buying and storing music and banished millions of CD collections to the basement. Subsequent launches, such as the iPod Shuffle or Nano are obviously color. They deliver variations on the same theme.

This means color and advance can help you think strategically about what you are really trying to achieve with new products and how to go about it. For example, you can analyze the competitive context in these terms. Is the market high on color, that is, are there lots of variants and models? If so, you will need to introduce a significant advance in order to gain a competitive advantage—a slightly more electric blue or an extra megabyte won't do it. Or perhaps someone else has just made a big advance into a new market (e.g., a hybrid engine) and the opportunity is to add your own version (i.e., add color).

Creating a genuine advance might take longer and require more investment, but it will yield a more dramatic and lasting impact. So if you decide to set out to create a new product that is an advance, you will know you need to be more patient and put more resources behind it. If, on the other hand, you are focusing primarily on color, then perhaps you can afford to be less cautious or risk-averse. You might use a more flexible, agile development process, take decisions more quickly and instinctively and get your product into the market quicker.

If you don't appreciate that color and advance are fundamentally different, it can cause problems. For example, a global drinks company I worked with would see any departure from the prevailing norm as a huge advance. As a result there would be ponderous international meetings, multiple stages of research, consultative documents, and so on. Yet Central Marketing was often outperformed by the smaller operations at the edge of the organization who regarded new drinks as no more than a colorful riff on a few basic ideas. That encouraged them to play around with variations and recipes, put new product out quickly, see what worked and get to market sooner. There is a credibility issue here, too. From the customer's point of view, presenting color (extra fiber, low-fat, boysenberry flavor) as if it were a major advance just makes you look foolish.

Thinking in terms of color and advance can also help you with targeting. Are you interested in attracting a whole new public (advance) or are you trying to cater to the needs of your existing customers (color)? If you are Mercedes-Benz and you see that the worldwide market for big cars is in decline, you know that you need to attract a new kind of customer. Thus the launch of the (smaller) A-Class was a new product advance for Mercedes in a way that the newest S-Class never is, however loaded with new technology it might be. Advance is not about technological sophistication, per se.

By contrast, if you have a loyal following eager for more of the same, then it might not be necessary to take much of a step forward. While the original *Star Wars* movie was a huge advance, the prequels simply added color—using new technology and computer graphics to add yet higher production values and, in this case, literally filling in the earlier details of a story the end of which we already knew.

Thinking in these terms can change how you do your market research. Do you want a richer, deeper understanding of all the nuances of your brand (color) or do you want to know what has changed with the arrival of a new competitor (advance)? Which is it? Often people mix these objectives in the same study, yet the two kinds of question might demand quite different methodologies. If it is a big advance, you might want to let them take it home and see how they get on with it in practice rather than simply hearing their knee-jerk reaction in a focus group. Being clear about what measure of each is important and would help to clarify many market-research briefs, which are often hopelessly muddled.

The construct would also inform what stimulus material you produce. If you want people to give you detailed feedback, then you need to make it as close to real as possible—you need to add a lot of color. If, on the other hand, you want to explore more strategic ideas (i.e., a big step forward) then you should actively avoid color—otherwise people will plunge straight into the detail and you won't get any response to your overall concept. Moreover, you might be able to get them to fill in their own idea of the color, which will give you new information and ideas.

Understanding whether what you have is color or advance will also help you interpret the findings. When Sony researched the first Walkman, people were quick to point out all the reasons it wouldn't work (many complained they would bump into things if they were listening to music in the street). This was because it was a genuine advance. When that is the case, you shouldn't expect people to be entirely comfortable. Thus classifying your development as color or advance will help you interpret what people say.

A few years back there was a wonderful exhibition on the history of the portrait at the Prado in Madrid. It traced the development of this form of painting from the early tenth century when portraits first began to appear in religious paintings through to Miro and Picasso. Following this timeline, the paintings were exhibited along the length of a long narrow gallery in the center of the Prado so that you literally walked the history of the portrait from its inception to the present day. However, at certain points you could branch off and reenter the permanent collection. So, for example, when you got to the portraits of Velazquez you had a choice—you could either continue along the history of the portrait, or you could take a deeper look at Velazquez and explore other works of his, which would give you a new context for seeing his portraits.

This exhibition was a physical expression of color and advance. The historical line laid out along one long gallery paced out the advance of the form (in this case the portrait). Where the collection was strong and the curators wanted to allow you to explore a painter in depth, you could delve into their work in another room—adding color. This was an ingenious way to invite the audience to navigate their own way through the gallery and connect the special exhibition with the permanent collection.

This example show how you can use the construct of color-advance to think about the use of physical space. For example, at a sales conference you might lay out material with the main thrust of your strategic story along the central axis of the space you are using, and then create side alleys off it with additional information that people can peruse if they wish. I once did something similar with a research debrief at *Wired* magazine, where we took advantage of the walls made of pin board (there to lay out the mocked-up magazine) to stick our presentation up around the room. The main thrust of the argument flowed horizontally along the walls (advance) and detail was added vertically (color). By making it all visible and literally walking them through it, our audience was able to direct us to what most interested them.

You could use this idea to disrupt the conventions of store design or office layout. Apparently IKEA's store design was inspired by another art museum—the Guggenheim in New York. Here, instead of discrete galleries, there is a single, continuous spiral passageway. This layout takes you past all the art (or furniture) on one single path. In other words you get an eyeful of color. In IKEA's case I assume the intention was to ensure you see everything, thus tempting you to buy more. I wonder if they haven't overdone it? In the IKEA stores I go to, I have noticed that more and more shortcuts (i.e., advances) are cropping up. Too much color and you simply can't take it all in.

Color-advance thus has many practical applications within organizations. It can also be a tool for personal growth. In everyday conversation most of us find either one or the other easier. If you find color easier, there is a chance that you will make too many digressions and people lose track of your story. On the other hand, if you are always advancing, you may not engage people as well as you might.

The opportunity here is to reflect on your own dominant style (it may be immediately obvious or you may have to ask someone). Once you have an idea which is your preferred style you can work on the other one. The skill is to be able to flex from one to the other. If you are unaware of your personal style, or find it difficult to move away from, then your story is less likely to be rewarding for the people you are talking to. As we have seen with other practices, a good way to start this process is simply through awareness—you don't have to try to change dramatically or suddenly (which can seem forced or false anyway). There are sophistications here too. You may find that you prefer one over the other depending on who you are talking to. For example, with your friends you might be all color and with your partner all advance. If so, you might have to finesse your practice to fit who you are with.

More than a few people have suggested that there are gender differences when it comes to color and advance—the common idea being that women have a style of expression which tends to be heavy on color, whereas men tend to gravitate toward advance. This fits the stereotypes of the gossipy housewife and the testosterone-driven executive, and like all stereotypes, there may be some truth in it. Certainly one (female) marketing manager told me a story about a team she led in which there was only one man. Apparently he habitually got frustrated that they weren't "pushing things forward" and he regarded anything that wasn't an explicit advance as a waste of time. The rest of the team thought he was very uptight. They were quite happy to spend time layering on the detail, adding color and complexity until, in their view, the appropriate advance naturally emerged from the conversation.

In this example, the stereotypical views seem to hold. Men, ever thrusting and eager to get on, are impatient with "irrelevant" detail. Women, meanwhile, are attentive to the details (particularly those to do with relationships) and see the men as simplistic. Conflict or difficulty occurs where the roles are too polarized. Yet these stereotypes don't always apply. When it comes to commitment, particularly getting married and having children, the roles tend to swap. In those circumstances men are notorious for resisting advance and women are more eager to get clarity (one way or another) and move on. Who plays which role may depend upon context.

In a personal relationship, which is a story just like any other, the original idea still holds—both color and advance are necessary. In a good relationship people will understand and respect the need for both, be aware of their own personal style and be able to flex and change when necessary—being sensitive to what the story needs. If people don't have the skills and the understanding to value and deal productively with the contribution of both color and advance, then their relationships are likely to become fraught with tension. If both people are too strong on one or other pole there will be something lacking—two excessively colorful individuals will rarely get anything done, and two excessive advancers will either get torn apart as they advance in different directions or fail to create enough detailed connections to hold things together (like worn Velcro). If people are strongly polarized or unable to flex, it will lead to misunderstanding. If there is no coordination between the desires for color or advance, this will lead to problems—imagine I want to move when you want to deepen your connections in the neighborhood.

The real skill lies in holding tension between color and advance in a productive way to cocreate a unique story (or relationship). Problems arise when people, apt to either color or advance, don't respect each others' styles or fail to see the importance of the other role in cocreation (and let's face it, nothing is more cocreative than a personal relationship). So by all means, use color-advance to improve your presentation skills or inform your company's new product development program, but don't neglect the opportunity for personal growth it can offer you as a tool for understanding the fundamentals of your most important relationships.

Enough color. Let's advance.

12 🌸 Getting Unstuck

Imagine you are a fruit salesman and you have a customer who is keen to buy cherries. Unfortunately the combination of a bad hailstorm and a plague of beetles means it has been a bad year. The few cherries you have are reserved for the expensive restaurants and you have to say no to many of your customers. Imagine you are a graphic designer and you have a client for whom you really want to do great work, but all you get by way of direction are vague ramblings about a "different look." Imagine you are interviewing someone and you can't find a way to get the conversation going; all you get are monosyllabic replies.

In each of these examples the flow of the interaction is stuttering. These specific examples might not be ones you face, but we all encounter situations where the flow grinds to a halt or slows down or becomes difficult to sustain. On Your Feet clients often ask us to help them with a conversation or relationship that has become awkward or stuck in some way. Approaching problems like these from an improv perspective gets you thinking about what is going on in terms of offers.

Everything may be an offer, but that doesn't mean offers are all the same. There are many kinds of offers and each kind has a different effect on the flow. My colleagues and I have developed a way of framing this called the "offer funnel," which is a tool that helps you understand how to use different kinds of offers. It is a refinement of the foundational practice. Much as color-advance is helpful for engaging an audience, the offer funnel is particularly useful when things get stuck.

It looks like this:

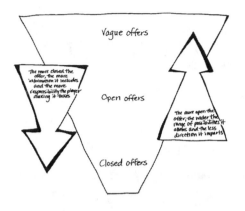

Broadly speaking there are three kinds of offers—vague, open and closed. At the top of the funnel are vague offers. As you might imagine, a vague offer doesn't contain much information. On stage, "Help!" would be a vague offer. It doesn't indicate what you need help with or why; just that you need some. In my business, statements like "we should meet" or "we want new ways to think" are vague offers. Since vague offers don't give much direction at all, they naturally sit at the wide end of the funnel—i.e., the top.

In the middle of the funnel are open offers. By adding some information to a vague offer, we turn it into an open one. For example, "I need help with my car, it won't start." Now we know the kind of help that is needed and something about the person as well (that they are a motorist, trying to get somewhere), so this offer is a bit more crafted. Nonetheless there are still lots of different options that such an offer suggests. Anything from "Jump in and we'll try and jump start it" to "Do you want a lift?" would fit. In the working context, the vague offer to meet becomes an open offer if I say "We should meet next week to talk about how we might work together." This gives you a better idea of what to expect and how to prepare, but there is still plenty of room to maneuver, which is why open offers sit in the middle of the funnel.

At the tight end of the funnel are closed offers. A closed offer contains yet more information than the open one and strongly suggests a specific response from the other person. For example, "I need help with my car, it won't start, so bring yours up alongside and we'll get the jumper cables connected." Short of blocking the offer altogether, there aren't many choices here; this offer takes you right to the jumper cables. A closed offer is not a block because it gives you a way to continue the flow, but the options are limited to some very well-defined alternatives.

You can see why we draw this as a funnel. The wide part at the top represents the offers that give people a lot of freedom and responsibility but little direction. At the bottom the opposite is true: you make an offer that narrows things down and gives other people little freedom or responsibility, but very clear direction. Understanding this spectrum helps you analyze what is going on and work out what to do next.

The categories of vague, open and closed offers are convenient rather than scientific. There is nothing absolute about them—you could invent other groups and while away many a happy hour debating which offer should be classified in which category.[1] However, experience suggests that three groups is plenty to work with. It is also important to notice that the funnel talks about offers, not questions. The offer funnel applies to offers of every kind, including statements and gestures.

Let's see how this works by going back to our fruit salesman. The problem he faces is a common one. The challenge here isn't just to sell something, but to sell a *particular* thing to a *particular* customer. The grocer wants the highly prized cherries that the salesman has to reserve for the restaurateurs. The salesman finds himself in an unenviable position—he is forced to say no to a customer. Moreover this happens

----

1   Doing so would be a fine example of what improvisers call "activity"—see Chapter 8. It might entail different schools of thought springing up, some favoring five categories while the more persnickety maintain that anything less than seven is insufficient. These schools would then bicker among themselves, publish learned papers, and fall out with each other. Freud apparently called this "the neurosis of the small difference."

repeatedly—all the special stuff gets held back for special customers—which makes the relationship with the grocer difficult. In essence, the question here is, how do you keep a relationship going with someone you need to say no to (it could be a parent and child instead of a salesman and customer)?

To the salesmen we worked with, thinking through this interaction in terms of the offer funnel gave them a new way to see things. They realized that the real problem was not saying no, per se, but their own tendency to go straight down the funnel without thinking about it and arrive quickly at the no with a bump. They found themselves giving an automatic or reflexive no, and the conversations they were having would sound like this:

Customer: "I want twenty cases of the picota cherries."

Salesman: "I am afraid we can't do that. Sorry."

But make an open offer instead of a closed one and you have a different conversation, like this:

Customer: "I want twenty cases of the picota cherries."

Salesman: "Wow, that's a lot."

Customer: "Is it?"

Salesman: "Yes, you see this has been a bad year, particularly in cherry orchards lower than seven hundred meters."

Customer: "So, what does that mean, can you get them or not?"

Salesman: "You know, there's another kind, the rabo corto, that come in season a little later and are less expensive and they can be just as sweet."

Customer: "I don't think so. It's picotas I want. Why can't you get them for me?"

Salesman: "It's the pests. There has been a plague of unicorn beetles this year which has affected much of the production."

Customer: "Well, could you at least get me a couple of kilos?"

Salesman: "No promises, but I can try. If you don't mind how they look, I could probably get some fruit that has been affected by hail. They taste just as good, and if you make smoothies…"

This feels very different. Even though there is still no immediate sale, both parties get something from the conversation. The customer feels seen, rather than snubbed, and the salesman maintains his position and keeps the customer sweet. All it took was some presence of mind and a few seconds of extra time.

The crucial moment is the first offer that the salesman makes in response to the question. That's where the trap of the reflexive no lies. The trick is to make an open offer first. That offer could be a comment or a question. In the example above, he could have said, "What makes you think your customers will go for the picotas?" or "How long do you think twenty cases would last?" or "You know, personally, I love picotas but they do affect my digestion a bit" and so on. It doesn't matter which particular offer you make, but it does matter what *kind* of offer it is.

The open offer creates a flowing conversation that might help him to sell similar lines (e.g., the rabo corto) as well as build and grow his understanding of that particular customer. It also feels much more positive. In reality this seemingly tiny shift in their behavior had a significant effect on their customer relationships. It's not rocket science, but the clients who faced this issue weren't selling rockets (or cherries for that matter).

Another example I gave was the designer with his vague client. This too is a common problem; in both our professional and personal lives we all give and take direction. There is a story about the Catalan designer Mariscal[2] that illustrates this particular issue. On one occasion a potential client approached Mariscal to design him a "Mariscal chair." What kind of chair? asked the designer. "Just a Mariscal chair," came the reply, whereupon the client was promptly shown the Mariscal door. Mariscal couldn't work with such a vague brief, flattering though it may have been that somebody wanted anything he might come up with. If you are famous like Mariscal, you can show someone the door. But what if you have to work with the vague brief? What can you do to get more clarity?

- - - - - - - - - - - - - - - - - - -

2   Outside Spain, Mariscal is best known for designing the mascot of the Barcelona Olympics in 1992.

Quite simply you need to move them down the funnel. The way to do this is to move down the funnel yourself. This is what Mariscal is trying to do by asking, "What kind of chair?" He wants to know who is going to sit on it, for how long, for what purpose and so on. However, in my experience such questions are often met with equally vague answers, so I have learned to make a more crafted offer myself—normally in the form of a proposal or outline for a workshop—quickly. Rather than agonize over getting it right, I concentrate on making a more specific offer for the client to respond to so that I get to learn what they really want. Notice this implies using another piece of practice—being willing to let go of the ideas in the proposal, which are primarily there to accelerate the process of learning.

Funnily enough, in my experience you often get hopelessly vague direction from clients who really like you. The high level of trust they have for your work can make them a little lazy, and they don't think in a very disciplined way about what it is they want to achieve. They figure that some of that cool stuff that On Your Feet does will be a help. Even if they are right that anything we do might help, bringing them down the funnel by making a crafted offer will enable us to give them more.

Understanding this enables you to give direction to other people more effectively. If you are aware that you need to give some open offers, it will be easier to get better work from the people you yourself brief, whether it's a travel agent or an architect. You may think it is generous of you to leave as much open as possible, but in fact it is just confusing. An open brief is the easiest one to work with, not a vague one.

And what about the conversation where you just can't seem to get going (my example was an interview)? In this kind of conversation you want to discover something. Either you want to learn about the person themselves (if it's a job interview, for example), or if you are doing research of some kind, you want to discover what they know, think, or feel about a particular subject, which implies that you want *them* to do most of the work. In either case, you don't want to supply too much information yourself, so you need to make offers at the top of the funnel.

In these circumstances it can be helpful to make an offer that is open to the point of being vague. When conducting qualitative market research I found that simply saying "So…," followed by a long pause, could be extremely productive. This is about as vague an offer as you can imagine. Nonetheless it does a good job in the circumstances. It implies there is something to be said, but excludes nothing. If you are willing to sit with a few seconds of silence, invariably someone will pipe up and they often say more revealing things than when they answer specific questions. You learn what's on their mind. There are many other occasions when you might want to elicit what people think without leading them—when planning a family trip, asking a friend for advice or canvassing opinions about the performance of a colleague, for example. In which case, a vague offer will do very well.

It can take a conscious effort to stay vague, particularly if you are attached to the idea of seeming impressive or efficient. Understanding that vague offers have their value can help you pause, hold off and leave space for the person you want to learn from. It can help you to feel fit and well about making a vague offer.

I remember being on the receiving end of this technique once. An interview for a job I desperately wanted began with a very vague offer. "Tell me about yourself," said the interviewer. For a second or two I was stumped. Such a vague question kicked me out of the exam mentality I had fallen into (with answers to the questions I thought would come up scrolling through the back of my mind). The question forced me to actually think, rather than regurgitate what I had prepared, which, I am sure, was exactly what the interviewer was after. He wanted to know a little more about me than the fact that I was smart enough to anticipate the stock questions. And although it felt uncomfortable for a few seconds, it led to a conversation about the wild orchards that grow on the old railway line between Stonehenge and Larkhill, the result of World War I troops throwing apple cores out the window of the transport trains,[3] which was far more interesting for both us and told him a lot more about me than the standard interview fare.

- - - - - - - - - - - - - - - - - -

3   I have heard that a similar phenomenon accounts for the chestnut groves around Cuevas del Valle, a village near where I now live, though the soldiers were Roman, the fruit was sweet chestnuts, and instead of a railway line, it was a Roman road (much of which is still there).

There is a pattern in these examples. At the beginning of a process or conversation, when you want to get going, vague offers are helpful. Thus at the beginning of a scene, an improviser might simply make a gesture, like opening a door. They won't define where the door leads from or to, if it's on a ship or in a bank, if it is a cupboard door or a fire exit, but opening a door literally opens possibilities that they know will become more defined as the scene progresses and more offers are made. Similarly, at the beginning of a meeting or on a first date, you might want to make vague offers that allow flow of some kind to be easily created and keep plenty of options open.

Once you get going, open offers are the sweet spot for cocreation. It is through the exchange of open offers that improvisers keep a story moving and developing. There is enough information there for the audience to be able to follow, but enough openness that surprise and discovery are always possible. Open offers have particular importance for relationships, which are cocreations by definition. If you give me an open offer you invite me to add my own ideas. This allows me to be seen and demonstrates that you are not trying to impose your view on me. Giving open offers demonstrates trust.

Nonetheless at some point you need to narrow things down and get to a conclusion, at which point closed offers assume more importance. For example, conversations with potential On Your Feet clients can rumble on and get stuck at the level of interest without turning into work. When this goes on for awhile (and it can be a few months), we find it useful to come down the funnel by making a closed offer. If I say, "We will be in London in June and could do a workshop for you on twenty-fourth, twenty-fifth or twenty-sixth," this will clarify things one way or another since the client is almost obliged to say yes or no. If they say yes then great, if no then I can cross it off my list and get on with looking for other new business, which saves me time and gives me focus.

There is a temptation to shy away from this—after all, you don't want to precipitate a no, do you? However, there comes a point where clarity is the most important thing. It would be dumb to make a closed offer in the first conversation with a client, but if things don't seem to be reaching any definition, then a closed offer helps. If they are going to say no anyway, it is better to know and move on.

Since closed offers tend to bring a conversation to a conclusion, you do need to be careful how fast you come down the funnel. Not so long ago we were asked to help a bank with a conference. Their request was extremely vague, yet we responded with a closed offer—a specific design with a specific cost. The bank didn't like the cost and sent us packing. We didn't get the chance to propose an alternative.

This is an easy trap to fall into. We made the mistake of being too specific, too quickly. If their brief was vague, we should (like Mariscal) have tried to bring them down the funnel and get more information (like the budget, for example) before we made what amounted to a closed offer. Or, if they weren't willing to give us more information, we could have made the proposal itself into an open offer, by including a series of options and a range of prices. How they responded would have given us the information we lacked, and at that point, we could have made an appropriate recommendation. As it was, we ended up moving far too quickly to an exchange of closed offers and the flow ended unsatisfactorily.

When you are a supplier, particularly of professional services, there is a tendency to feel that you have to provide solutions or answers, which leads you to make closed offers. But if you are to do a good job for someone, you need them to play their part, too. It isn't just a question of jumping when they say so because they are the client. The offer funnel can help you navigate such circumstances. Had we spotted their request as a vague offer, we would have known to make an open offer next.

Vague offers are most effective when you want to get going, open offers when you want to cocreate, and closed offers when you want to conclude—they correspond to beginnings, middles and ends. There are lots of beginnings, middles and ends to work with, not just because each of us are simultaneously involved with lots of different processes, but because nested within any one there are little flurries of flow, each of which have their own beginning, middle and end. (Early in the Second World War Churchill famously referred to the Battle of Britain as not "the end, or even the beginning of the end, but the end of the beginning.")

What improvisers do is move up or down the funnel, varying the kind of offers they make, in order to open up or close down the story, according to what they feel is needed. Their skill in doing so enables them to give the story shape, even though they are creating it as they go. They often start with an offer from the audience, a relationship, for example. Imagine the suggestion is "siblings." This is very open—it doesn't tell us what age they are or how they get on, so the actors will make offers that bring them down the funnel, like this:

"Sixteen years making ball bearings and I have never seen such amazing results. You know, Doug, I think we should expand the family business, maybe go public. That way we'd become rich, and I might even be able to get a girlfriend like you."

This brings the audience way down the funnel. Doug could add something about the results or Fred's chances of getting a girlfriend, but pretty soon we will need something else. We have already reached a little end because the funnel literally narrows you down, so the actors will need another beginning. You can create that easily enough by making a vague offer. Again, this is pretty simple:

"What was that?"

It could be a gunshot, the sound of footsteps or Doug's tummy rumbling. This allows the actors to change tack, introduce a new idea or get new energy into the scene. The natural process of improvising a story is one of oscillation up and down the funnel. You start high with something very open or vague that allows you to quickly generate momentum. Open offers then start to shape and direct the story, bringing you further down the funnel until a particular section or idea reaches some kind of conclusion. To create new impetus you then go back up, opening yourself up to new possibilities, inputs and ideas. There are lots of little beginnings, middles and ends nested within the larger structure of the story and the process is one that cycles up and down, which you can draw like this:

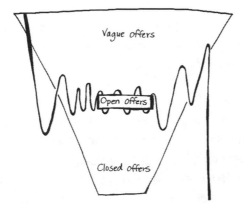

When you get stuck, see if you can identify what is going on in terms of the offer funnel. If you think the flow could do with an injection of new ideas or energy, try coming up the funnel and making an offer that is open or even vague. In a tense moment with a friend or a partner, where nothing you say seems to please the other person, try being vague. Instead of trying to leap to a solution (for example, "Shall we go out for lunch then?"), it might work better just to say, "I would like to do something to help." By being vague you allow them to define what that could be, thus avoiding the risk that you guess wrong.

With difficult conversations, like negotiations or sales, try and stay in cocreative territory by making open offers. Don't come down the funnel too quickly unless you are happy to end something. If, on the other hand, you are struggling to reach a conclusion of any kind, try coming down the funnel and deliberately making more closed offers to see if you can precipitate a result.

When you are leading or managing a team you can think in these terms about which kind of offers it would be helpful to make. If you want to give people a lot of responsibility, your offers should be vague. If you want them to tightly follow your direction, more of your offers should be closed. Remember, everything you do is an offer, so you can also think about how the physical or organizational offers you make affect your team. Is the physical offer open or closed (i.e., do you stipulate where they all sit or allow them to organize themselves)? What kind of offer do the rules or operating procedures of the team constitute? Are they vague, open or closed? What would you like them to be?

You could also label or indicate to others what kind of offer you are making and why. For example, "I know this is a bit vague, but I just want to get the conversation started…" or "If we had to close this down now, what conclusion would we draw?," etc. And above all, understand that sooner or later what goes up must come down (and vice versa)—natural and effective communication has a cyclical nature. Get comfortable and skilled with such an ebb and flow—you need to be able to yo-yo.

There is one insight in particular that I owe to the offer funnel that I would like to leave you with. Thinking in these terms has made me aware of how often people assume that the more work something takes, the better it must be. The Protestant work ethic, if that is what it is, runs broad and deep. That seems innocent enough; after all, what harm can it do if people work a little harder than perhaps they ought? Yet is that really so?

Imagine that you and I work as facilitators and we want to find a way to share knowledge more effectively across our team (which is diverse and geographically spread out). I volunteer to lead the project and set to work. I start by doing some research and come up with a framework for the kind of information I think we will need to collect. I can't decide if it's more sensible to organize this by theme or by author, so I spend some time trying out two different versions.

I can see merit in both, so I design a matrix that will allow us to search by either. Along the way I start to wonder about what kinds of things we should include—should it be little tips, tricks and games or are we talking only about comprehensive models and frameworks? I really feel I need to get clarity about this before I can go much further because I want to get this right, and it takes me a while before I find enough time to think it through. Just as I reach the conclusion that we should focus on the substantial stuff, I get an e-mail from Frank reminding me to include the *Thief's Dilemma* in the "box of tricks." His precise choice of words stops me in my tracks. Frank thinks of this as "a box of tricks." Yet I had decided to exclude tips and tricks. Obviously I will have to add an explanation of what should be included and why—otherwise everyone will have different ideas about the kinds of things they should contribute.

I also realize that while Frank knows the *Thief's Dilemma* very well, I always have to bone up on it, so I decide I should include some background reading. Time passes. I am aware that people haven't seen anything from me yet. Perhaps I shouldn't have promised it in a month? Now that over two months have passed the pressure is mounting—what I come up with had better be good...

In the meantime, you begin to wonder what is happening. As you recall, the project was meant to be about *sharing* knowledge, so you are miffed that you haven't been asked to contribute. Moreover, when I finally present it, my approach is very text-based, which makes it hard to capture models that primarily rely on visuals, which are important to you. Since your input was never sought, you feel excluded. You are also skeptical—what I have done feels more like an attempt to parade knowledge of my own than something designed in the spirit of sharing. Since I have invested so much time in it, your comments feel like criticisms to me. I am loath to change the system I have invented partly because I have become attached to it. I also need to justify the delay.

Oh dear. I have been waylaid by trying to make a highly crafted offer. I want to do something good that will reflect well on me, yet the task here was to facilitate learning *between* people. I could have started sharing much sooner, it was more important to get going than to get it right. I could have made an open, or even a vague offer—like asking everyone to volunteer one tool they thought useful—and a simple pattern might have emerged from the initial contributions people made. This would have served the project (and ultimately, me) better since my colleagues would have felt included.

This is easy to miss. The tendency to complicate things is seductive because it makes us feel that we are grappling with issues of importance. We often worry that people might think we are slacking unless we produced something polished, but more often than not, that's just a shadow story. Not everything has to be as finished as we sometimes assume.

There is a lovely example of this within our own body. Have you ever had the experience of turning your head just in time to see and avoid something you were about to bump into? If so then you probably thought this was lucky. Not a bit of it. You turn your head because cells called "looming detectors" tell you to. These cells notice objects that approach. "Something coming!" they scream. That's all they do—they won't tell you whether what's coming is big or small, pretty or scary, tasty or prickly. But what they do, they do quickly—so quickly in fact that there isn't time to inform the conscious mind, which is why it feels lucky that you turned your head. Their action brings into play other cells which *are* good at recognizing size, shape, color and the rest. This is a kind of leadership behavior. If you insisted on knowing what it was before you devoted resources to turning your head, the danger would be upon you before you could react.

One of the things that this tool in particular, and improvisation in general, demonstrate is that you don't necessarily have to work as hard as you think. As Kevin Kelly explains in *New Rules for the New Economy*, "Releasing incomplete 'buggy' products is not cost-cutting desperation; it is the shrewdest way to complete a product when your customers are smarter than you are."

The offer funnel can deepen your appreciation of the value of cocreation and of the power of leaving things incomplete. You don't have to wow them with the brilliance of what you have already made, you can impress (or engage) someone by involving them. What's more, by involving them earlier there is a greater chance that what you end up with is a better fit with what they need. Sharing responsibility can make your life easier, make people like working with you more and produce more effective results more quickly, which seems like a pretty good result for doing less.

13 ⏱ The Dance of Status

In 1996 *Toy Story* took the world by storm. It was the first full-length computer-animated film, and nothing like it had ever been seen before. A decade or so later, after dozens of computer-animated films have been released, it is apparent that the real genius of *Toy Story* was the quality of the story, not the technology it was rendered on. At the heart of that story is a battle between Woody, the cowboy, and Buzz Lightyear, the space ranger, for top spot among the toys and in the affections of Andy, their owner.

Woody starts as favorite. But when Buzz Lightyear turns up with lasers, wings and hi-tech features, Woody's position becomes vulnerable. Buzz's gizmos impress the other toys, but he's so full of himself that he also appears a bit arrogant. The rivalry escalates until Woody finally shows some humility, whereupon Buzz comes to his rescue; they become friends and help each other to be reunited with Andy and the other toys.

Childish fantasy though this may be, it's a familiar story—you see similar behavior in the office, with similar consequences. Sheriffs and space rangers aren't the only ones that indulge in this kind of sparring—the same can happen to executives, teachers, army officers or brands. Just like Woody and Buzz, this can make life difficult for themselves and for the people around them.

Improvisers have a novel way of understanding how people position themselves, relative to one another. It is a practice called "being sensitive to status." Once you understand the dynamics of status, office life never seems quite the same again, so be warned. The basic idea is that as well as the stable social position that you occupy (which you might call "rank"), there is another variable in play, which improvisers call "status." By status they mean the position you occupy at that very moment in that particular conversation; it is established through your actions, not given by your job title, so it changes constantly.[1]

Imagine you get lost. It doesn't matter whether you are a banker or a baronet, the moment you stop to ask someone the way, your own status sinks and that of the knowledgeable local rises—even if they are a beggar. Your formal positions (baronet and beggar) haven't changed, but the status in your relationship has, which may explain why men (who, in general, like to be high status) are often reluctant to ask the way.

Status, as improvisers understand it, is not something you are born with or struggle long and hard to acquire, it is something that you constantly create through how you act in the moment. It is a temporary, fleeting, almost volatile quality. You can embody high one instant and low the next. It will vary when you talk to your mother, your sister or your daughter, even if they are all in the same room at the same time.

This idea was first articulated by Keith Johnstone. He felt that the stories his improvisers created would often seem flat. Without a script it was very easy for them to fall into cliché and stereotype, which is not very engaging for the audience. Johnstone noticed that in ordinary conversation there is a fluid, dynamic, never-ending negotiation of pecking order that is woven into everyday relationships but was missing from his improvisers' scenes. He coached his actors constantly to raise or lower themselves, relative to the other characters on stage, and all of a sudden, the conversations felt a lot more realistic.

- - - - - - - - - - - - - - - - - - -

1   This distinction would be easy to make in Spanish. In (Castilian) Spanish there are two verbs to be, *ser* and *estar*. *Ser* is used for things that are permanent, including where you are from (and which football team you support). *Estar* is used to for things that are deemed to be temporary, for example, whether you are hungry, hot, or married. A Spanish improviser would thus use *estar*, not *ser*, for status because it is something that fluctuates and changes, not something that stays fixed.

You may not be aware of it, but in any and every conversation most of what you say (or do) will affect the level of status you play, and in turn that will affect how people hear, understand and respond to what you say. For example, you might challenge a client, which would have the effect of raising your status, or defer to a subordinate, which would lower you. These dynamics are universal but normally we don't pay attention to them. If you do, new options and possibilities open up to you. By changing your physical actions, gestures and speech you can vary or modulate the status you adopt. This is not a Machiavellian ruse and does not mean pretending to be something you are not. The point is that by understanding the upside and downside of high and low status positions you can make conscious choices rather than trotting out your habitual or conditioned response.

The idea that status is malleable creates a new way to motivate or connect with people. Great leaders do this instinctively. They know when to bellow and when to whisper; when to project impregnability and when to allow their own frailty to be seen. An adroit grasp of status can help prevent a leader from being taken prisoner by his or her position. What you discover when you start playing around with status is that contrast and counterpoint engage people. The art is to be able to vary and flex the status you use according to the circumstances. Imagine, for example, you are welcoming a group of new people to the company. You might say something like this:

> "Good morning and welcome to Maelstrom Inc. This morning I am going to give you an introduction to the corporation, to how we do things and the results we have achieved. I am going to explain the Maelstrom Way, which will give you an idea of what it is that makes Maelstrom different from our competitors."

This would be confident, assertive and high status. Or you could say:

> "Hello and welcome to Maelstrom. This morning I am going to tell you a little about us. I am going to talk about some of the mistakes we have made, what we have learned from them and how this learning process has made Maelstrom what it is. This should give you an idea of what we are about, how we have done things up to now and how you can contribute."

This is frank and open and low status. The two statements say much the same thing but they feel different. The first is more imposing, the second more welcoming, but neither one is intrinsically better than the other. The context and the audience would determine which is more appropriate.

This might seem obvious but the vast majority of businesspeople feel the high-status position is intrinsically superior. Indeed, they often find it hard to see low status as anything but weak, and in competitive environments many people will habitually try to avoid it, which is both a shame and a loss. Low status has some gentle and important virtues. It invites people to contribute, it creates empathy and charm, and can disarm tension. Skillfully incorporating low status into your repertoire doesn't mean abandoning positions of knowledge, power or authority, it simply means being able to flex. While in excess this can feel weak, when used well it promotes a more open, participative climate that builds trust and is conducive to creativity. This is an important quality, don't you think?

The downside of high status is less obvious to most people but is important nonetheless. We may assume that leaders need to display strength, power and certainty regardless, but the classic role of power and authority is limiting (and exhausting) if you try to live there permanently. The tension that results isn't engaging or motivating for people around you. Energy is wasted or dissipated in conflict, and people (quite naturally) want to see you fall.

High status thus has the negative side of "exclusive," as well as the positive, i.e., it quite literally excludes people, which distances you from them—part of the reason that "it is lonely at the top." This can make it harder to exchange ideas, build trust or motivate someone. Aloofness can also come across as arrogance, and since high status doesn't readily include others, the high-status player often has to rely on his own will and energy. Habitual high-status players don't see this as a consequence of their own behavior, instead they see others as lackadaisical and feel that "I am the only one who ever gets anything done around here." I don't mean that high status isn't important and valuable, it just isn't the whole story.

These costs and benefits can be summarized in a four-box grid, like this:

	Low Status	High Status
Value	break down barriers diffuse tension create sympathy inclusive charming endearing	efficient controlled order others confident powerful credible
Cost	unconfident weak low credibility uncomfortable powerless can seem inept	overbearing sets you up for a fall arrogant exclusive not participative high responsibility creates conflict

This raises a question. What kinds of behavior qualify as high or low, and what can you do to shift your level of status? Here are some examples of things you can say that will raise your status:

1. Invoke authority.

The authority figure might be a person, a publication or a company. (Keep in mind that what constitutes an authority will vary according to the context, too.) But you might say something like:

"As Einstein (Daddy, Spielberg, etc.) says…"

"In *The Harvard Business Review* (*British Medical Journal*, the *Odyssey*, etc.)…"

"At Nike (Head Office, Tassajara, etc.)…"

2. Be definitive.

This is the second high-status gambit. It doesn't even matter if you are right, being definitive alone can be enough to raise status. Examples of how to be definitive would be:

"There are two important points here…"
"The real issue is…"
"What we need to decide is…"

3. Draw on exclusive experience.
> If you have access to experience which others lack, it will raise your status. You
> might phrase statements about that experience like this:
> "When we tried that last time we found that…"
> "We discussed this at the executive board and…"
> "When I was in Nigeria we saw that…"

You can probably work out the low-status plays for yourself—they are in effect the opposite of the three suggestions above.

1. Self-deprecation.
> Displaying humility by putting oneself down is perhaps the most obvious way of
> lowering your own status:
> "I'm an not an expert here…"
> "I really don't understand technology…"
> "From what little I know…"

2. Make uncertainty explicit or express doubt.
> This is the counterpoint to being definitive. It may require confidence to do this,
> but in terms of status, it still lowers you.
> "I am not really sure about this…"
> "I guess you could argue that…"
> "I am in a quandary here…"

3. Raise others.

Since status is relative, by raising the status of others you inevitably lower your own:

"You know more about this than I do..."

"Mary is a difficult act to follow..."

"I felt lucky to be working with such amazing people..."

This list isn't exhaustive but it should be enough to give you the idea.

I should emphasize that status isn't just a matter of what you say. How you move and hold yourself will contribute enormously to your status position, and there are many ways to change status physically that you can also play around with. This applies to space and objects, as well as people. When you walk into a room you play a certain level of status in relation to the space around you, even if it's empty. You might stride around like a king or shuffle like a librarian. You might pick up a book with awe, familiarity or contempt, each of which will change your status in relation to the object. To embody high status independently of the content of what you say, you can:

Speak in a clear, even voice (more than a loud one)

Hold your head very still (and move it only slowly)

Make precise movements and gestures

Don't touch your head with your hands

Make your "um's" and "er's" very long, e.g., "uuuuuummmmmmm"

Seek and hold eye contact

If standing, have one foot point out

Pause before you speak

Conversely, to lower your status:

Fluctuate how loudly you speak

Move your head while you talk

Touch your head with your hands

Make imprecise movements and gestures

Say "um" and "er" often and quickly

Look down or away (break eye contact)

If standing, turn one foot in

Make quick glances, then look away

Answer questions immediately

If you want to test how strong physical cues can be, try holding your head absolutely still while talking to someone. See how you feel and how they react—the effect of such a seemingly small change can be quite striking (and curiously enough, it even seems to work on the telephone even though the person you are talking to can't even see you!).

We once had a client who very deliberately used physical cues to establish the status he wanted. Kevin Carroll worked for Nike and his job was to stimulate people across the whole organization, yet he didn't have a department so he needed people to come to him. We noticed that in his office, he had one high chair and one low chair. We asked him about it and he explained that it was quite consciously done on his part. As he put it, "I like to get lower than people, it is a way of getting them to feel comfortable coming in here."

Sometimes you may need to win over skeptics and invite people in at the same time. This implies playing both high and low status in the same breath. This is a situation we often face at the beginning of a workshop; there will be some people in the group who think playing games is a waste of time and unless we can quickly demonstrate our worth, they will be dismissive and unreceptive. Other people will be terrified by the prospect of improvising, so what they need is the welcoming gentle touch of low status to invite them in and allay their misgivings.

If I am present and listening I will pick up on these expectations before the workshop begins. If so, then I might sit on the floor while participants sit above me on chairs. From this lowly position I can mention some impressive companies I have worked with (like Nike or GE) and follow that by explaining that I have no special talent or training in improvisation. There are multiple channels open to you (the physical, the verbal, the paralinguistic and so on) and you can use each of these in different ways to establish the status relationship you are looking for.

Let's have a look at how you might use this four-box grid of status as a tool. Imagine you work for Maelstrom—a British multinational in a high-technology business that is expanding quickly into new markets. As part of the leadership team you need to visit new markets and meet with managers in each new country you are moving into. On one trip you have to visit France, Albania and Spain and give the same presentation in each place. The material is fixed; however, you can alter *how* you present it. How might you use the status grid to think about this?

France is an old, wealthy country, where even a farmworker can regard himself as an intellectual. Moreover, for a thousand years or so they have been remarkably keen on taking the British down a peg or two. The French are likely to see you as low status anyway so if you play low it would merely make it easy for them to dismiss what you say. You want to gain respect, which means raising your status, so you want to be definitive, quote authoritative figures and sources and draw on experience to which they do not have access.

In Albania the opposite might be true. You not only come from headquarters, but from the country that gave birth to Winston Churchill and David Beckham, no less. So in Tirana, if you don't lower your status you might come across as intimidating. It will be difficult for them to feel they can make a contribution, and you will feel they are lacking in initiative and ideas. So you should play low, admit ignorance about something (Albania itself might be a good candidate), invite their opinion, and be less definitive.

In Spain, where I live, you would need a mix of both. Spaniards are routinely impressed by foreigners while at the same time being extremely disdainful of them. This might seem contradictory but then Spain is a country of contrasts. Ideally, before the meeting, you would establish your ability to play low status by swearing like a trooper, staying out drinking until absurd hours and gleefully admitting your ignorance. Then in the meeting you can happily play high status and reaffirm your Johnnie-foreigner credentials. The high-status presentation without the low-status drinking would invite accusations of arrogance. Yet if all you know is how to enjoy yourself, why should they bother to listen to you? I have deliberately used exaggerated stereotypes, but the point is that you can use the grid to adjust what you do and say to a particular audience (whether it's a particular nationality or a particular department).

However the idea isn't simply to pitch your status at one level and stay there. While it is a good place to start, skillful conversation is a dance where levels of status shift constantly (it was emulating this dance that allowed improvisers to make their scenes authentic). Take the following conversation between two colleagues, with the flows of status made explicit (in parentheses):

Richard: Hello, Mick, it's good to see a familiar face. How is the Australian market? *(Lowers his status by admitting he is glad to see someone he knows.)*

Nick: It's Nick, actually. (Lowers Richard more by pointing out his mistake.) Australia? Oh, really well. We sorted things out down there. *(Raises his own status by hinting that there is more to his life than Australia and by saying everything is going well.)*

Richard: Nick, yes, of course. Sorry. You were definitely the right man for the job. *(Continues low by flattering and elevating Nick.)*

Nick: Well, thank you. You know I've moved on, I am heading up Asia-Pacific now? *(Raises his own status even further.)* How are sales in the U.S.? Not so good, I heard. *(A put down, lowering Richard.)*

Richard: Well, we did have a tough first quarter, but things are booming now with the new X1 and the X0 on the way. *(Raises his own status by showing that Nick is out of date, by saying things are going well, and by laying claim to something new, the X0.)*

Nick: I can't wait to see the X0. What's it like? *(Lowers his own status and elevates Richard by accepting that he hasn't seen it and asking for information.)*

Richard: Can't say much, you know, but its very, very cool. *(Stays high by refusing to elaborate.)*

Everything is loaded with status, whether you mean it to be or not, and you can see how quickly things shift. In this snippet Richard starts low and ends high. Nick does the opposite—he starts high and ends low. This is easier to see if we turn the conversation on its side, like this diagram:

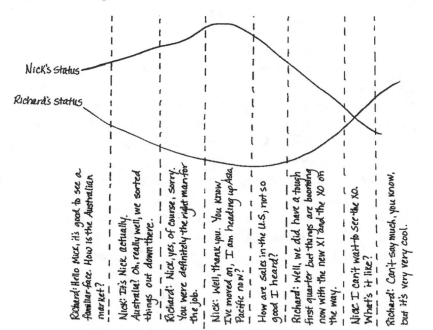

Nick's status

Richard's status

Richard: Hello Nick, it's good to see a familiar face. How is the Australian market?

Nick: It's Nick actually. Australia? Oh, really well, we sorted things out down there.

Richard: Nick, yes, of course, sorry. You were definitely the right man for the job.

Nick: Well, thank you. You know I've moved on, I am heading up Asia Pacific now?

How are sales in the U.S, not so good I heard?

Richard: Well, we did have a tough first quarter but things are booming now with the new XI and the XO on the way.

Nick: I can't wait to see the XO. What's it like?

Richard: Can't say much, you know, but it's very very cool.

Going back to the Maelstrom example, whichever country you were in you would be aware of the overall note you wanted to strike (high in France, low in Albania, a mix in Spain), and then as you went through the presentation you would be sensitive to your audience, looking for offers that tell you what was needed at each particular point to keep them with you. Once you have impressed the French, do you then need to soften your position a little and lower your status to invite them into a conversation? Are you in danger of underwhelming the Albanians and could you beef up your presentation with a little more high status? And so on, as the presentations unfold, you can adjust and shift what you are doing, which, no surprise, requires you to practice being present and listening.

I would love to see people apply these ideas to their written marketing materials. Most marketing is high status. The assumption is that if you want to make something desirable, you need to dwell on its positive attributes and maybe even exaggerate a teensy-weensy bit. This seems reasonable enough. However, if everyone makes the same assumption, high status becomes the norm and everyone's material is peppered with monotonous superlatives. "Claim inflation" sets in and people on the receiving end quite naturally become cynical. In a linguistic version of the tragedy of the commons, the result is that everyone sounds the same, no one has any credibility and the language is devalued in the bargain.

This reminds me of Mandy Rice-Davies—a call girl who was involved in a scandal with John Profumo, British Minister for War in Harold MacMillan's 1960s government. When told that Profumo denied meeting her, she replied, "Well he would say that, wouldn't he?" High status marketing elicits a similar response: "Well they would say that, wouldn't they?" If everyone sings their own praises, it is not only tiresome but ineffective, so marketers would do well to come down off their high-status pedestals every now and then.

They rarely do so because there is something of a taboo around playing low status. I have often heard marketing directors say "It would too much of a risk" or "Our market is too competitive for that." Yet the real risk is going unnoticed. Being prepared to lower your status is a very powerful thing, *especially* in a highly competitive environment. It not only makes you stand out, but it makes you more credible (and likeable) as well. Tesco has become Britain's most successful supermarket while using the humble slogan Every Little Helps. To punctuate the high-status babble, you don't need to plunge to great depths of self-deprecation; all you need is a counterpoint.

It is the contrast that counts. If most advertising were gentle and humble, then a resolutely high-status claim would be refreshing. Something like this happens in the realm of technical support. Most technical support is surrounded by disclaimers and caveats that quietly lower both expectations and status. You can see the prevailing logic at work here—playing low status limits the amount of responsibility you take. Into the breach steps The Geek Squad, a specialist tech-support company that positions itself as a technological *Men In Black* and makes prodigious high-status claims. Their book is called *The Geek Squad Guide to Solving Any Computer Glitch*; an ad for new "agents" has the headline "Recruits wanted for world domination"; and e-mails carry mottos like "Serving the public, policing technology, protecting the world." When I interviewed the founder Robert Stephens a few years back, he was particularly fond of being definitive. He would say things like "The hard drive is history" with incredible certainty, which made him sound authoritative (it matters little that the hard drive is still with us). In the meek and evasive world of tech support this high-status position stands out. Stephens is a natural showman who, in the most unlikely of areas, has created a fantastically engaging property. He knows how to get an audience's attention—as anyone who has seen him on stage will testify.[2]

However, this isn't simply a good piece of marketing theater. Robert is also a shrewd leader who knows that his business depends upon getting and keeping good people, and he understands those people extremely well. Many of these status plays (such as the genuine diecast "special agent" badges) are directed at the internal audience and the primary goal is to make those special agents feel truly special so they stay with the company. It has worked well enough to get Geek Squad agents into Best Buy stores across the United States.

Wherever a brand or company speaks, you have the opportunity to shift status to achieve the effect you want. Take airlines, for example. Flying is a high-technology and potentially dangerous business. In fact it is remarkably safe, but reassurance remains very important to customers. Unsurprisingly, airlines normally play high status. Hence

- - - - - - - - - - - - - - - - - - - -

2   I once introduced Robert at a conference. The audience was rolling in the aisles and the next speaker came up to me and said, "Well, thanks for nothing. How do I follow that?" That speaker was Malcolm Gladwell, bestselling author of *The Tipping Point* and *Blink*.

captains with somber uniforms and impressive stripes of gold braid. (Imagine how you might feel if they wore T-shirts?)

Yet on one flight to San Francisco, as we began our descent the pilot said, "Those of you on the left of the cabin have a great view of Yosemite. At least, I hope it's Yosemite because if it's not, we are lost." In a playful moment the pilot abandoned the high-status convention of his profession. This gentle nod toward low status made me feel warmer toward the pilot and the airline; it didn't make me worry about his navigational skills. Airlines like Southwest (or Alaska) have built a whole brand personality out of breaking the industry routine around status.

Nonetheless you need to stay sensitive to context. When 9/11 created a massive tilt to the platform of air travel (to use terms from Chapter 8), captains and airlines made some interesting status shifts. The normally homely Southwest clearly felt that they needed to add some (high-status) reassurance. When flights resumed they announced that "You are still safer on this flight than you were traveling to the airport, even allowing for terrorist activity." They invoked authority (i.e., statistics, research, data) to do this—one of the tactics we identified earlier—and momentarily abandoned their fun-loving, low-status position.

A captain on one of the large airlines did the opposite and adopted a "we are all in this together" position. It was the first flight from Denver to Dulles (Washington, D.C.) after the tragedy, and he made a lengthy announcement to the passengers once the doors were closed. He said that he could be sure there were no bombs or firearms aboard because security checks for those were exhaustive. However, relinquishing the normal position of high-status authority, he explained that not even he could be sure of much else. He acknowledged that there were still risks and that most of these came from other passengers. He explained how to use pillows and blankets as protection against someone armed with a sharp instrument, and finally, asked all passengers to introduce themselves to the person next to them. Instead of people being filled with fear, the cabin erupted in cheers.

Like improvisers, these pilots are being sensitive to status. They are shifting or changing a familiar pattern in a way that engages, pleases, entertains or in some other way satisfies their audience better in the particular circumstances they face. On the phone lines, in its advertising or through its salesmen, any organization can put the practice of being sensitive to status into action. It is a tool you can use to engage your audience and is particularly useful when the patterns of status are very predictable.

Disrupting those predictable patterns can allow you to have new kinds of conversation. For example, one (financial) company we worked with felt that their formal structure was stifling. Given their industry, they couldn't get rid of the hierarchy, so they decided to create an additional structure of a very different nature. They formed groups of about a dozen people from different levels and functions called hubs. Everyone was assigned to a hub. Each hub included a senior manager, but their role was simply to act as a conduit back to the leadership team—they were not in charge. Everyone was an equal member, so this created the opportunity for people to free themselves from the hierarchy and shift their status so that new relationships and connections became possible. The hubs quickly became powerful sources of ideas, opportunities and information. They created very strong emotional bonds and people came to regard their hubmates as family. The power of creating a space where the normal rules of status didn't apply was impressive.

This has a historical parallel. In seventeenth-century London the hubs were the coffee houses. The normal rules of rank and position were suspended—anyone (male) could enter and be treated equally. Such places consequently became hot beds for the exchange and scrutiny of new ideas in much the way that the internet (another space where your position depends on what you say, not who you are) is today.

In general, most of us—individuals as well as organizations—display a predictable pattern. We normally have a natural preference for playing either high or low status and feel more comfortable one way than the other. Over time we find what works for us and we tend to stick to it. We develop a personal style.

This does not mean you only play high or low status. Personal styles are more interesting than that. You might play high status at work and low status at home. For example, Alex Ferguson rules Manchester United with a rod of iron, but at home its clear that his wife takes the lead. Personal styles are like a patchwork quilt. Overall, the quilt may have a particular tone, but look closely and you can see patches of different colors and texture that make up the whole. However, if within any given context you are unable to modulate or shift into a different register, you limit how effective you can be. For example, a tendency to play low status can be a weakness when it comes to negotiating fees or sending back food in a restaurant.

As with color-advance, becoming more aware of your personal style can help you understand what is going on in your relationships and what is limiting you. You can then either set about trying to change these limitations or learn to be happy living with them. For example, either you get better at playing high status to negotiate better fees, or you choose to stay comfortable (low status) and accept that you are not going to make as much money. What do you want—more money or an easier life? Whichever you choose, you are better off making that choice consciously.

Though flexibility is the key, in business that principally means discovering a deeper appreciation of the gentle virtues of low status. Business tends to attract and promote the pushy behaviors, so the chance that there is a shortage of high-status behavior is remote.

Not only is there an imbalance, but that imbalance is becoming more important. As Marshall Young at Oxford University's Saïd Business School is fond of reminding people, "Each pair of hands comes with a free brain." (And, I would add, a free heart.) Thus the modern leader's job is to inspire and motivate other people to take initiative and contribute their own ideas as much as it is to issue directions or orders. A quick glance at the grid shows that playing lower status is what creates empathy, connection and a climate of creativity. Allowing yourself to not know the answer, to be happy with ambiguity, to invite people in, to leave ideas unfinished so that others can contribute—these behaviors, which are increasingly important in a collaborative knowledge economy, all require you to become comfortable with low status.

This gives us another chance to work on that twenty-first-century psychological chore—letting go of the idea that leaders must always be certain and commanding.

Uniform high status is neither necessary nor desirable. Vulnerability, doubt and uncertainty are, in this way of looking at things, a necessary note that a sophisticated leader, now more than ever, needs to be able to hit. That may seem like a difficult thing to do, but if you have the presence of mind and the humility to admit you don't know all the answers, it might actually help you find them. As Mark Twain put it, with one of the most elegant modulations of status you can imagine, "I was asked a difficult question and I was delighted to be able to answer at once—'I don't know,' I said."

Postscript

A word of warning: once you start noticing status it is easy to get obsessed. You can end up paying more attention to how people say things than to what they say, in which case meetings might start to sound a little like this:

Ted: Hello, everyone. I am going to say thanks for turning up because that makes me look important.

Frank: No problem, Ted. I will suck up to you early on just in case you do well. I can always distance myself from you later.

Ted: So, did you get a chance to look at what I sent out? Asking that keeps me at the center of things.

Linda: Yes, I did, and to make myself look smart I will ask you about a detail on page seven.

Marcel (boss, entering): Sorry, everyone. I was held up by a meeting with people far more important than you and apologizing allows me to draw attention to that.

Frank: Good, good. One thing, if I take over the conversation I get the chance to parade my knowledge, which is good. I say that there are three main points—which makes me sound like I have a firm grasp of the situation, even though I don't know what those points are. The drawback is that I get carried away with the sound of my own voice, and though that keeps me center stage, it gets difficult when I realize I have no idea where I am going. So, to save myself, I will throw in some numbers (63 percent), a reference to the *Harvard Business Review* and link back to Marcel, who I can thus toady up to, right Marcel?

Marcel: Well, the only thing that matters here is what I think, so I don't even have to pretend to listen to any of you. The nub of the matter is the one thing that I can think to say on the subject (which is the thing I always say). This coffee really is awful.

Ted: The real issue here is whether we get to talk about something that makes me look smart or something that makes Frank look smart.

Marcel (yawns): I suggest we set up a task force. I won't give you any detail about what that task force should do so that if it doesn't work I can blame you.

Ted: Marcel, I know you have really stiffed us there, but I will get back at you one day, you useless old windbag. In the meantime I will volunteer, but with enough caveats so that later, if necessary, I can blame Frank. OK, Frank?

Frank: Absolutely Ted, I know you are out to shaft me, but I would do the same to you, so I will sound positive so you don't suspect I am plotting to shaft you first.

Linda: I am a bit confused, but I guess I will just make the same noises as Frank and Ted since they seem to do well around here.

Marcel: Good, looks like I can get out of here now and skate on to the next meeting with nothing new on my list. Thanks, everyone.

PART 4

Improvisation and the Joy of Uncertainty

14 ♡ *Homo sovieticus* and Other Control Freaks

Improvisational practice is not grand or complicated. It is not obscure, technical or difficult to grasp. It only takes a few minutes to understand an idea like everything's an offer, yet the practice could last a lifetime. You don't need to keep up to date with the latest advances in improvisational theory because there won't be any worth worrying about. Lengthy study or clever debate, however much you might enjoy them, are not necessary. Returning to the same idea or asking the same question time and again is what makes a difference. Look for an offer, find one, use it, see what happens, look again. Over time repeated practice commits the learning to deep, unconscious memory and integrates it into who you are.

This simplicity is a strength. Nonetheless adopting the practice is no pushover: simple is not the same as easy. Improvisation isn't easy because it forces us to question some of our most cherished habits. Innocent though it may look, it is, in fact, quite radical—it suggests a way of behaving that is quite different from what we are used to. It obliges us to think about how we think.

How much of a challenge this can be came home to me one afternoon in a pine forest near the border of Lithuania and Belarus. I had been running an off-site meeting for an advertising agency from Vilnius and we had finished early. Though the weak Baltic sun was low, there were still a few hours of light remaining so the group I was with decided to stop on the way home and go searching for mushrooms. As we wandered around looking for *Boletus edulis* Igor Tolkaciovas, one of several Russians in the group, approached me. Igor was not your average advertising man—before joining the agency he had trained as a Soviet fighter pilot (and before that as a Franciscan monk). I had learned over the previous few days that he wasn't short of colorful opinions, so when he got me in his sights, clearly eager to say something in particular, I was curious to know what it might be.

Igor made up for his limited English with an extraordinary determination to communicate fueled by implausible quantities of coffee and cigarettes. Trembling from the concentration (or the caffeine) he said, "Me, I, too much still *Homo sovieticus*," and paused for effect, no doubt enjoying my confusion. "Control is…," he paused again, searching for a word only to find help quite literally at hand. He pointed at the cigarette smoldering between his fingers and said, "addiction."

We found a nearby colleague to translate and I learned that Igor attributed the difficulty he had experienced with improvisation to the centrally planned Soviet regime he had been brought up in. He felt that living his formative years in a highly controlling culture had left an indelible mark. It had never occurred to me that the Soviet Union, though defunct, might still be making its presence felt in this intensely personal way.

Yet though Igor was undoubtedly unusual, *Homo sovieticus* was remarkably familiar. I have seen plenty of people in London or Los Angeles struggle in much the same way. Improvisational exercises are designed so that no one can determine what happens; however, like Igor, many people find this difficult to accept and quickly start to tell other people what to say or do. Rather than allow something to emerge, they try to coerce or compel other people to conform with their own idea. This happens fast. Many people have so little tolerance for uncertainty and ambiguity that they will get visibly agitated within a matter of seconds.

This habit is woven tightly into everyday behavior. When one of my clients wants to go through the plan for a workshop with a fine-tooth comb, asking detailed questions about what happens after the break on the second morning or what the concrete output of a specific exercise will be, *Homo sovieticus* (or his western equivalent) rears his head. Such conversations happen frequently because people focus their attention on what they *can* control—in this case, the running order. They may imbue it with importance *because* they can control it, but a running order is not important in itself (except perhaps as a defense against anxiety). It is the equivalent of a military plan that "won't survive first contact with the enemy" or, in this case, the participants. An effective workshop will evolve and develop as it unfolds. The plan should be a springboard, not a leash.

Other people try to determine the result instead of the process. More than once I have been asked to specify in advance "precisely what we will get" from a creativity course. This is like asking me to take you exploring—but only to places you know. Creativity necessarily involves discovery and surprise; it cannot be installed step by step like a piece of software. Nonetheless such a question is regarded as sensible and prudent even though it forms part of the generally accepted management practice that Marshall Young (at Oxford University) described as a "myth."

I see this tendency in myself. I can easily catch myself trying to predict and control what is going on. For example, no matter how many workshops I lead, I still have to fight the knee-jerk reaction to adhere to a script or plan, especially when things get tricky. Even though I know that it is better to allow the participants to affect what happens, rather than trying to determine everything myself, I have to make a conscious effort to act on this. My desire to be in charge can quickly take over.

Clearly *Homo sovieticus*, as Igor dubbed him, is not a peculiarly Soviet phenomenon. He wields great influence over the way business is organized and conducted all over the world. While the centrally planned Communist regime may have had a particularly strong addiction, we all have something of a habit. It is this habit that makes improvisation a challenge. Instead of making his presence felt through a five-year plan, *Homo sovieticus* shows up in our enthusiasm for standardized tests and scores, status meetings, benchmark studies or comprehensive reports. He lurks behind language like "future proof," with its tantalizing promise of controlling that most unruly of territories—the future. We are taught to measure, test and statistically analyze everything from personality types to advertising ideas without questioning how appropriate or helpful it really is.

We get attached to controlling measures like head count even if they are only of tangential importance. We value uniformity and regularity as ends in themselves and we design organizational systems and structures to reinforce and promote this behavior. The pursuit of control has become our default setting. It shows up even in trivial actions like a visit to McDonald's where we expect the french fries to conform to a single, consistent ideal. As gardener and writer Michael Pollan says, "What is that if not a control thing?—and not just on the part of McDonald's."[1]

Yet it is hard to loosen our attachment to control. This is not surprising. Its deep embrace is a result of how spectacularly successful it has been. It is hard for anyone born in the modern era to imagine quite how opaque, mysterious and cruel the world must have seemed three or four hundred years ago (though a trip to the poorer parts of today's world might yield some insight). Hobbes's famous observation that life is "nasty, brutish and short" was depressingly accurate.

Newton's equations allied with the development of the experimental method based on observation, changed that. Suddenly it became possible to acquire systematic and certain knowledge that allowed you to predict and control the unruly forces of nature. Thus wildness seemed to become tame. This was a magnificent achievement and allowed people to harness and manipulate material like never before. It seemed that physics had discovered the inner secrets of the universe—the very mechanisms on which it depended.

The success of this project delivered colossal material progress. The industrial revolution, prodigious economic growth, hygiene and sanitation, vaccines, antibiotics, the car, the moon landings, the personal computer, the internet, the skinny soy vanilla latté and all the other paraphernalia of modern life followed. Hundreds of millions of us live in a level of comfort and security that no medieval king could have dreamed of. Reasonably enough, we place great store by prediction, regularity, certainty and precision.

- - - - - - - - - - - - - - - - - - -

1   This quotation is from *The Botany of Desire*. Both this book and his later *In Defense of Food* contain wonderful observations on the control mentality.

However, over time the default setting can become the only setting. *Homo sovieticus* is oblivious to the fact that the control mentality has costs and consequences, yet as psychologist James Hillman says, "Ideas we have and do not know we have, have us."[2]

In this context, the improvisational practice is a jolt. It makes visible both the automatic nature and the strength of our attachment to control, which has become an ideology. People frequently display a mixture of puzzlement and exasperation that the improv games prevent them from doing what they normally do. They remonstrate with me or take issue with the rules rather than question their own thinking. A game might work perfectly well and produce a pleasing result quickly, yet people are often offended by the mere fact that they can't control it.

This faithfully reflects what happens in organizations. As long as there is a process that feels predictable and serious, all is assumed to be well. If there is a thick report, a dense set of numbers or a long presentation to go with it, so much the better. This buttressing activity becomes an end in itself and what really matters is lost from sight. When faced with any difficulty people redouble their efforts to control things. If that doesn't work, the rationalization is that they didn't try hard enough. In workshops, if people offer a recipe for improvement it will almost always involve concentrating power in an individual (or a small group) and adding more rules, normally prescriptive ones. They try to create a system that dictates what happens.

This is a laborious way to act. Trying to create a system to control an improv game (or any other human activity, for that matter) is slow and ineffective. It reduces the chance of producing anything creative quickly and easily to zero. Pressure on the people trying to run the system rises, as does the sense of frustration and boredom felt by everyone else, who doesn't get to participate. In other words, familiar problems are quickly recreated.

It is important, therefore, that we start to see the connections between our desires for control and the difficulties we often find ourselves grappling with. We need to become more aware of the costs and consequences of control—and there are plenty.

----

2   James Hillman, *Kinds of Power* (New York: Currency Doubleday, 1995).

For example, detailed plans create pressure, tension and stress. It was this tension that led Gary to take up improvisation in the first place. As a budding actor at college he found the process of learning and reproducing predetermined lines and moves terrifying. The script felt like a narrow path along a sheer cliff face. One false step and he would be lost. The anxiety this provoked made it very hard for him to deliver a good performance, so he turned to improvisation where the freedom available released him from this pressure.

Spelling out each step of the way in a plan or script gives you a point of reference, which is meant to be reassuring. However, as soon as you have a fixed reference point, you create a right answer, and as soon as there is a right answer, there are plenty of wrong ones. If I play a game with one particular point in mind and the game doesn't make that point, it follows that the game has gone wrong and I have failed. But it is my attachment to the script that creates the failure. In business a great deal of importance is attached to making plans. Yet I wonder how much of the pressure and stress that creates is really productive?

Trying to control everything is exhausting. People will often expend a disproportionate amount of time, energy and attention trying to control a situation without even asking themselves if that will help. For example, I worked with one group who insisted on exploring every possible interpretation of the rules of a game before they started to play. The net result was that we spent nearly fifteen minutes discussing something that only takes two minutes to do. They were a clever group of people but this wasn't a clever thing to do. It would have been much more efficient to learn through doing rather than trying to anticipate every eventuality. In the time they took to talk about it, we could have played the game several times, accumulating learning from each iteration. The action would have created better communication and yielded more information than talking.

The clients I mentioned earlier, the ones who wanted to anticipate what was going to happen in a workshop, were doing something similar. While such conversations may feel reassuring, they are mostly a charade. No amount of detailed analysis will tell you in advance what is going to occur and it is easy to waste a lot of management time this way. Trying to control everything will certainly keep you very busy with reports and meetings, but what else does it really achieve?

Plans can also put a ceiling on your aspirations and steer you away from novelty. Had Gary and I stuck to the plan in the Three Lions Bakery, we would have talked about a T-shirt rather than allowing an improv-based consultancy to emerge. Improv games are often improved or new ones invented when people misunderstand or reinterpret the rules, but the group I mentioned above, who wanted to catalog every possibility in advance, put themselves in a state of mind where innovation simply wasn't going to happen.

Never is this more obvious than when you travel. Imagine you make a once-in-a-lifetime trip to Paris and you plan thoroughly to "get the most out of it." You research the best restaurants and memorize the floor plan of the Louvre to make sure you don't miss any great masters. Let's say your plan comes off perfectly. If so, then you get exactly what you imagine in advance but nothing more, and you miss the homeless Moroccan musician's extraordinary guided tour of Pigale. Package tours work this way. You have the security of knowing exactly what you are going to get, but you cut off any other possibilities. There is little joy in such certainty. The confusion, uncertainty and disruption necessary if you want to get somewhere new are neutered by an overemphasis on certainty and control.

Moreover, when everything is perfectly regular, something important is lost. Good wine, for example, is the result of variable conditions. In La Rioja (Alavesa) a breeze blows from the Sierra de Cantabria at sunset, cooling the vines, which develops the character of the grape, and the resulting wine, in a way that an even temperature would not.[3] In music, rhythm is irregular. Nirankar Khalsa, a jazz percussionist (to the sound of whose music this book has largely been written), says that the difference between a

- - - - - - - - - - - - - - - - - -

3   My wine-making friend Juan Carlos López de la Calle reserves derision for fruit like bananas and avocados that are grown in even temperatures, which he says are bland and boring: "A flat temperature creates a flat taste—which is completely useless if you want to make anything interesting."

metronome and a musician is that a metronome delivers an invariant mechanical beat whereas a musician stretches and compresses time, playing around with it, moving off center only to return at the opportune moment. "That" he says, his eyes wide and his smile broad, "is what we call rhythm."

Irregularity isn't just an aesthetic quality. Take a more fundamental rhythm—the rhythm of a heartbeat. In the winter of 1916, in the middle of the First World War, my grandfather William Emmanuel Flew was rejected as unfit for active service because of an irregular heartbeat. For another seventy years that supposedly "dickey" heart kept going strong (though it would beat a little faster with irritation if you asked him about the episode). Cardiologists now recognize that a healthy heartbeat "is full of strange little flourishes and incongruous leaps."[4] A certain irregularity, it turns out, can be healthy.

A relentless emphasis on control can also lull you into a false sense of security. If all your energy and attention is directed to trying to predict and control what happens, you may not respond well when something unexpected does occur. In Chapter 4, I mentioned the disastrous summer of 1996 on Everest. One of the teams which suffered most was New Zealander Rob Hall's Mountain Adventure. Hall and his team were pioneers in taking nonprofessional climbers to the summit of Everest; a feat that requires meticulous preparation and enormous skill. Nonetheless that year Hall himself and a number of his clients were among the sixteen climbers killed.

Filmmaker Matt Dickinson was on the mountain at the time and became only the fourth person to film on the summit of Everest. He maintains that the cause of the calamity was not the storm that blew in, but the Mountain Adventure team's attitude. To make the point, he shows one of their advertisements which boasted "100 percent success on Everest." The implication was that the team could control everything necessary to guarantee a result. That belief influenced the promises they made and the decisions

- - - - - - - - - - - - - - - - - - -

4   David Whyte, *The Heart Aroused: Poetry and the Preservation of the Soul in Corporate America*, (New York, Doubleday Business, 1996).

they took so that when a storm blew in, they ploughed on with fatal results. How often do people in business forge ahead regardless because it says so in the plan?

Dickinson says this blind spot is remarkably common. Having filmed more than fifty extreme expeditions, he told me that "there is always an avalanche or a sandstorm or whatever," and yet people are invariably surprised when something occurs which they hadn't planned for. But plans are always incomplete. If you accept, as Dickinson says, that "the mountain is always in control, not you," it leads to a different response with different results. The team he belonged to hunkered down instead of soldiering on and made a successful summit attempt once the weather had cleared.

Perhaps the gravest cost of our desire for control is the effect it has on people around us. While most of us would like to be able to be in control ourselves, few of us want to be controlled by others. When you are dealing with machines, this doesn't matter (a car doesn't resent the driver), but people bridle when you try to control them. "Control freak" is not a compliment.

I remember being witness to a particularly vivid demonstration of this. I was working in the Madrid office of an Anglo American multinational when one day, James, a director in the London office, called to tell me how a forthcoming presentation to an international client ought to be delivered. I dutifully reported his instructions to my Spanish boss, Fernando, who picked up the phone and called James back. They had a brief conversation. Eight words to be precise—enough for Fernando to display an impressive command of colloquial English. "Hello, James, it's Fernando…fuck off, you prat!" he barked and slammed the phone down.

This was pretty brutal, even for a Spaniard, but Fernando was sick of being told what to do by the people in London and wasn't shy of making that obvious. He dared to say what most of us feel when we are ordered around without consideration for our ideas or point of view. A few moments later Fernando's phone rang. It was James calling to eat a large serving of humble pie.

In relationships, giving too much priority to control, regularity and predictability is counterproductive. You can't sustain the interest (let alone the affection) of a colleague, customer, audience or lover through control. Uncertainty, not control, opens the door to surprise, discovery and delight. The fresh thought, the new insight, the unlooked-for caress—all require some measure of doubt, ambiguity or unpredictability. In human relationships, control only works for the person wielding it and only in the short term. Over time it builds resentment and erodes motivation. It makes people less likely to take initiative or volunteer their own ideas. Good leaders do an awful lot more than order people around.

The negative consequences of trying to exercise control can pass unnoticed. It is therefore important to realize that if you insist on trying to determine and control everything, you will pay a price. As we become more aware of these costs, we may start to realize that improvisation is not as risky as we might have imagined.

In reality, there is little we *really* control anyway. You can control a car but not traffic. Weeds and pests simultaneously become immune to our chemicals and our desires to control them and invade crops drenched in ever-increasing doses of pesticides. Superbugs prosper among the antibiotics in hospitals, and (just like children) managers in local markets always want to do things their own way. As one executive put it, "You're deluding yourself if you think you can control Kazakhstan from Minneapolis." For all its accomplishments, indeed, perhaps because of them, the modern world is far from stable. If anything, we know rather less about what is coming next and how it will affect us, than our ancestors did. Rather than eradicate mess or mystery, our technical prowess has shifted it. The extraordinary progress of science and technology means that we can predict within a few minutes when the several hundred tons of metal, rubber and plastic that we call a Boeing 777 is going to land in London after a journey of thousands of miles, but we could never predict the conversations that the people on board the aircraft might have—the deals that will be done, the ideas that will occur, the romances that will flower.

We cannot even control our own selves. Most of the extraordinary things your body does are beyond your conscious control. As neuroscientist Paul Broks puts it, "There are many features of my body over which I have no direct control…there are millions of physiological processes going on inside me that I scarcely know about, let alone control."[5]

Your immune system is more complex than the entire internet. What chance is there of controlling that? In many ways our mind is like an uncomprehending guest in a beautiful palace we call our body.

Not that the mind itself is under any more conscious control than the body. This is easy to demonstrate. Think of a word (any word) and for the next sixty seconds concentrate only on that word and nothing else. Not associations, connections or memories the word leads you to. No lists, idle fantasies or tangential trains of thought; just the word.

How did you get on? If you were really able to control your thoughts a minute shouldn't prove difficult. Yet I defy you to say your mind didn't wander in spite of your conscious attempts to control it. This isn't really surprising—the vast, bubbling vat of interconnected cells which underlies the mind is naturally turbulent. Even meditation is not so much the ability to control the windswept ocean that we call mind, as an attempt to observe it, as if from a high cliff.

If we cannot really control our own bodies or minds, what chance is there that we can control anyone else's? Frankly, nowadays we frequently find that we can't even control the direct offspring of the control mentality: machines. This isn't something that only befalls bloated government IT projects or an elderly gentleman baffled by his mobile phone. I once met a production engineer at a microchip factory who told me how even the best technical experts in the business can be humbled.

In microprocessor plants like the one where Kevin worked, the environment is cleaner than an operating theater—temperature, humidity, airborne particles (i.e., dust) and just about anything else that can be measured are maintained within precise limits. It would seem that everything is perfectly controlled. Then one day a shift in the

- - - - - - - - - - - - - - - - - -

5   Paul Broks, *Into the Silent Land: Travels in Neuropsychology*, (New York: Atlantic Monthly Press, 2003).

production schedule required a machine to be switched from one process to another. Even though it was designed to do both jobs, it crashed. The engineers consulted manuals and experts, checked and rechecked procedures, to no avail. A special team of technical wizards were called in. They worked round the clock and into the weekend and still found nothing. In desperation, late on Sunday afternoon, one of them suggested, "Let's just leave it alone." Exhausted, depressed and their pride more than a little dented, they all agreed. When they came in on Monday morning, to everyone's surprise and confusion, the machine worked. Even with an extraordinary array of technical knowledge on hand, the old trick of switching it off, waiting a bit and switching it back on again was what finally worked. I asked Kevin what he made of this. "Well," he said, rather self-consciously, "you could say the machine took a little while to get used to the idea of changing."

Strictly speaking the failure was due to what are called "parasitic capacitances." This means that charge is stored in electrical circuits in an unexpected way which prevents the machine from working properly. Leave it long enough and the charge leaks away, making it possible to establish the normal pattern on start up (in a sense, the machine does "take a while to get used to it"). There is an underlying material cause but the phenomenon cannot be predicted. Long before they develop independent intelligence, machines behave in ways we can't control, and the more complex they become, the more they seem to resemble their owners, with mood swings, refusals to cooperate and behavior that varies for no obvious reason. An element of wildness creeps back in.

Though we rarely acknowledge it, our ability to plan, predict and control is clearly limited. We can disturb or influence, sometimes even shape or direct, but the panorama of events we can determine is much more limited than we like to imagine. No amount of wealth or power changes this. When fire breaks out at her castle, even the Queen of England feels like a pawn in the game of life, as Elizabeth did in 1992, a year so plagued with unexpected misfortunes that she dubbed it her "annus horribilis." How much power does the president of the United States really wield, when the negligent actions of a single drunken supertanker captain can disrupt the price of oil and send the sprawling mass we call the world economy into a spin? The intrinsic uncertainty of things isn't just a personal matter. Many epoch-marking events, from the fall of the Berlin Wall to great scientific discoveries, are completely unforeseen, even by the experts.

This is not because we don't know enough. Science itself is telling us that uncertainty and unpredictability are intrinsic properties of anything complex. In those complex systems, tiny, immeasurable differences get amplified and produce consequences that can never be foreseen, however much information one might have. Myriad interactions between zillions of highly interconnected parts inevitably produce something new, different or unexpected. This is the world in which we live and work.

In a stable environment, with good information and few variables, the command and control approach is very powerful. It suits (or requires) a centralized, engineered environment. In such circumstances *Homo sovieticus* is in his element. But increasingly, the circumstances we face are far from the simple stability that is appropriate for command and control. Working harder to introduce more systems, more measures, more rules and more precision is of limited value. We have to act with partial information that is changing faster than our ability to perceive it. We face complex predicaments, not problems attributable to a single cause. Moreover we have to be creative to survive—survival depends upon being able to generate enough novelty to exploit a changing environment.

In the organic world this has always been true, and as our technology becomes more complex, it applies, progressively, to the mechanical world as well. It should come as no surprise that organizations, which include layers of human complexity in addition to their technical complexity, cannot be managed effectively with the mechanical model that consciously or unconsciously was so widely applied in the last century. This can be hard for us to see, let alone accept. As a senior British police officer said when asked (in private) if he was "in control" of the police force, "Of course not—but we can't tell anyone that." It has become taboo to admit that we are not in control.

We have come to believe that without control, order is not possible. This belief is what makes improvisational theater seem impressive—we are amazed that a coherent story can be produced with no one in control. But in natural systems as well as improv ensembles, this is completely normal—order does not arise from a central control or conscious design. A single cell of yeast has the same number of component parts as a Boeing 777 and, like the airplane, is incredibly ordered. The Boeing was consciously designed by using human brains that have no central control. The yeast, which is only five micrometers across, built itself and can also reproduce. *Homo sovieticus* might not like to admit it, but plenty of order and value can be created without anyone being in control.

Improvisational practice, however, invites you to challenge this taboo. Rather than prescribing a recipe for more control, with all its attendant huff and puff, it suggests ways to work with what there is. This enables us not only to cope with, but thrive on and enjoy uncertainty. It encourages you to think less, or to think in a different way, by using your body, your intuition and your instinct, rather than your intellect alone, thus giving you access to a different layer of your own intelligence. This isn't easy. Breaking a habit that is constantly being reinforced not only requires effort and patience, it means being willing to upset those people who are deeply attached to the idea of control, some of whom, like *Homo sovieticus*, may be deep inside us.

15 🦴 Yes, And…

Imagine you are a native English speaker who has been living and working in New York for a number of years, and you feel you know the city pretty well. Then one day you wake up to find you have miraculously acquired the ability to speak Spanish. You start to notice things you hadn't before: signs advertising Argentinean cuts of beef or cheap phone calls to Ecuador, the latest episode of a Venezuelan soap opera blaring from a shop window. You catch snatches of different conversations and smile at the lyrics of a song you have heard a hundred times but never understood. The group of young men on the street corner is anything but intimidating now that you know their animated banter is about babies and baseball, and as you wander by, you join in their conversation. When you know Spanish, New York reveals another side of itself, and opportunities that were previously hidden become available to you. As Joseph Jaworski said, "We do not describe the world we see. We see the world we can describe."[1]

Learning to work with improvisational practice is like learning Spanish in New York. It adds a whole new dimension to a world you already know. The familiar English-speaking city is still there, but nestling within it is another layer of experience and a new set of possibilities that the second language gives you access to. For example, when you start to describe events in terms of offers (rather than prob-

- - - - - - - - - - - - - - - - - - -

1   Joseph Jaworski, *Synchronicity: The Inner Path of Leadership*. San Francisco: Berrett-Koehler Publishers, 1998.

lems), it shifts your understanding of what is going on and what is possible in a fundamental way. It not only gives you more choices and options, but makes you feel different about the fact that you can't control what is happening.

Learning a second language of any kind gives you two very valuable things—a new resource and a new perspective. The resource is very obvious. You can read books, visit places, meet people, have conversations, appreciate culture or order food that you would not be able to otherwise. Similarly, learning to work in an improvisational way gives you a new resource to apply in situations that you currently find hard to deal with. When time is in short supply, resources are scarce, you need new ideas immediately or things are changing quickly, you may well find this language more effective than the language of planning and control.

However there is more to it than that. When you speak only one language it is easy to assume that everyone sees the same world. When you learn a second language it becomes obvious that there is more than one way of saying (or seeing) anything. For example, one of my favorite Spanish words is *chollo* (pronounced "choy-o"). I could translate this as "a pushover" or "a stroke of luck," but neither quite captures it. Not only are there nuances of meaning but the sound and feel of the word itself has an effect which cannot be expressed in English. Languages can be translated, but they are not reducible to one another.[2]

Learning a second language thus gives you perspective in much the same way that having two eyes allows you to see depth. Knowing many languages may give you other advantages, but perspective comes with the step from one to two. When you constantly experience that there is more than one way of seeing things, it forces you to accept that you are not in sole possession of the single truth and this foments a more pluralistic worldview. Curiously enough, this may mean that those who speak English—the global lingua franca—as their mother tongue may be at a disadvantage, not an advantage.

- - - - - - - - - - - - - - - - - -

2   You might say that each and every language has a certain *je ne sais quoi* or a unique *weltanschauung*. The *New Oxford American Dictionary* lists both these phrases (which it defines as "a quality that cannot be described or named easily" and "a particular view or philosophy of life," respectively), implicitly acknowledging that the French and German phrases add something their English translation does not.

Since they have no need for a second language, they miss the perspective it brings and can easily end up with a monotone, Anglo-centric view (a complaint I have often heard at international meetings).

Something similar happens with the language of control and certainty, which is as dominant in our thinking as English is in our speech. It is so prevalent that we become dismissive of anything else. Yet other approaches cannot be rendered in the language of control any more than *cholla* can be properly expressed in English.

This problem is exacerbated by the kind of reasoning that control relies on—commonly known as "or" thinking. This built-in logic, much beloved by *Homo sovieticus*, divides everything sharply into two classes: good or bad, right or wrong, one of us or one of them. Such logic tends to disregard a method like improvisation—certain, rational knowledge is what counts, ergo any method that doesn't produce it is useless.

By contrast, improvisation is based on "and" thinking. The practices encourage you to notice, accept and work with what is already there, not to evaluate or block it. Thus improvisational practice is itself a "yes and...." It accepts and adds to what you already know, rather than replacing it; it is a complement, not an alternative. You can think of the practices of improvisation as a kind of vitamin supplement to leaven a diet of too much control. You don't live on vitamins alone, but they enable you to make better use of the rest of what you eat.

It follows that developing your ability to improvise does not mean you have to abandon the idea of planning or analysis. As I discovered when building my house, you need to be able to plan and creatively adapt—our house was the product of both, not one or the other. Juan Carlos López de la Calle at Artadi says that "making a good wine is *always* very methodical and it is *always* very intuitive." Generals know their plans won't survive first contact with the enemy, and yet they still make them. If you are able to "sense and respond" to what needs to happen beyond the plan, the plan itself will still serve you (which is infinitely preferable to you being in service to it).

This makes obvious sense. Learning a second language wouldn't add much perspective if you promptly jettisoned the first one. This might seem self-evident, but we are very accustomed to thinking in terms of alternatives. I remember one occasion soon after meeting Gary when I was preparing a training course for a rather conservative company in Chicago. I was keen to include some improvised games, but apprehensive about how people might react, so I asked my friend Scott Dawson, Dean of the School of Business Administration at Portland State University, for advice. "What do I do if a game doesn't work?" There was a long pause while Scott rocked back in his chair and gazed out of the window at distant Mount Hood, which was bathed in an orange glow from the afternoon sun.

"Can it *not* work?" he replied.

I assumed that either he hadn't understood my question or he had been distracted by the view.

"Of course it might not work; it might be a complete disaster. They might just sit there and refuse to play," I blurted out, giving voice to my fears.

There was another lengthy pause.

"Would that be it *not* working," he asked gently, "or would that be it working in a way you hadn't expected?"

Now it was my turn to pause. As I did so, Scott took the opportunity to add a little color:

"Even if they refuse to play, you can still use that. You could ask them why there was resistance to doing something different and that might provoke a conversation they really need to have."

This was news to me. I had only seen two alternatives: one good, one bad, either it worked or it didn't. It hadn't even occurred to me that success might consist of finding a way to use whatever happens rather than trying to ensure that something particular does. This was a revelation to me and the phrase "can it *not* work" has become something of a personal mantra. It helps me remember that there are always more than two possibilities.

Such a sharp divide might be useful in science, but in normal human affairs it sets one possibility, idea, person, point of view, religion or ideology against another: The law of the excluded middle (to give it its proper name) is, by its very nature, divisive. Hence President Bush's declaration in the wake of the attacks of September 11 that "you are either with us or against us." The dichotomy forces you to identify "good guys" and "bad guys," which was precisely Bush's intention. However, as events have shown, such divisiveness also tends to promote conflict. But it is not unique to one particular point on the political spectrum. The same polarizing idea anchors the environmentalists' call to arms: "Either you are part of the solution or you are part of the problem."

I want to resist such sharp distinctions. Reality as we experience it is not black and white, but gray, fuzzy, shifting and contradictory. Who you hire or fire, who you befriend, what you invest in, where you choose to live, which product to give prominence to—these are rarely either/or decisions. Most of what we are interested in lies in the middle, which is precisely what the law of the excluded middle ignores.

It may seem rather cheeky to question such a basic piece of logic, but this so-called law is not like the laws of physics. You can't choose to see gravity working upwards; it holds universally, which is what makes it a law. However, the law of the excluded middle is a logical convention, not an observable fact. There is nothing inevitable about excluding the middle, and we can choose a different set of conventions if it suits us. Indeed, many eastern traditions (such as Buddhism or Taoism) do exactly that. Even in the West, "fuzzy math" and "fuzzy logic" have proved extremely useful in figuring out previously unsolvable problems precisely because they start with a different premise.

Thus I would encourage you to include rather than exclude. To say "and" as well as "or." Say yes to planning and say yes to improvisation as well. Rather than pitting one idea against another to see which one wins, try adding them up to see where they take you.

When I was five years old I asked my mother, who taught languages at the local secondary school, to teach me French. I saw this as a lengthy task, but one that wasn't essentially difficult (after all, I was nearly six). I imagined that a language was a long list of words and learning a new language simply consisted of memorizing the equivalent French word for all the English ones. I had no idea of grammar or of the irreducible poetry inherent in any language, and it didn't not occur to me that in different languages the same idea might be expressed in a different way. I failed to realize that there is more to learning a language than swapping one set of words for another.

The same is true of improvisation. Because it is a genuine "yes and…" you need to do more than learn a few new terms or buzzwords; you have to develop an altogether different way of acting. This can be hard to appreciate. I remember one occasion when On Your Feet got a brief from one of the world's top consulting companies, a firm which prides itself on hiring exceptionally smart people. They knew that their Achilles heel was the "soft stuff." Their clients told them that despite doing excellent analysis, the results suffered because they were not so good at building rapport. Happily for us, the consultants concluded that improvisation could help them develop that ability. However, by the time they briefed us, they had already developed a measurement system and a mathematical quotient they planned on using to plot their course to better soft skills. They were doing what they always did (and do very well), but they reminded me of the Englishman abroad, who when he fails to make himself understood, simply repeats what he said but louder.

Like learning a language, learning to improvise requires more than acquiring a new vocabulary. It is not a mechanical or purely intellectual task. You have to be willing to be a novice, venture into the unknown, make mistakes and sound stupid, just as you do when you learn a language. These are quite important changes—in a sense you have to change your idea of who you are. This is a particular stretch for anyone whose identity is invested in sounding smart, which includes most people who do well in business.

This ought to sound familiar: letting go, being willing to be changed, using and learning from mistakes, working with the unknown and so on are precisely the ideas we have been exploring in this book. Thus the practice of improvisation is self-supporting: it both requires and produces the same kind of change in your behavior.

The kind of knowledge this develops is also different from and complementary to the kind of knowledge that we traditionally regard as important. Rather than grand concepts or sophisticated analytical tools, improvisation helps develop intuitive or tacit knowledge.

Increasingly this kind of knowledge is being recognized as important. A retired NASA scientist recently commented to a friend of mine that nowadays NASA wouldn't be able to build a Saturn V rocket. Despite having all the plans, they lack the informal knowledge that only lived in the heads and hands of the people who had the experience. They could start from scratch and build another rocket, but not a Saturn V. The power and potential of any organization lies not just in the individuals, but in the rich web of connections and relationships between them. The informal, human connections are at least as important as the formal structures.

Because tacit knowledge derives from personal experience, it is hard to standardize, measure or break down into smaller pieces. This can make it seem mysterious. For example, Basilio, one of our builders, has an ability to find mushrooms that is almost magical (the ability, that is, not the mushrooms). The intelligence he displays is remarkably precise: from hundreds of meters away, he will bound off to a particular spot, stop suddenly, bend over and there they will be. The etiquette of mushrooming means you don't ask about specific locations because they are often fiercely guarded secrets, but I was interested in learning how Basilio does it, so one day I asked him, in general, what kinds of things one needs to look out for. He was perfectly happy to talk about it, but even so, the conversation which unfolded was quite bizarre:

Rob: How do you know where you'll find Delicious Milk Caps (niscalos)?

Basilio: Well, you have to find a spot that looks promising and search there.

Rob: Right. And how do you recognize a promising spot?

Basilio: Because it looks like there will be Milk Caps.

Rob: I see. And what kind of things are you looking for?

Basilio: Um. (long pause) Pine trees…(There are several million pines around here.)

Rob: What kind of pines?

Basilio: The ones that look like there will be Milk Caps.

And so it went on. Basilio wasn't being deliberately evasive. It was very clear to him, but he couldn't put it into words. I thought this was just a quaint local story until one evening, at Templeton College, Oxford, a particularly fine cream of mushroom soup prompted me to relate the anecdote to Marshall Young (then Dean of the College). "That's just like Sir John Templeton," he said. Since Sir John Templeton is a billionaire investment tycoon and founder of an Oxford college, I was struggling to see the connection. Marshall helped me out.

"If you talk to Sir John about investment, he will talk in a similar way. Ask him how to make money and he will say, 'Well, you buy at the bottom of the market and sell at the top.' Push him as to how you know when something is at the bottom of the market and he will say something along the lines of, 'Well, it's at the bottom when it won't go down any more.' And so on. It's exactly like your friend with the mushrooms."

Like Basilio's ability to find sought-after mushrooms or Sir John Templeton's investment decisions, improvisational knowledge is intuitive and visceral. This might make it hard to get a handle on, but as science itself is discovering, this doesn't mean it isn't real. Psychologist Guy Claxton dubs the kind of rational, conceptual thought which happily delivers verbal explanations as our "hare brain." He contrasts this with our unconscious, intuitive capacities which he calls the "tortoise mind." By definition the tortoise mind is invisible and mysterious and doesn't give reasoned explanations. Which allows the hare brain to assume that the tortoise mind is only good at low-level functions like regulating heartbeat or digesting food.

Nonetheless Claxton shows—with experimental data of exactly the kind that is compelling to the hare brain—that when you are under pressure, even specific tasks (like counting the number of objects that fall in one quadrant of a grid) can be performed more rapidly and effectively by the tortoise mind. As Claxton puts it, intelligence increases when you think less.[3]

Studies of people that face complex or chaotic situations, like firefighters or stock traders, show similar results (as Malcolm Gladwell describes in *Blink*). Intuitive

----

3   Guy Claxton, *Hare Brain, Tortoise Mind*, (Hopewell, NJ: Ecco Press, 1999).

knowledge works where business-school-style rationalizations break down, and it is that kind of knowledge that improvisational practice develops. At a conference in Singapore, someone asked Laura, a professional improviser on our team, how she chose which offer to accept on stage. Her answer was "feel."

Even if it flutters below the threshold of consciousness (or perhaps because it does) this kind of knowledge is extremely useful. Most of the time there is so much complexity, change and unpredictability that we cannot really analyze effectively. Reason is a limited tool. Life is not a laboratory and most of the decisions we make, even technical decisions based on robust data, include a good dose of "feel." Such feel (which a psychologist might call "pattern recognition") can only be developed though experience and practice, something the business world, with its high turnover rates and relentless pace does little to promote. It is a skill that involves the heart and the gut more than the intellect, but it is a skill nonetheless, not an innate gift. Even in business bodily skills count for more than we think. George Soros, another billionaire investor, makes investment decisions, according to his son, because his back starts killing him. If we only listen to rationalizations we ignore the wisdom of the tortoise mind which, by definition, shows up in these indirect ways. We need, quite literally, to broaden our body of knowledge, hence the importance of a complementary method like improvisation which takes some of the mystery away and provides a way to practice systematically, developing new skills and a different kind of knowledge. Naming, listing or representing the practices in a diagram (like the triangle on page 46) provides an anchor for the hare brain to cling to, but we also need to work with the tortoise mind.

There are any number of reasons why you might learn Spanish. You might want to retire to Costa Rica, do business in Latin America, learn to tango, have a better night out in Madrid or get to know another side of New York. The same is true for improv as a second language. You may want to develop your soft leadership skills, play more easily with your kids or help your organization get better at innovation. Personally I was drawn to it because it seemed to make sense of my everyday experience and help me get more out of it.

Whatever your personal interest, there is a growing body of literature from journalists, academics and consultants which suggests that the kind of skills improvisation develops are becoming absolutely vital. As long ago as 1994, Kevin Kelly, editor-at-large of *Wired* magazine, explored "the new biology of machines, social systems and the economic world," all of which, he said, is "out of control." *New York Times* journalist Thomas Friedman describes a "flat world" where creativity and collaboration are vital to anyone and everyone. Eddie Obeng (founder of the consultancy firm Pentacle) coined the phrase "the world after midnight" to describe an environment in which change occurs faster than our ability to perceive or analyze it. Gary Hamel talks about strategy as an emergent process, Meg Wheatley about self-organizing systems and Professor Ralph Stacey suggests that organizations have no separate existence; they are nothing more than webs of relationships among individuals.

These thinkers (and others like them) all have different vantage points, but I believe there is a common pattern. In a nutshell, I see that certainty is becoming less important than creativity. We are not so much living in an age of change, but living through a change of age. This does not mean that the juggernaut of rational, scientific and technological progress which began in the seventeenth century is about to end. There will be new areas we can parse into digestible pieces and reorder in a methodical way to suit our purposes—nanotechnology springs to mind. However, the massive web of interconnections that this very technology is creating will amplify the inherent unpredictability we face. A lot more is going to happen that we won't expect. Certainty will remain the pot of gold at the end of the rainbow: it recedes before the pursuit. As routine mechanical tasks are outsourced or automated, individuals and organizations need to become increasingly creative to survive, as Norman (the CEO of Big Technology Inc. we met in Chapter 1) knew only too well. Our livelihoods increasingly depend on how we respond to changing circumstances, which means being able to embrace uncertainty and work with it, rather than ignoring it or trying to do away with it.

This change is happening fast. In the 1960s when Robert McNamara joined the Kennedy Administration from Ford, he brought with him a generation of managers known as "the best and the brightest" whose fervent belief in an analytical and statistical approach drove the strategy that the United States (under Lyndon Johnson) pursued in the Vietnam War. No one would try such a thing today, partly because of what happened in Vietnam. We know that analysis alone is not sufficient to grapple with the complexity we face.

Even physics, the "hardest" of the "hard" sciences has had to accept that when we look deeply into what the world is made of we don't find any stuff at all, just patterns and relationships between phenomena we might describe as either particles or waves, depending on how we look. Science paints a fuzzier picture than we had imagined. Given that, it is not surprising that people are reappraising the importance and relevance of the arts to our everyday life and work. As novelist Margaret Atwood says, "'The arts'— as we've come to term them—are not a frill. They are the heart of the matter because they are about our hearts, and our technological inventiveness is generated by our emotions, not by our minds."[4]

Improvisation is one particular art whose relative importance is growing fast. If it is a language, then it's the new English. Thirty years ago speaking English was helpful; today it is vital. The same is true of improvisation—the skills and abilities it develops are gaining in importance every day and are necessary for people in almost any walk of life.

However, it doesn't stop there—the improvisational practice explored in this book is not the final word. One of the beautiful things about this way of working is that as more and more people start to play around with the ideas improv rests on, it will naturally spawn a series of mashed-up, hybridized "yes and"-ed ideas that are simultaneously surprising and fitting. The fact that you don't know where it will end simply means that it's a great place to start.

- - - - - - - - - - - - - - - - - -

4   Margaret Atwood, "Scientific Romancing" (Kesterton Lecture, Carleton School of Journalism, Ottawa, Ontario, January 22, 2004).

16 🐟 Going Native

Turn off the trans-peninsular highway in Baja California Sur at the sign marking kilometer sixty-four, about half way between Los Cabos and La Paz, and you will come across a most unlikely sight. There, nestled in the barrio of Las Palmitas, amid the corrugated iron shacks and the luscious tropical plants, is a bright blue concrete hemisphere standing some eight feet proud above the red, dusty earth that surrounds it. This is the top of the "hoody"—a vertically oriented bowl that forms the most striking and visible feature of a skate park of terrifying proportions. As well as the over-hanging hoody, there is a cavernous bowl with towering sides of smooth cement, much of it vertical, capped by a "blood wall" with a total drop of nearly seventeen feet. It is enough to challenge the best skaters in the world and would look more at home in Santa Monica or some other skateboarding mecca. So what on earth is it doing in the tiny Mexican village of Pescadero?

This was the question that David Keating found himself asking in March of 2003. He had come to Baja to surf, only to find himself staying just down the road from this outrageous structure. David needed no encouragement to go and have a closer look— as a filmmaker he is, by his own admission, "somewhat predatory" when it comes to sniffing out stories and as he fell into conversation with a tall, athletic gringo who was working on the site, that predator instinct was up. Justin Armour turned out to be the owner and driving force behind the project and David's instinct was right—there was indeed a compelling story lurking beneath the curves of reinforced concrete.

Another unlikely story was about to begin. The meeting between David and Justin sparked a creative process that led to the making of a seventy-minute documentary film entitled *KM64: Birth of a Skatepark*. Like Robert Rodriguez, David also had virtually no budget and a small town in Mexico. Unlike Rodriguez, David was quite consciously affected by "the ideas improvisation rests on." The notion that this film could be made at all, as well as the way it actually was made, were both influenced by David's experience collaborating with On Your Feet. As he puts it, "Improv infected the process from beginning to end, and this enabled us to achieve things that, in the conventional way of seeing things, ought not to be possible." Thus we can use the story of the making of *KM64* to paint a picture of what it can look like if you take these practices to heart.

This chapter is dedicated to telling stories which show how the improv practices can play out. Telling stories invokes the imagination and sparks off ideas about how we might use the practices ourselves. Some of those stories (like *KM64*) have been directly influenced by the work of myself and others in On Your Feet. Some have nothing to do with us. This is quite deliberate. My aim is not to brag about On Your Feet's success, but to simply bring the ideas to life in as vivid a way as possible so that you can make your own connections.[1]

Given that, I won't limit myself to stories about the past. We all face new situations which continue to change and evolve even as we engage with them, so we cannot assume that everything we need to learn has already happened. Story is a wonderful way to imagine what could happen and investigate some of the possibilities and consequences without leaving the safety of the armchair. This isn't as unconventional as it might sound—scenario planning, which was developed by Royal Dutch Shell in the 1970s, is effectively a way of exploring the future using stories, rather than trying to make predictions. Therefore what follows, starting with the story of the making of *KM64: Birth of a Skatepark*, is not intended as only tips for budding film directors or skatepark builders. My aim is to provide inspiration, not evidence.

- - - - - - - - - - - - - - - - - - - -

1   If you want to find more stories or share a story of your own, check out www.everythingsanoffer.com.

The story of *KM64* began not in Baja California, but a thousand miles further north. As a friend and collaborator of On Your Feet, we had invited David to join us in Arch Cape on the Oregon coast for a five-day intensive improv session. Wanting to make the most of the journey from Ireland, he decided to add a surf trip to Mexico on the back end of it (thereby using what he had). Google threw up Pescadero Surf Camp and though it crossed his mind that this could be hideous, he made a booking anyway reasoning that "we could always move on." He was very open to whatever might turn up, good or bad (i.e., he stayed out of judgment and was willing to be changed).

When he turned up at the skate park he heard Justin's story, which, in brief, went like this. Having retired from professional football, Justin had set out with his wife to travel for a year, only to be waylaid in Baja California by the idea of building something to help the local kids. When Justin bumped into Geth Noble and Stefanie Moller—a couple of skate park designers who had gone to Baja on vacation—this turned out to be a skate park of stupendous proportions.

David had only his hunch that this story could be made into a workable film—there was no proposal, no budget and no screenplay—but he was nonetheless willing to act upon it.

"To be blunt, this seemed like a huge offer and I didn't know who the offer was coming from: from Justin, from inside me, from my wife, from the universe, whatever. But it was an offer nonetheless."

So after just two meetings with Justin he decided to return to Baja with whatever backing, equipment and crew he could muster back home in Dublin in time for the opening ceremony, which was only a couple of weeks away. David, the producer Jorgen and the cameraman Eric, filmed in Pescadero for a week. Post-production was done in Ireland, on a stop-start basis, but ten months later and for a similar outlay to *El Maria-chi*, the seventy-minute documentary *KM64* was complete.[2] I asked David what he had learned from the experience. Here is what he said:

- - - - - - - - - - - - - - - - - - - -
2   You can find out more about the film at www.everythingsanoffer.com.

The way we worked on KM64 was really very, very different to normal film-making, to the extent that most people in film would simply say, "You can't do that." KM64 demonstrates that if you strip away the layers of assumptions, that simply isn't true.

For example, everyone in the business says that you can't set out to make a film without having nailed the script, the story, the funding and so on. Clarity is deemed to be absolutely necessary before you can even begin. Yet it depends what you are clear about. We were very clear that there was a story here, even if we didn't know how it would unfold. And, yes, I was haunted by that, but not paralyzed. I was also fascinated by it. If you have a low tolerance for ambiguity, then you will be slow to act and miss opportunities. There is a cost attached to the normal way of doing things too, which people often don't see or acknowledge.

We were willing to embrace the unknown. We decided from the get-go we were going to trust in the process, to consciously hold onto the belief that we would find what we needed when we needed it as we went along, that it would emerge. This sounds naïve, but what it does is force you to look for it. What this meant practically was always having the camera on hand, not shooting to a plan and being prepared to turn over when anything interesting happened.

Despite the fact that it was going to have to be an interview-based film, we made no formal arrangements whatsoever of who, when or where to interview. Everyone says you absolutely have to have a shot list, but really its only of marginal relevance. We didn't prepare set-ups or lighting or the questions we would ask. This allowed interesting conversations to happen, and we made sure we were ready to shoot them whenever or wherever they occurred. We got some of my favorite footage because it just got interesting, and though we weren't planning to do that, we did it anyway.

Eric tuned in to this immediately. As conversations were evolving or emerging I would be trying to catch his eye and find a chance to whisper,

"Eric, camera on," and invariably he would reply, "Already on." He didn't wait for my say-so; he trusted his own instincts. This kind of rapport was more important than pure technical ability.

The informal way of working meant that there was never a single instance of asking someone "would you mind moving…" Instead we would move. That caused some technical problems but also created some great success. What we got was people saying the things they really had energy for. It is far more compelling when you can capture the way people really talk. There was one particular chat in the car where we got an unusual shot that we would never have set up like that had we had the chance, and that gave it a certain freshness.

In filmmaking you always need faith. With a feature, that comes from the long and tortuous preparation. You get endorsement and investment at every stage. From the first draft of the screenplay, improvements and additions, casting, financial backing, people agreeing to work for you, and so on, so this is what gives you belief. Here it came from a small group of committed people and a sense of urgency. What we discovered was that trust was as much a result of this way of working, as it was a precondition.

My wife just said, "You have to do this." She never really said anything different; she just repeated it when necessary and never deviated, which was enormously different from what normally happens in the film world. What it did was add energy rather than sap it. It built confidence instead of undermining it. In a way, I guess it shows the creative power of delusion.

Working this way was no scarier than filmmaking normally is. There were concerns and I was tired as you always are making a film. Yet on KM64 we were also constantly trying to figure out where we were, so we were very focused on the here and now. Camera, batteries, tape. What was going to happen on any particular day was impossible to predict or understand, so we tried to get into a rhythm that allowed us to pick up clues as to what might *be interesting; we were always trying to make sure we were present to offers. At the time it felt fantastic. The constant possibility of surprise and discovery of something great just happening was always there, and a lot of the stress and strain of the normal routine wasn't.*

KM64 hasn't (yet!) got the response I might have hoped for, and sometimes I wonder if it was worth it. But then I have the feeling that the story hasn't quite played out yet...Also, to me, it is important not to get distracted by other people's responses. When I think of the process and what it felt like at the time, it makes me feel proud. We made something out of nothing. I feel we did a beautiful thing. There were very practical gains as well, though. I continue to use all of what I learned on KM64 in the work I am doing now making feature films. For example, through KM64 I came to a deeper appreciation that you don't solve a problem with a pen and paper. You solve a problem by getting some pictures, some music, and putting them up there where you can see them, actually working them. This thing about practice, about getting physical, about having a camera in my hand, has become really important to me.

I have also noticed how I am at my best when I let the people I am working with have direct access to me—when they can be close enough to see my face and really hear my voice; when they know I am paying attention to what they do. This means they pick up on the nuances that I might not be able to express very articulately, and just as importantly, it shows that what they do matters to me. This is easy to forget—nowadays with video you can get caught up in watching the monitor and end up ignoring the actors. On my current project I make sure that everyone has my mobile number so they can text me or call me when they need to. This might sound obvious, but in the film world its quite radical because normally things are very hierarchical. I want to shorten the chains of communication so that people can easily check in with me. I think KM64 taught me that this kind of direct contact can make my life as a director easier, not more difficult.

There are plenty of parallels here with any complex undertaking, and the story suggests a number of questions that are relevant to any endeavor, such as:

What do you need to be clear about?

In the film business, the conventional wisdom is that you need to be certain about the script, the budget, the shots you want and so on. David had none of these and still made a film. What would happen if you let go of all the conventional certainties that are there to help people feel comfortable and worked without your equivalent of a script? Could you let go of the pretest, the pilot study or the committee approval and gain some flexibility and agility as a result?

Are you haunted by uncertainty or paralyzed by it?

David recognized that the uncertainty of the venture "haunted" him, but it didn't "paralyze" him. This sums up beautifully the way improvisers relate to uncertainty. By trusting the process and allowing ideas to emerge, David was able to find and make something out of opportunities that he otherwise would have missed completely. If you are willing to tolerate or encourage not knowing or uncertainty—rather than trying to eradicate it as soon as it appears—what might you stand to gain? How and where could you allow yourself to be haunted but not paralyzed?

What kind of preparation do you really need?

"Camera, batteries, tape." David and Eric did prepare for each day of shooting in Pescadero, but they prepared in a different way than they normally would. Rather than refer back to a script, they would prepare by thinking about what had just happened and how the story was emerging, and this would help them think about what to do next. This didn't make detailed planning redundant, they still needed a charged camera loaded with the right stock (e.g., for shooting in water), but they also needed an open attitude. What would happen if your preparation focused on using what had just happened rather than on the original plan?

What skills are most important?

Rapport was more important than pure technical ability. Where is a narrow focus on technical prowess limiting you? What other, lateral abilities do you need to have, and how can you recognize them, recruit them and reward them?

What obstacles or barriers can you use as offers?

The interviews weren't set up or organized, which would seem like suicide for an interview-based film. Yet many of the freshest scenes emerged by moving the camera around the person being interviewed, not the other way round. Where could you use the obstacles to get more creative instead of trying to sweep them out the way?

What would happen if you made do with less?

Everyone always feels the budget is too small. Is that really a fact, or is it just a feeling? In theory, you can't make a film for the money David had. In practice, you can. Whatever you are short of, why not try using whatever little you have rather than use the shortfall as an excuse to stall, wait or procrastinate.

Have you forgotten your actors?

As a film director it is easy to get caught up in watching the monitor. But it is the actors who deliver the performance that makes a difference to the end result. Ask yourself whether you are being distracted by technological sophistication or some other seductive complexity. Are you paying more attention to the plan or the people? Who do you really need to attend to?

Inspiration is often unexpected. *KM64* itself was inspired by improvisation, which is a form of dramatic art very different from film. In turn, the story of how a motley cast of characters came together to create a skate park at KM64 on the trans-peninsular highway in Baja California provoked a partner at PricewaterhouseCoopers to rethink what "diversity" meant in an international firm such as hers. The unexpected construction of a skate park leads to an improvised film, which gives new insight to a Transfer Pricing specialist. Who would have scripted that?

Technology underlies the high speed of change of modern society, but it also holds up a mirror to those changes. A snapshot of current happenings in the online world suggests that things are moving rapidly in an improvisational direction. When I first started thinking about this book, Wikipedia and its millions of entries was just a gleam in

Jimmy Wales' eye. YouTube's meteoric rise only began in February 2005. Even that wizened old stalwart, Google, has only been around since 1998—less time than tiddly On Your Feet. The fact that such recent examples already seem like ancient history adds weight to the argument that flexibility and agility are abilities we need to have deeply incorporated into our everyday behavior.

Each of these giants, in their own way, reflect elements of improvisational practice.

Wikipedia did not come about because of a technical innovation—all the software it used had been around for years. The new idea was that you could make something on a large scale, based on the principles of openness and trust. Jimmy Wales, the founder of Wikipedia, says, "The design of Wikipedia is the design of community."[3]

In that community you can see plenty of improv-style behavior in play. Wikipedia is entirely cocreated. It is self-corrected by the community, not controlled from the center. Rather than judge, evaluate, exclude or edit contributions before they are made, problems are addressed once they occur (and normally very quickly). In other words, all offers are welcome and anyone can make one. A large community of thoughtful users and a small group of volunteers pay close attention to changes and edits, and systems exist (like the All Recent Changes page) to enable this, so some blocking occurs. However, the assumption is that most contributions will be improvements, and they are. Far more is accepted than blocked, resulting in the largest and fastest-growing encyclopedia in the world. In terms of accuracy, the result isn't substantially different from a traditional, expertly sourced encyclopedia. Studies have shown that Wikipedia is, broadly speaking, as accurate as *The Encyclopedia Britannica*. What Wikipedia shows is that there is more than one valid way to compile a reference work and that openness and participation can provide a powerful engine of growth on a large scale.

Google and YouTube provide some further examples of how important collaboration and participation are in the online world. The way Google searches the Web is

----

3   Lecture, The Long Now Foundation, April 2006.

based on the behavior of its users. Though Google has a lot of clever mathematicians, in a sense, their work piggy-backs on the searches we all make. Everyone who uses Google helps to make it work better and Google takes advantage of "the wisdom of the crowd."

YouTube is another current example of what cocreativity (or "crowd-sourcing," in the jargon) can do. Since YouTube simply provides the means to "broadcast yourself," its creative and production department effectively runs to several hundred million people. Users don't just make the films, though. They also decide how they use the site, which in turn influences how it evolves.

People who work in internet broadcasting have little choice but to behave in an improvisational way. Chris Abel is one of the founders of the Bike Channel, (www.bikechannel.com) a specialist internet broadcaster whose motorcyclist users currently download about one hundred and fifty thousand films a month (a statistic that will be out of date before this ink is dry). On a daily basis Chris receives news of competitors (or suppliers) he has never heard of, which means there is absolutely no chance of doing a conventional competitive analysis. He points out that in this environment anyone that claims to know too much arouses suspicion. "We have to talk confidently about our stuff, but it has to be done with humility, which is part of being flexible." In other words, running the Bike Channel requires a sensitivity to status and a willingness to play low. It also inverts the normal relationship with certainty. In the conventional world certainty inspires confidence. Here it raises doubts. Nonetheless, as with *KM64*, uncertainty is no excuse for inaction. As Chris points out, "People forget that if you shoot from the hip you still aim, and you start to adjust that aim as fast as you can. That's what we have to do." This means being permanently willing to make offers, be changed by what people do with them, and be "fit and well" about whatever happens as a result.

The joy of a cocreative relationship is that you don't have to do all the work, which is one of the things that makes improvising on stage far easier than it looks. When you know that you don't necessarily have to finish a thought, know the answer or deliver the punch line, all you have to do is follow the practice and you can trust that somehow, someone will finish it for you and almost certainly in a way that you wouldn't expect. The YouTubes of this world show that the same kind of thing can happen in other spheres of life. If you want to do less work, ask yourself how you can let your customers (or your suppliers) shape things themselves. The implication is that you have to stop trying to control them. Most business organizations (still in thrall of *Homo sovieticus*) find this difficult, but it is vital work.

At the 2006 TED conference, Sir Ken Robinson suggested that "creativity is as important now in education as literacy, and we should treat it with the same status." He pointed out that children entering education in that year would finish their working careers in the year 2065. "Despite all the expertise on show, nobody has a clue what the world will be like in five years' time, and yet we are meant to be educating them for it." The current system, he maintained, is better designed to produce university professors than to prepare people for the challenges that lie ahead. "As children grow up we start to educate them progressively from the waist up. And then we focus on their heads. And slightly to one side."

If he is right then improvisational practice has a double claim to form part of the educational curriculum. On the one hand it teaches a creative method that generates new ideas and on the other it gives people the skills to adapt and change—something which will be crushingly necessary in this unpredictable and accelerating world. What might happen if an inspired Minister of Education took Sir Ken Robinson's contentions to heart?

> *"The idea of a lifelong career is past its sell-by date," said Margaret Yun, Minister for Education. "I'm hardly at the cutting edge," she admitted, "but even I have been an academic and an entrepreneur, as well as a politician. We need to prepare our children for an age of unprecedented change and introducing improvisational skills to the national curriculum is an important part of that. We need initiatives like this if we are to develop our national competitiveness."*
>
> *It was a brave decision and the media had a field day. "Comedy educational policy," screamed the headline of one newspaper. But the decision was*

based on a pilot program that had been running in a half dozen schools for a number of years to great acclaim. Jerome Taylor, headmaster of one of the participating schools, explains: "We don't do physical education to try and make the kids into professional athletes, we do it because it is healthy and good for you. Improvisational skills are similar. We help the kids to acquire some habits that are healthy, which will be incredibly useful in later life and let them have some fun at the same time."

The kids seem to agree. "At first we just thought it was just a bit of a laugh, but after a while you find you start to use the stuff all over the place," said Leo Richards, who studied improv for his final two years. "When I left school there were so many things that were different, so much to adapt to, and yet it was easy for me, all those habits of seeing things as offers and stuff just seemed normal. I didn't even have to think about it. I reckon that of everything I learned at school, it's what I use most, every day, and I don't think that will ever stop."

The program also had an unexpected benefit—on staff. Jerome Taylor explains: "The better teachers always adapt what they are doing to that group of kids at that moment, and the weaker ones basically deliver the same stuff in the same way in every class. The emphasis we were giving to improvisational skills challenged and encouraged the staff to become more flexible and imaginative in their teaching. Some of the more accomplished pupils started to teach impromptu improv skills to some of the teachers, which was a neat inversion of the normal order and started to make the place feel more like a learning community than a school, and the whole thing snowballed."

This invented story allows us to explore the idea of improv in education in an imaginative way. Rather than arguing for or against it, you can simply play around with the idea and see what you learn or discover as a result. For example, the parallel with physical education or the fact that such a move would have unexpected effects on teachers.

I can also see some of my own assumptions, for example, that such a program would need to be institutionalized, hence my depiction of an announcement by a minister. But what if individual schools picked up the idea for themselves and started incorporating improvisation into other subjects, such as English, drama, social studies, business studies or physical education—networking informally among each other to share learning? Not so long ago, when the subject came up at a conference, a few head teachers demonstrated a surprising readiness to entertain the idea. What if they just took the offer and committed to it, *KM64*-style, without waiting for policy to catch up?

Stories are a good way to explore or invent the future (i.e., to make strategy). This is a technique that we use very consciously in On Your Feet. Allowing yourself to have fun with an idea and take it to the extreme can tell you far more than staying close to reality.

It is a very simple idea. There is a permanent and open invitation to everyone connected with On Your Feet to write stories about the future. This could be anything from a small extrapolation of the current reality to a huge imaginative leap or complete fantasy (one such story involved the western seaboard of the U.S. breaking off and docking in the Mediterranean). Anyone can offer a story at any time. The stories are periodically collated and circulated, just as they were written, without editing or polishing. That's it. There is no obligation to write stories or minimum number required or review committee, so everyone can join in the conversation. Often one story will provoke a flurry of stories and conversation then things lie fallow for a while.

Let me show you how this can work, by writing one now. Here goes…

The book Everything's An Offer *had a curious effect. Over the course of a few years, over five thousand copies were distributed. However, it also led to other new On Your Feet products. From working on the podcasts of the book, Brad became very accomplished with the medium and audio bulletins became a new strand of On Your Feet's business. In the book line, the "cook-books" that Julie developed and edited (a kind of field guide) in the wake of Rob's book became another highly profitable line. And Rob developed a highly unusual improvised speaking product, born out of what he learned in the process of writing rather than out of the text itself.*

There's one. Which, by the way, I wrote without censoring in about three minutes. Let's try another:

Everything's An Offer was the last significant thing Rob ever did for On Your Feet. His energy ran out when the text was finished and he had none left to get the thing published. Gary's promises that he would take charge of the production side turned out to be barren—the success of the new improv vehicle Super Project Lab distracted him and took up all his extra energy. Moreover, Julie voiced some misgivings about some of the material, so Gary was pulled in two directions. While everyone made encouraging noises, nothing much happened and Rob felt he had run out of road. His appetite for On Your Feet started to wane and he began to put his efforts into White Leaf—a leadership retreat based around the cultivation and culture of olive trees—instead.

Well. Look at that. Same start point, same process, different result.

It is remarkably easy to do and you can see how the process is driven by the practice. I simply notice an offer—in this case the end of the book—accept it and add to it via "yes and"-ing, using any other offers that occur to me along the way and staying out of judgment about whether or not these are appropriate. As a result, much of it comes as a surprise, even to me.

So what do we learn? The first story invites me to think beyond the book itself. It encourages me not to become too attached to the text and encourages me to practice using "yes and…" with my colleagues to see how the book might act as a springboard to other new ideas, which is a timely reminder.

The second of these two stories is what we call a story of anxiety. I didn't plan to write one of those, but that was what emerged. We discovered this category of stories by looking at the stories we were collecting. We noticed that many of them centered on a worry or concern. At first this puzzled us, but we quickly realized that it is entirely natural to have doubts and fears. We found that having a mechanism which allowed these doubts to emerge was a boon—it legitimized them and enabled us to raise issues that we might otherwise bury, avoid or simply be unaware of—which is particularly useful with a group of people that rarely meet.

Consider how different this approach is from a planning process. These future stories are a way of allowing us to make visible ideas that might otherwise not surface. Which is very different from trying to make predictions. I would contend that creating stories about possible futures is a form of strategizing. It certainly helps us identify issues. Sometimes simply acknowledging the feelings that the stories bring up is enough, on other occasions we might have to take action to address an issue directly. Sharing stories helps us communicate better, on many levels, very quickly.

Occasionally a story will turn out to come true, but more often than not this is because the story itself sparked off a chain of action that brought it into being, not because someone was gifted with a crystal ball. Sharing stories helps us to create the future, not just explore it. It also helps us track the past. The collection of stories becomes our shared history—which makes up for some of the shortcomings of a virtual, networked organization.

Such a technique isn't only appropriate to a small and idiosyncratic group like On Your Feet. An open-ended, collaborative, story-gathering method can be of great value to a large extended organization. Consider the following story, for example.

Gaucho is an outdoor clothing and equipment brand from Argentina with strong roots in Mendoza in the Argentinean Andes. As the company spread worldwide, the understanding of what the company is really about inevitably got diluted. They used stories to fill the gap. Like most companies they had come up with a list of words to define what they stood for, but they were deeply dissatisfied with the results of using the words alone. "One of the biggest difficulties we had was translation," says Gonzalo Redondo, head of Gaucho's culture team. "I don't mean between Spanish and English, but much deeper than that. What made a lot of sense here in Mendoza either didn't make sense in Chelsea or Chueca, or meant something completely different to the people there.

"We do have a list of values, but the words are a beginning, not an end. We think of the values as labels for big buckets full of experience which we describe with stories. Sometimes the stories revolve around objects, what anthropologists I think call artifacts, which we also collect. My job is to be a story carrier. This has two parts to it. When I go into a facility, a factory or a store, I tell people stories. We have many of them in a book, on our intranet and the Web-TV site, but I prefer to tell them out loud. For example, there is one I love about Marcelo Sidicaro. Marcelo comes from a family of real gauchos, and gauchos ride their horses without shoes, so the bottoms of their feet become hard, like leather. Marcelo is now production director at our biggest factory in La Consulta but he often goes without shoes, even in meetings with investors.

"I tell this story to give people an example of what we mean by the word 'independent.' The power of story is amazing. When I tell you Marcelo's story it is like you have seen him in a meeting with no shoes, and you go on and tell someone else and they say, 'Wow, is that the kind of place I work at?' And that leads to the second part of my job. I don't want the people in the Chelsea store to take their shoes off, that's not the point. But once I have told them about Marcelo, I invite them to tell me stories of what 'independent' means to them. I collect these and the best ones we incorporate into our fund

of stories. We stick them on the Web site, put them in the book or film them and post them on gaucho.tv. This makes for a dialogue, not a monologue. The stories we collect give us two things. They tell us if those people are understanding what we mean, and second, they help us deepen our own understanding so that we get an idea of "independent" that is bigger and deeper. This is really important to us. I mean, if one of your values is 'independence,' it doesn't make much sense to be always telling people what to do does it?

"I used to work at a big American company. We used a list of words which were just the same as all the other big companies—you know, 'imaginative,' 'customer-focused,' all that kind of stuff. And at the same time we were telling employees that they had to be innovative and creative. Most people seemed to think it was normal but it seemed nuts to me, which is why we do things in a different way at Gaucho.

"I think I have the best job in the world. I get to go round the world, hearing and telling some amazing stories, which in turn spark more stories. And this work isn't only fun, it's important—it makes a real difference to how well we do and to how everyone feels."

This story is, in fact, imaginary. There is no Gaucho and, in reality, La Consulta is a sleepy village of a few thousands souls surrounded by vineyards. But before you cry foul, let me explain that I deliberately chose to use a fictitious story here for two reasons. The first (but not the most important) was confidentiality. Real examples which are just as colorful do exist—we have heard stories about people turning goods trains around or skiing through a snowstorm to fulfill a promise—but often, because they say a lot more about an organization than any annual report or PowerPoint presentation, people aren't too keen on us making them public.

The second reason was that I wanted to push the idea. In my experience few organizations realize the true value and power of the stories they have, let alone the ones they have yet to find. Almost any organization will prove to have some great stories, yet few people are aware of them and fewer still know what to do with them. In order to show what *could* be done, I wanted to portray an organization that really committed to using story as an open-ended, interactive, noncontrolling way of entering into dialogue about the identity of an organization with the people who make it what it is.

I think it is both a shame and waste that organizations don't act on the power of story in the way Gaucho does in the story. Companies devote a huge amount of time, energy and resources to devising and disseminating visions, missions and values because they know how important it is to try and get people aligned. Yet all too often this gargantuan effort doesn't seem to make any difference to what people in the organization do or how they feel. If they put even a fraction of the energy into stories, they would see a much greater return, especially if they facilitate a two-way dialogue. Hearing stories tends to trigger more stories, so the process feeds itself.

To make this happen you have to give stories importance, make them accessible and make them real, but that isn't any more complicated than making a book of them, offering prizes for the best ones or posting them on a Web site. The fact that the Gaucho story is so plausible just goes to show how easy it could be.

It makes me smile to realize both how much I have learned since I met Gary in the Three Lions Bakery and how much I have still to learn. A recent session at the Saïd Business School brought this home to me. A participant (on a leadership program) either failed to hear or completely misunderstood an instruction for a game. As a result, an exercise which depended on a message being passed along a line was about to crash completely.

I stood to one side of the room watching, and as the flow of the game began to stutter and it began to break down, I could feel the heat of people's gaze. They were looking to me to see whether this was right or if it was working. I could feel anxiety rising and an inner voice started to whisper that I could step in and correct what was happening. I was on verge of doing so when something inside me shifted. My breathing slowed, I felt very grounded and suddenly it became obvious to me that I didn't have to listen to the voice. I smiled involuntarily, my body relaxed and everyone around the room understood, as clearly as if I had said it out loud, that everything was just fine. I would even wager that at this point some people thought I had set up the disruption on purpose.

In reality I had no idea that it would occur or what would happen next, but I knew and trusted the feeling that it would lead somewhere interesting, which it did. It opened the door to a fabulous few minutes. We laughed and learned so much. The breakdown in communication that had happened in the game gave us a real experience of the issues leaders face and led to a great conversation. What the group was able to observe and create together was far more powerful than anything I might have prepared beforehand. This was the joy of uncertainty coming home to roost.

This, for me, is how the practice makes itself felt. I notice more of what is going on inside me. If I get caught up with trying to stay in control or stay with what I know or constrain what is happening, I am more likely to become aware of it. That awareness enables me to let go of those concerns and pay more attention to what can be learned, what is new or what is most productive for the group or the process. I look for the offer—which is a shift away from thinking and toward sensing and feeling what to do.

It is hard to tell this story without making it sound like I am the hero of the piece. That really isn't true, if only because there are plenty of occasions when I still don't manage it. Even in this episode I came very close to intervening—you can never assume you have really learned the lesson, all you can do is keep practicing.

If you do, the pay-off can be considerable. At such moments I stop worrying about my own performance or reputation. It's a rush, but I don't feel any hurry. Sometimes everything feels so good, so fitting, that I literally jump up and down. The fact that this looks silly doesn't occur to me; I am enjoying myself too much to worry about that.

Every day we have a choice about how we react to the uncertain and the unknown.

Power lies in knowing that vulnerability is not the same as weakness, not in becoming invulnerable. Improvisers are able to stay open, keep changing and be creative because they are happy to make themselves vulnerable. The practices provide them with a kind of mental skeleton that enables them to stay in that fruitful territory which lies on the edge of chaos.

There is still plenty that can shake, surprise or wrong-foot you, even if you become a skillful improviser, but instead of seeking to control events, you choose how to respond to them. You become more practiced and thus more skillful at working with uncertainty. Rather than gloss over the moments when something "goes wrong," you find yourself relishing them because you know that these are the occasions when you stand to gain the most. Just like in the improv theater, these are the moments which seem like magic.

Being able to make sense and meaning out of what feels like chaos is critical to our personal satisfaction and growth. The importance of developing creativity, flexibility and adaptability goes beyond our material needs. These are qualities which enable us to feel that we are "participants in our own future, not observers of our fate."[4]

Such qualities will also shape our collective future. A truly sustainable society cannot be planned, it will have to emerge. We need to do more than control ourselves. Banning plastic bags won't stop environmental destruction or lift people out of poverty or prevent political instability. Parsimony is not a creative force. The ecological damage our industrial civilization is wreaking merely emphasizes how sorely we need new ideas in every nook and cranny of our society. These ideas will enable us to have a symbiotic relationship with the natural world we are a part of, rather than consume or despoil it.

The beauty is that all kinds of undiscovered, strange and lovely ideas that could unleash unimaginable shifts are all around us if only we can learn to see and use them. If we choose, we can see everything as an offer dripping with untold promise: even the back of a T-shirt.

- - - - - - - - - - - - - - - - - - -
4   Attributed to British Politician Tony Benn.

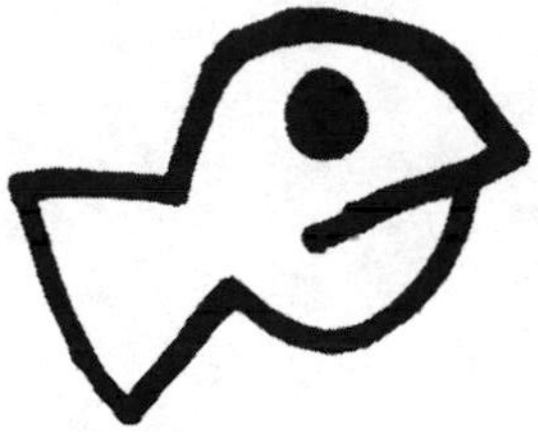

🐝 Epilogue

When I started writing I imagined that despite the subject matter, the book itself would not be very improvised. A book seems a far cry from the playful, cocreative method of improvisation. Yet as the process unfolded I came to realize that I was using many of the very ideas, thoughts and tools I was writing about. Since at school we were always taught to "show your workings," I thought I would take a page or two to explain how some of the ideas in the book have been used in the process of its own creation.

Another lesson I was taught at school—that you should plan your essay before you write—seemed even more important for something of this scale. However I found it impossible to first nail a structure, then fill it in. Instead, structure seemed to emerge from the writing itself, bending any plans I had made out of (or into) shape. Ignoring the ghosts of English teachers past, I decided to commit to what felt natural and allowed myself to play around more, adopting an emergent style of working where the structure would evolve with the material.

This felt more like a journey of discovery than the exposition of a thesis. Offers were everywhere—ideas or connections would occur as a result of a conversation with my wife, a passage in another book, a newspaper article, game of football, phone conversation, workshop or something welling up from my own unconscious. My job became to accept these offers, connecting them and combining them, allowing the ideas to lead me, rather than the other way around (letting go of many a shadow story in the process). As a result, there are many ideas in the book that I didn't know I had (or *could* have) and I learned much of what is here as I went along.

I also found myself applying the practices very explicitly during the act of writing. Like most people my internal censor is able to spit out immediate criticism which can be paralyzing. Letting go of such instant judgments was a necessary and liberating practice. When I got really stuck, deliberately looking for a new offer or breaking a routine were both enormously useful. Two particularly effective ploys were to do something physical (living in the countryside there is no shortage of physical work to be done) or call a colleague to get another perspective.

When you write on a computer (an Apple Powerbook G4, to be precise) it is easy to rattle off a lot of words quickly and sometimes such flow is wonderful. However, on occasions I found it helpful to slow down and give much deeper attention to what I was writing. By being really present to the words, noticing their weight and shape, I could make more sure-footed progress than I would by rushing ahead.

Being present and letting go of judgment were also crucial in the dark moments, of which there were many. "I can't do this, this is beyond me, why am I so slow, this is all a waste of time" are insistent thoughts and require some kind of antidote, which the practices provided, in no small measure. The idea that "if it isn't fun, it isn't working" also helped me avoid wallowing in the pain and drama of the difficult moments, which felt seductive and heroic, but tended to be extremely irritating for those around me.

The thought of starting anywhere and paying more attention to getting going rather than getting it right came into its own when facing a blank screen. Often, once I generated some flow in this way, I would find it heading quite productively in a direction I had not anticipated. The passage that got me going in the first place might then be jettisoned, having already played its role, exercising the muscle of letting go.

That muscle needed exercise—it was absolutely vital when editing (which happened throughout). In part this was necessary to cut down the sheer volume of material, however, letting go of particular passages, phrases, jokes or segues was also important. Loosening my attachment to these fixed points let in some daylight and almost always made the process easier and the result better. Not that blocking didn't play a role. I deliberately gave myself a lot of other opinions to listen to, and there were occasions when it felt important to stick with my own view. However, as suggested in Chapter 6, I tried my best only to do so for a good reason.

Color-advance I used in several ways. I am apt to polish, excessively, a small amount of text. The idea of color-advance helped me spot this. I took the idea further and invented a way to use different colored font to force myself to advance. When reworking text, I would change the color as I went, say from black to blue, and forbid myself to do anything further to the blue type while there was still black remaining. Color-advance also provided a useful overarching framework to track whether I was getting lost in detail or skating over things. My colleagues used it to give me direction, too—they pointed out that if I were telling a personal story, it made it more engaging if I included some personal color—sharing not just what happened but how it felt at the time.

Playing around with status helped me find the tone of voice in which I wanted to write. When a passage grated, it was often because I had slipped into a higher register of status than I wanted. Later on in the process, I refined this understanding and Amanda Blake helped me to recognize that the low-status "voice of doubt" could undermine what I was trying to say, so I tried to be careful with that.

The making and marketing of the book has also been shaped by the practice. We consciously chose to publish this book ourselves. (I say "we" because this production was full-on cocreation.) Nowadays technology allows you to put your own creative work out in the form that you want, easily and (relatively) cheaply, which was so fitting an offer that we simply had to accept it.[1]

Doing so allowed us to play around, move fast and include ideas from many different people (for example, via an online spreadsheet we got input on the title from all over the world). We were thus able to use what we have, whether it was our network

- - - - - - - - - - - - - - - - - - -

1 Technology also allows us to garner contributions and reactions from others and put those back out into the world, so if you want to share a story or idea visit www.everythingsanoffer.com and there will be space or a link for people to post their own stories.

or Gary's imagery. This was far more fun than trying to drive the book towards a particular idea of "success" (e.g., volume sales). And perhaps more importantly, it gives us the opportunity to learn. This book is an offer, not an answer, and putting it out in the world allows us to see what other offers it generates in turn, for us or for others. By choosing this path, we may not sell as many, but who knows what adventures it might unleash.

Beyond these specific applications of the practice there is a deeper sense in which the book itself reflects the ideas it endeavours to explain. Early on in the process an agent said to me:

> There is a view in the publishing industry that there are only two kinds of book—how-to books and philosophy—which if you think about it, means that there isn't much between *The Beverly Hills Diet* and Immanuel Kant's *A Critique of Pure Reason*.

I decided to mash the two kinds and produce something that is both philosophical and practical, personal and professional. Just like On Your Feet's business, this book is a "yes and…." This may break the conventions of publishing but it is true to the spirit of improvisation—making unlikely connections and combinations is at the heart of the practice and thus at the heart of the book.

For further installments, feedback, podcasts, T-shirts, connections, links and so on visit www.everythingsanoffer.com.

Thanks

While a singer-songwriter's name might be conspicuous on the cover of their albums, their creations are inspired, shaped and accompanied by a colorful crew of musicians, producers, technicians and tea boys who get cute credits in the sleeve notes. I think of this book in a similar way. Though I have written the words, it has truly been a cocreative endeavor, on many levels, thus the list of thanks and acknowledgements is as varied as those you see on the back of an album.

That starts with my influences—those thinkers and writers whose ideas opened me up to some of the possibilities explored in this book. It was the work of Fritjof Capra and Margaret Wheatley that first set me off on the trail of complexity and emergence, and I was delighted to discover, in a workshop in Sundance run by the two of them together, that Meg Wheatley's *Leadership and the New Science* was itself inspired by Capra's *Tao of Physics*. Without the understanding I gleaned from those books I may never have seen anything worth exploring in improvisation at all.

Paul Hawken's book *The Ecology of Commerce* and the course of the same name (held in June 1997 at Schumacher College in Devon, England) also made a big impact on me, not least because of the people I met there. Nonetheless, the book that had the most influence on me was without a doubt Kevin Kelly's *Out of Control*. I continue to be amazed that this wonderful mash-up of technology and ecology was published in 1994. It still seems ahead of the curve to me, and I regularly revisit my well-thumbed copy. Whenever I do so the dog-eared pages always seem to offer some new idea about how to work with complexity. Sincere thanks and profound respect to Mr. Kelly.

Edward Espe Brown helped me to see the connections between improv and Zen (another connection brokered at Schumacher College). I have enjoyed Ed's teaching, friendship, company, sense of humor and food for over ten years, and that has been a great privilege.

In the world of improv theater, it is to Keith Johnstone that I owe a debt. His approach, while focused on the theater, seems to reach far beyond it, making it simple to apply his ideas to organizations and personal life. In addition to Johnstone, my touchstone in the world of improv theater has been Gary Hirsch, painter of T-shirts and co-founder of On Your Feet, who, since the first day I met him, has been able to make instant connections between the world of stage performance and everyday life.

Gary, however, has done far more than provide stage expertise and artwork. He has not only illustrated but illuminated this book, and it is only right that his name is on the cover. His influence and his ideas are implicit, if not explicit, on every page of the book. He has accompanied me on every part of this journey, giving his energy and attention freely, supporting or challenging as the moment required, living proof that it is perfectly possible to have a fabulous working relationship with someone thousands of miles and nine time zones away. That said, his handwriting is awful, so thanks for Laura Faye Smith for the calligraphy on the diagrams.

The rest of my On Your Feet colleagues have also played a great part. Julie Huffaker added her customary rigor to a sprawling first draft and, as the author of three books herself, a wealth of tips and tricks to help me manage myself. Lizzie Palmer and Brad Robertson never wavered in their unstinting enthusiasm for both the book project and the text itself, however boring or obsessive I became about it. More importantly, they, together with Gary, Julie and everyone else who collaborates with On Your Feet (including Laura, Daryl Olson, Mame Pelletier, Shelley Six, Suzy Bolt and Kay Scorah), created the opportunity for the book in the first place. Without the innumerable workshops, speeches, conferences and consulting jobs that they have created, designed and delivered over the course of more than a decade, there would have been nothing to write about.

That particular thank you needs to be extended to include all the clients and participants brave enough to take part in or commission all that work. By now this runs into tens of thousands of people, but let two who made a particular contribution stand for all of them—Andy Davies (to whom I owe the comment "the company paid for that, but it was for me") and Jonathan Daly (who coined the phrase "accepting is not submission"). To those two and thousands of unnamed others, thanks. Thanks also to everyone who contributed to the online poll for the title. It was a great help not only to get your opinions and ideas but, as ever with cocreation, made the responsibility of the decision less burdensome.

As the opening story demonstrates, this adventure, like so many, turned on particular connections being made. Two particular connectors stand out. Without Robin Lanahan (née Joannides), I would never have been in Portland to buy a T-shirt, let alone meet Gary. Without Nick Smith, I would not have been introduced to Templeton College, Oxford (now under the auspices of the Saïd Business School). Being able to ply this work in such august surroundings has been a great source of learning for me, which I owe to Richard Marshall (bless him) and Marshall Young, whose faith in alternative approaches I deeply appreciate. Working on the Strategic Leadership Programme has also brought me into contact with a wonderful group of people from whom I have learned a great deal and whose support, enthusiasm and insight has been invaluable. That group includes Tracey Camilleri, Ron Emerson, Mike Harper, Harald Knudsen, Helena Molyneux and Kurt April. Kurt also offered me the opportunity to write about these ideas (in a series of articles commissioned for *Convergence* magazine) and effected an introduction to Elaine Rumboll at the University of Cape Town, who in turn gave me the chance to experience a southern hemisphere perspective.

Authors Jay Griffiths, Andy Jackson, Conrad Keating and Adam Morgan all gave me useful tips and advice about writing. (Adam also supplied numerous possible titles and boundless enthusiasm.) Thanks also to Neil Penny who, in Mrs. Cornish's class at

Harnham Junior School, circa 1973, first showed me what fun writing could be.

Amanda Blake unwittingly but graciously allowed me to volunteer her for the job of editor, a role which she has played with great perspicacity, sensitivity and diligence (fire that choir). Detailed feedback was generously given by many of the aforementioned folks (namely Gary, Julie, Lizzie, Brad, Elaine, Kay and Amanda), but also by James Gardener (despite the fact he barely knew me), Lucy Harris (despite the fact she has had to put up with me her whole life) and Olivia Knight. I had been warned that this was too many readers, but I have no hesitation in saying that everything each of you said was useful.

In terms of putting the ideas into practice, particular thanks are due to David Keating, who had the commitment to use these ideas to make a film. For doing so, for the film *KM64* itself, for sharing so freely the learning that resulted and for endless, brilliant conversations, I will always owe you a pint.

Closer to home, I live surrounded by a practical example of how fundamental improvisation can be in the form of our house, a creation that would not have been possible were it not for the consummate improvisational talents of Jose Luis and Basilio Moreno and Tomas Villegas. Gracias, tios, de verdad.

On a more practical note, a word of thanks also to the people at Apple that developed Spotlight. Without it I would have gone mad trying to find scraps of text among the mayhem of my filing system. Also to Nirankar Sing Khalsa, Cristian Reyes and Werner Glaser—this book has largely been written to their calming music (the album *Ciclos*—for links to their music, check out www.everythingsanoffer.com).

Finally, love and thanks to Bruno, Mateo and Pablo, and above all to Beatriz for the joy and delight they bring to the improvisation that is my daily life.

Many of the people listed above (and plenty of unnamed others) have helped me see and use the mistakes I have made along the way as offers. Thus any that remain are purely my own responsibility. Nonetheless I take heart from the fact that even these can be regarded as lurking offers, waiting to be pointed out, corrected, used or construed in an original way by someone, somewhere. And who knows what that might lead to?

Further Reading

Here are some of the other books that have informed and influenced this one.

Abrashoff, Michael D. *It's Your Ship: Management Techniques from the Best Damn Ship in the Navy*. New York: Business Plus, 2002.
How to command by giving up control.

Broks, Paul. *Into the Silent Land: Travels in Neuropsychology*. London: Atlantic Monthly Press, 2004.
Neuroscientist gets philosophical about questions of self.

Capra, Fritjof. *The Web of Life: A New Scientific Understanding of Living Systems*. New York: Anchor Books, 1997.
A new scientific framework for understanding life. One of the more accessible scientific books but still scientific.

Claxton, Guy. *Hare Brain, Tortoise Mind: How Intelligence Increases When You Think Less*. Hopewell, NJ: Ecco Press, 1999.
We know more than we think.

Csíkszentmihályi, Míhaly. *Flow: The Psychology of Optimal Experience*. New York: HarperPerennial, 1991.
———. *Creativity: Flow and the Psychology of Discovery and Invention*. New York: HarperPerennial, 1996.
Fascinating and inspiring studies of creativity, flow and their relationship to happiness.

Friedman, Thomas L. *The World is Flat: A Brief History of the Twenty-first Century*. New York: Farrar, Straus and Giroux, 2006.
An exploration of (rather than attack on or defense of) globalization.

Hock, Dee W. *Birth of the Chaordic Age*. San Francisco: Berret-Koehler Publishers, 1999.
Chaos and order makes the oxymoronic "chaord." From the man that turned a banking crisis into the world's most successful credit card (VISA).

Hurst, David K. *Crisis and Renewal: Meeting the Challenge of Organizational Change*. Boston, MA: Harvard Business School Press, 2002.
Shiva comes to Canada. Hurst argues that creation requires destruction and uses ecosystems and a hostile take-over for a Canadian steel company as examples.

Jackson, Phil. *Sacred Hoops: Spiritual Lessons of a Hardwood Warrior*. New York: Hyperion, 2006.
There's more to life than basketball, but then there's more to basketball than basketball.

Johnstone, Keith. *Impro: Improvisation and the Theater*. New York: Theater Arts Book, 1987.
Classic text on improvisation, includes some wonderful thoughts on what is wrong with conventional education.

———. *Impro for Storytellers*. New York: Theater Arts Book, 1994.
Rich in games and stories for any budding improv junkies but with some particularly interesting ideas about how to create action that are very widely applicable (see the chapter entitled "Making Things Happen").

Kelly, Kevin. *Out of Control: The New Biology of Machines, Social Systems & the Economic World*. Reading, MA: Perseus Press, 1995.
Complexity, ecology, creativity, the evolution of evolution, Borgian Libraries and warring robots. It's all here...

Kleiner, Art. *The Age of Heretics: A History of the Radical Thinkers Who Reinvented Corporate Management*. New York: Currency Doubleday, 1996.
History of "corporate" heretics from Pelagius to the present day.

Kosko, Bart. *Fuzzy Thinking: The New Science of Fuzzy Logic*. New York: Hyperion, 1993.
Science isn't as scientific as you might think.

Lewis, Thomas, MD.; Amini, Fari; Lannon, Richard. *A General Theory of Love*. New York: Vintage, 2001.
Poetic take on the science of emotion by three doctors.

Pert, Candace B. *Molecules of Emotion: The Science Behind Mind-Body Medicine*. New York: Simon & Schuster, 1999.
A double story of the discovery of endorphins and the struggle of a woman scientist in the National Institutes of Health.

Pollan, Michael. *In Defense of Food: An Eater's Manifesto*. New York: The Penguin Press, 2008.
A wonderful attack on the reductionist idea of "nutritionism."

———. *The Botany of Desire: A Plant's-Eye View of the World*. New York: Random House, 2001.
Are we using plants or are they using us?

Rodriguez, Robert. *Rebel Without A Crew: Or How a 23-Year-Old Filmmaker With $7,000 Became a Hollywood Player*. London: Faber and Faber, 1996.
Consummate lessons in how to use everything as an offer.

Saul, John Ralston. *Voltaire's Bastards: The Dictatorship of Reason in the West*. New York: Vintage, 1993.
Where the age of reason went wrong.

Schumacher, E. F. A Guide for the Perplexed. New York: Harper Perennial, 1978.
It's not you, it's the map.

Soros, George. *The Crisis of Global Capitalism: Open Society Endangered*. New York: PublicAffairs, 1998.
One of capitalisms winners says it's all going wrong.

Wallace, Danny. *Yes Man*. New York: Simon Spotlight Entertainment, 2006.
An idle comment from a complete stranger can change your life.

Weiner, Jonathan. *The Beak of the Finch: A Story of Evolution in Our Time*. New York: Knopf, 1994.

Evolution happens even faster than Darwin thought.

Wheatley, Margaret J. *Leadership and the New Science: Discovering Order in a Chaotic World*. 3rd ed. San Francisco: Berret-Koehler Publishers, 2006.

Management consultant on complexity trip plays poet.

Whyte, David. *The Heart Aroused: Poetry and the Preservation of the Soul in Corporate America*. New York: Doubleday Business, 1996.

Poet on complexity trip plays management consultant.

Zeldin, Theodore. *Conversation: How Talk Can Change Our Lives*. Mahwah, NJ: HiddenSpring, 2000.

Oxford academic sets out to change the way we talk to each other.

Index

Robert Poynton

One Saturday late in November 1996, Robert's career as an advertising and marketing consultant was interrupted by a T-shirt. T-shirts are not meant to have career-changing properties, yet the purchase of this particular T-shirt was a pivotal moment. It introduced him to improviser Gary Hirsch and led to the creation of the consultancy firm On Your Feet, a collaboration between business and the arts which uses methods and tools derived from improvisational theater.

For over ten years Robert has been designing and leading programs and workshops for clients such as Philips, Orange, JWT and Starbucks. He regularly teaches (and plays snooker badly) at Oxford University's Saïd Business School and at The Graduate School of Business at the University of Cape Town. He lives in central Spain in a solar-powered house with his wife, three sons and a Real Madrid season ticket. This is his first book. His wife is hoping it will be his last.

Gary Hirsch

One Saturday late in November 1996, Gary's career as an artist and improviser was interrupted by a phone call from a marketing and advertising guy with a funny accent. Marketing and advertising, yet alone funny accents, aren't meant to have career-changing properties to free-spirited artistic types, yet meeting Robert Poynton was a pivotal moment. It lead to the cocreation of On Your Feet, a thirteen-year (and counting) collision between the arts and business.

Gary grew up in Cleveland Heights, Ohio, having lots of nightmares. His father asked him to illustrate these vivid dreams, and he has been doing so ever since. Gary's paintings, illustrations and public works can be seen in galleries, homes, streets and torsos worldwide (and at www.doodlehouse.com). He has just completed illustrating his first children's book called *Dare*. Gary has been performing improvisational theater for over twenty years. He lives in Portland, Oregon, with his wife, two children, and performs there with the improv theater company Super Project Lab (www.superprojectlab.com).